RapidWeaver 5 Beginner's Guide

Build beautiful and professional websites with ease using
RapidWeaver

Joe Workman

BIRMINGHAM - MUMBAI

RapidWeaver 5 Beginner's Guide

First published: September 2012

Production Reference: 1040912

Published by Packt Publishing Ltd.
Livery Place
35 Livery Street
Birmingham B3 2PB, UK.

ISBN 978-1-84969-205-2

www.packtpub.com

Cover Image by Asher Wishkerman (wishkerman@hotmail.com)

Credits

Author

Joe Workman

Reviewers

Gilberto De Faveri

Will Woodgate

Acquisition Editor

Wilson D'souza

Lead Technical Editor

Hithesh Uchil

Technical Editors

Merin Jose

Ankita Meshram

Project Coordinator

Vishal Bodwani

Proofreader

Aaron Nash

Indexer

Monica Ajmera Mehta

Production Coordinator

Nitesh Thakur

Cover Work

Nitesh Thakur

About the Author

Joe Workman is an indie software developer who develops popular applications for Mac OS X and add-ons for RapidWeaver. Joe released his first RapidWeaver Stacks add-on to the Mac community back in 2008. He has grown since then to become the largest RapidWeaver add-on developer with over 125+ add-ons available.

Joe has developed many popular Mac utilities, but his flagship application is DomainBrain. DomainBrain helps users get all their domain-related data out of their brains into a centrally managed location.

Joe was born, raised, and still currently lives in the SF Bay Area with his beautiful wife and three kids, although he had some wonderful years living in Goiania, Brazil, and London, England. He loves photography and coaching his son's soccer team.

For more about Joe and his products, head over to his website at http://joeworkman.net.

Acknowledgement

I want to dedicate this book to my wife Francsica and to the best three kids that a dad could have. They make my life a complete joy. Every second of my life is devoted to making them happy. I love you infinity demais!

I want to give a huge thank you to Isaiah from YourHead Software. If Isaiah had not pushed me into selling my first piece of software back in 2009, I would never have become the full-fledged indie development shop that I am today. I am forever grateful for his mentorship and being a great friend.

Dan Counsell and Nik Fletcher over at Realmac Software have both been instrumental in both getting this book complete as well as creating the amazing community that allows me to be in business. Nik has been a life saver behind the scenes where he makes all the magic happen, while Dan is a true visionary behind Realmac that I can only hope live up to someday.

While I was off busy writing this book, someone had to hold down the fort. So a huge thanks goes out to Tron Sutton and Rob Ziebol for their amazing work. They have the privilege of handling all the support tickets for all my products and any special projects that I may throw at them. They are a godsend. Thanks guys!

So last but definitely not least, I want to thank all of my customers for making this happen. I would not be where I am three years later without your support, praise, and ideas. I hope that I have returned the favor to you over the years in turn with some great support, awesome products, and a plethora of free updates (even though I've been told that I am crazy for doing so).

Now go forth and make your websites great!

About the Reviewers

Gilberto De Faveri is the lead Cocoa developer at Omnidea, which he co-founded in 2006. Omnidea is the company behind RapidCart, RapidMaps, and many other popular RapidWeaver plugins and Mac utilities. He loves late-night coding sessions and Trappist beer, not in this order.

Will Woodgate originally trained as a hydrologist, and graduated from university in 2006 with a degree in environmental science. It was while Will was putting together a website for a water resources project, that he discovered RapidWeaver. A short time later, Will was busy developing new RapidWeaver themes and offering these designs free via forums for others to use, in hobby form.

In late 2007, the 'ThemeFlood' website was opened, and theme development grew to become a fulltime business. Not only does Will now provide a number of innovative off-the-shelf RapidWeaver themes, but he has since diversified into developing custom RapidWeaver themes and stacks. Alongside working in partnership with other RapidWeaver developers and documenting several plugins, Will also maintains his own blog with many topics on RapidWeaver (http://www.willwoodgate.com/).

www.PacktPub.com

Support files, eBooks, discount offers and more

You might want to visit www.PacktPub.com for support files and downloads related to your book.

Did you know that Packt offers eBook versions of every book published, with PDF and ePub files available? You can upgrade to the eBook version at www.PacktPub.com and as a print book customer, you are entitled to a discount on the eBook copy. Get in touch with us at service@packtpub.com for more details.

At www.PacktPub.com, you can also read a collection of free technical articles, sign up for a range of free newsletters and receive exclusive discounts and offers on Packt books and eBooks.

http://PacktLib.PacktPub.com

Do you need instant solutions to your IT questions? PacktLib is Packt's online digital book library. Here, you can access, read, and search across Packt's entire library of books.

Why Subscribe?

- ◆ Fully searchable across every book published by Packt
- ◆ Copy and paste, print and bookmark content
- ◆ On demand and accessible via web browser

Free Access for Packt account holders

If you have an account with Packt at www.PacktPub.com, you can use this to access PacktLib today and view nine entirely free books. Simply use your login credentials for immediate access.

Table of Contents

Preface

RapidWeaver allows users with any level of expertise to build beautiful and professional looking websites. The novice user will love the drag and drop, what you see is what you get interface. Advanced users will love that they can get down and dirty with some code when they need to.

This book covers all aspects of developing a website with RapidWeaver. Whether you want a family website to display photos from your latest vacation or a small business that is looking to increase your web presence, this book has got you covered. If you have a Mac and want a website, you need this book.

This book dives into all the components required to build a website with RapidWeaver. The first half of this book builds upon itself and shows you all of the basic building blocks that you will need to develop great websites. It starts off with a basic tour of RapidWeaver and gets you building your first webpage in the first chapter. The book progresses onto how to customize the look and feel of your website with themes and adding simple webpages with text and images all the way to blogs and photo galleries.

The second half of the book dives into more advanced topics that can really help you take your websites to the next level. These include e-commerce, blogs, managing web content outside of RapidWeaver, Search Engine Optimization, and even a little programming. By the end of this book, you will have a solid foundation that will allow you to build powerful websites.

What this book covers

Chapter 1, Getting Started — In this first chapter, we are going to hit the ground running. We are going to go from zero to a deployed website by the end of this chapter. This means that we are going to see an in-depth review of every setting.

Chapter 2, Touring RapidWeaver — In this chapter, we are going to step back a bit and take a tour of the RapidWeaver interface, preferences, and inspector windows. We are going to review every nook and cranny throughout the interface.

Chapter 3, Theming Your Site — In this chapter, we are going to review all the aspects of applying themes to your website. We will, specifically, look at topics such as choosing and managing themes, saving theme styles, customizing themes, and more.

Chapter 4, Styled Text Page — In this chapter, we will be reviewing the Styled Text page. The Styled Text page is an extremely versatile page type. You can add images, audio, video, and file downloads all without knowing an ounce of code! The Styled Text framework is not limited to just the Styled Text page. This means that everything that you are about to learn in this chapter can also be applied to most of the other RapidWeaver pages and plugins as well.

Chapter 5, Stacks — In this chapter, we will be reviewing the Stacks add-on of RapidWeaver. We will not only learn how to install and work with Stacks, we will also review its toolbars and settings, templates, and the default stack elements that ship with this add-on.

Chapter 6, Basic Page Types — In this chapter, we will be reviewing a few common page types and elements that are used throughout web design. Some of these are out-of-the-box page types that ship with RapidWeaver, and others are third-party developer plugins or stacks.

Chapter 7, Multimedia Pages — Websites would be pretty boring if they did not have media. So, in this chapter we will learn how to add images and videos, and also learn how files can be shared on our website.

Chapter 8, Blogs, Podcasts, and Going Social — In this chapter, we will learn how to create blogs and podcasts. We will also learn about integrating Wordpress, Tumblr, and social networking sites such as Facebook and Twitter, to our website.

Chapter 9, E-Commerce — In this chapter, we will learn how we can easily build our own online store using RapidWeaver. There aren't any page plugins which ship with RapidWeaver that allow you to do this; however, we will see how we can build our online store by simply copying and pasting some freely available code snippets.

We will also briefly review a few third-party add-ons that provide a robust and easy-to-use interface. As online sales is an enormous topic, we will be focusing on the easiest way to get your online store up and running quickly.

Chapter 10, Search Engine Optimization — Search Engine Optimization (SEO) is the black magic of web design. Essentially, it's the process that you need to go through in order to get the search engines to recognize your website and make sure that your web pages are provided as results to people who are searching on Google, Bing, Yahoo, and others.

In this chapter, we are going to be reviewing topics such as increasing popularity with search engines, the technical basics of SEO. We will also learn about plugins such as Sitemap, Meta Mate, and others.

This chapter also covers the analytics services that will allow you to track tons of various metrics about who is visiting your website.

Chapter 11, Advanced Weaving — In this chapter we are going to try to cram in as many tips and track as we can. Some of these are RapidWeaver-specific topics; however, most are going to be about general web design, followed by the summary of this chapter.

What you need for this book

The primary requirement for this book is Apple Mac OS X 10.6.8+ and RapidWeaver 5. The author refers to lots of optional software throughout this book, which may be installed as and when required.

Who this book is for

If you are a novice wanting to build your first website or an experienced user looking for a better way to develop your existing websites, then this book is for you. This book is perfect for iWeb users who are looking for something better. It's also great for advanced users who use applications such as Dreamweaver, and are looking for a simpler way to develop websites without sacrificing the ability to get into the code.

Using this book, you can build entire websites without writing a single line of code. But if you know a little web programming, then you will be able to take your websites to the next level.

Conventions

In this book, you will find several headings appearing frequently.

To give clear instructions of how to complete a procedure or task, we use:

Time for action – heading

1. Action 1
2. Action 2
3. Action 3

Instructions often need some extra explanation so that they make sense, so they are followed with:

What just happened?

This heading explains the working of tasks or instructions that you have just completed.

You will also find some other learning aids in the book, including:

Have a go hero – heading

These set practical challenges and give you ideas for experimenting with what you have learned.

You will also find a number of styles of text that distinguish between different kinds of information. Here are some examples of these styles, and an explanation of their meaning.

Code words in text are shown as follows: "The content that is placed between the <div> tags will be magically moved into its proper location that is defined by the theme."

A block of code is set as follows:

```
<div id="myExtraContent1">
    <!-- Your content goes here -->
</div>
```

New terms and **important words** are shown in bold. Words that you see on the screen, in menus or dialog boxes for example, appear in the text like this: "Simply select the text that you want to make as your heading and from the **Format** menu, select any heading from 1 to 6".

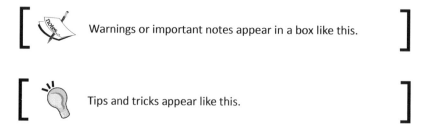

[Warnings or important notes appear in a box like this.   ]

[Tips and tricks appear like this.   ]

Reader feedback

Feedback from our readers is always welcome. Let us know what you think about this book—what you liked or may have disliked. Reader feedback is important for us to develop titles that you really get the most out of.

To send us general feedback, simply send an e-mail to feedback@packtpub.com, and mention the book title through the subject of your message.

If there is a topic that you have expertise in and you are interested in either writing or contributing to a book, see our author guide on www.packtpub.com/authors.

Customer support

Now that you are the proud owner of a Packt book, we have a number of things to help you to get the most from your purchase.

Downloading the example code

You can download the example code files for all Packt books you have purchased from your account at http://www.packtpub.com. If you purchased this book elsewhere, you can visit http://www.packtpub.com/support and register to have the files e-mailed directly to you.

You can also obtain the project files used throughout this book at http://rapidweaverbook.com.

Errata

Although we have taken every care to ensure the accuracy of our content, mistakes do happen. If you find a mistake in one of our books—maybe a mistake in the text or the code—we would be grateful if you would report this to us. By doing so, you can save other readers from frustration and help us improve subsequent versions of this book. If you find any errata, please report them by visiting http://www.packtpub.com/support, selecting your book, clicking on the **errata submission form** link, and entering the details of your errata. Once your errata are verified, your submission will be accepted and the errata will be uploaded to our website, or added to any list of existing errata, under the Errata section of that title.

Piracy

Piracy of copyright material on the Internet is an ongoing problem across all media. At Packt, we take the protection of our copyright and licenses very seriously. If you come across any illegal copies of our works, in any form, on the Internet, please provide us with the location address or website name immediately so that we can pursue a remedy.

Please contact us at copyright@packtpub.com with a link to the suspected pirated material.

We appreciate your help in protecting our authors, and our ability to bring you valuable content.

Questions

You can contact us at questions@packtpub.com if you are having a problem with any aspect of the book, and we will do our best to address it.

1

Getting Started

Let me first welcome you to this book. If you are reading this book, I assume that you are interested in learning how to build websites. Or maybe you already own RapidWeaver and you are hoping to pick up some tips and tricks. Let me assure you that this book is for both audiences.

In this first chapter, we are going to hit the ground running. We are going to go from zero to a deployed website by the end of this chapter. This means that we are going to see an in-depth review of every setting. Therefore, you are probably going to have a lot of questions. Happily, these questions should be answered in the remaining chapters of this book.

To be more specific, the following is what we will learn about in this chapter:

- ◆ What is RapidWeaver?
- ◆ Installing RapidWeaver
- ◆ Creating our first web page
- ◆ Publishing our website on the Internet

So strap your seat belts on and let's have some fun!

What is RapidWeaver?

RapidWeaver is a web development and design application for Mac that was developed by Realmac Software. It allows you to build stunning, professional websites very easily. RapidWeaver has both the novice and professional web designer covered. If you don't know (or don't want to know) how to code, RapidWeaver supports full code-free creation of your website; from blogs to site maps, photo albums to contact forms, you can build your entire website without a single line of code!

Without a doubt, RapidWeaver appeals to the aspiring novice web designer. However, it does not forget about the geeky, code loving, power users! And in case you were wondering...yeah, that includes me! RapidWeaver gives us geeks full access to peek under the hood. You can effortlessly add your own HTML or PHP file to any page. You can customize the look and feel with your own CSS file. For example, maybe you would like to add your own JavaScript for the latest and greatest animations out there; not a problem, RapidWeaver has got you covered. We even have full access to the amazing WebKit Developer Tools from directly inside the application. As RapidWeaver has all of these advanced features, it really serves as a catalyst to help an aspiring, novice web designer become a geeky, code loving, power user.

RapidWeaver's theme engine is a godsend for those users who are design challenged. However, it's also for those who don't want to spend time developing a site theme as they can leverage the work that some amazing theme developers have already done. Yeah, this includes me too! RapidWeaver ships with over 45 stunning themes built-in. This means that you can have a website that was designed by some world-class web designers. Each theme can be customized to your liking with just a few clicks. If you ever get tired of how your website looks, you can change your theme as often as you like. And your website content will remain 100 percent intact.

Once you have your website fully constructed, RapidWeaver makes it very simple to publish your website online. It will be able to publish to pretty much every web host around through its native support for both FTP and SFTP. You will be able to publish your website for the world to see with a single click.

iWeb versus RapidWeaver versus Dreamweaver

RapidWeaver is most commonly compared with both iWeb and Dreamweaver. While there are definitely direct feature comparisons, we are trying to compare apples with oranges. RapidWeaver is a great tool that falls somewhere between iWeb at one end of the scale and Dreamweaver at the other end.

Apple's iWeb was their first foray into personal web development software. In true Apple fashion, the application was extremely user friendly and developed beautiful websites. However, the application was really geared towards users who wanted to create a small website to share family photos and maybe have a blog. iWeb was not very extensible at all. If you ever wanted to try to steer outside the bounds of the default templates, you had to drive directly into full custom HTML. One of the biggest downsides that I came across was that once you choose the look and feel of your site, there was no going back. If you wanted to change the theme of your website, you had to redo every single page manually! For those of you who love the drag-and-drop abilities of iWeb, look no further than the RapidWeaver Stacks plugin from YourHead Software (covered later in this book).

Apple has acknowledged iWeb's shortcomings by pretty much removing iWeb from its lineup. You cannot purchase iWeb from Apple's Mac App Store. Furthermore, if you look at Apple's iLife page on their website, all traces of iWeb have been removed—if this is not a clear sign of iWeb's future, I don't know what is.

Now, let's jump to the opposite end of the spectrum with Adobe Dreamweaver. Dreamweaver has a much steeper learning curve than RapidWeaver (not to mention a much steeper price tag). Dreamweaver has a lot of capability for site management and can be used collaboratively on projects, and is designed to play well with Adobe's other design software. The Adobe Creative Suite with Dreamweaver is the package of choice for very large organizational websites being developed and managed by a team, or for complex dynamic sites. I am talking about websites such as `www.apple.com` or `www.nytimes.com`. For individual and small to mid-sized business websites, I can't think of a reason why one would prefer Dreamweaver to RapidWeaver.

So as I stated at the beginning, RapidWeaver provides a perfect middle ground for novice web designers and geeky code lovers!

It's more than an app

So far, I have talked about the RapidWeaver application itself. However, RapidWeaver is so much more than just an application. The user community that has been built around the RapidWeaver product is like nothing I have seen with any other application. The RapidWeaver forums hosted by Realmac are by far the most active and useful forums that I have seen. Users and developers spend countless hours helping each other with tips and tricks on design, code, and product support.

It's a worldwide community that is truly active 24/7. You can find the forums at
`http://forums.realmacsoftware.com`.

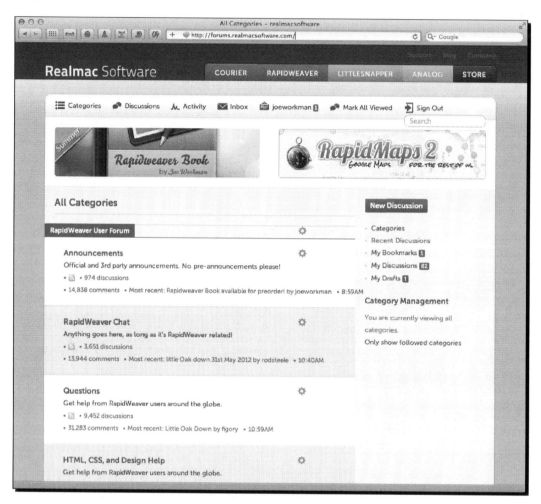

A part of the success of the strong RapidWeaver community is the strong third-party developers that exist. RapidWeaver provides a strong and flexible platform for developers to extend the application beyond its default feature set. There are currently three primary ways to extend your RapidWeaver application: Themes, Plugins, and Stacks.

As you may guess, third-party theme developers design custom themes that go above and beyond the themes that ship out of the box with RapidWeaver. With the number of amazing theme developers out there, it would be impossible not to develop a site that fits your style and looks amazing. We will cover themes in more depth later in this book.

RapidWeaver ships with 11 page styles out of the box. We will be reviewing all of these page styles throughout this book:

- Blog
- Contact Form
- File Sharing
- HTML Code
- iFrame
- Movie Album
- Offsite Page
- Photo Album
- QuickTime
- Sitemap
- Styled Text

However, RapidWeaver plugins can create even more page styles for you. There are a plethora of different page plugins from calendars to file uploads, and shopping carts to image galleries. I will be discussing various plugins throughout this book that will help you make your websites shine!

To illustrate the power of RapidWeaver's platform, YourHead Software developed the Stacks plugin for fluid page layout. The Stacks plugin created an entire new class of third-party RapidWeaver developer: the stack developer! A **stack** is simply a widget that can be used as a building block to construct your web page. There are stacks for just about anything: animated banners, menu systems, photo galleries, or even full-blown blog integrations. If you can dream it up, there is probably a stack for it! If you have visited my website, then you should know that my origins in the RapidWeaver community are as a Stacks Developer. I think that Stacks is amazing and should probably be the first plugin that you should consider acquiring. Just as with plugins, I will make sure to mention stacks throughout this book that will be useful in developing your website.

Realmac Software has added a section on their website in order to make it easier for users to explore and locate useful third-party add-ons. So make sure that you go check it out and peruse through all the great themes, plugins, and stacks! You can browse the add-ons at http://www.realmacsoftware.com/addons.

Installing RapidWeaver

In order for us to be able to build our first website, we need to download and install RapidWeaver 5 first. If you already have RapidWeaver installed, please feel free to jump to the next section. As with many third-party OS X applications today, there are two ways to obtain RapidWeaver: the **Mac App Store (MAS)** or directly from Realmac Software's website. Let's go through both options, and get you up and running.

The Mac App store

The Mac App store has become a very popular delivery channel for software. It allows you to browse through thousands of third-party applications and purchase them directly within the app. Another benefit is that it takes care of all the licensing for you, so you don't have to worry about storing your license keys any more.

Follow these simple steps in order to obtain RapidWeaver via the MAS:

1. Launch the Mac App Store application on your machine (requires Mac OS X 10.6.8).

2. Search and locate RapidWeaver using the search box at the top right-hand corner of the App Store.

3. Once you are at the RapidWeaver page (shown in the preceding screenshot) simply click on the **Buy** button.

4. Enter your username and password and the MAS will take care of the purchasing and installing RapidWeaver for you.

5. Open your `Applications` folder, locate RapidWeaver, and double-click to launch it.

6. You can drag RapidWeaver onto your dock for quick access in the future as well.

RealmacSoftware.com

If you do not have the App Store application on your machine or you just prefer not to use MAS, you can purchase RapidWeaver directly from Realmac Software. You can also simply download the trial version of RapidWeaver if you just want to check it out.

You can use the trial version for as long as you like. However, it is limited to just three pages.

1. Head over to the RapidWeaver product page: `http://www.realmacsoftware.com/rapidweaver/overview/`.

2. Click on the **Download** button to get your trial copy of RapidWeaver.

3. Once the download is complete, open the ZIP file found in your `Downloads` folder.

4. Drag `RapidWeaver.app` from `Downloads` to your `Applications` folder in the Finder.

5. Open your `Applications` folder, locate RapidWeaver, and double-click to launch it.

6. When you first launch RapidWeaver, you will be given the following three options:

   - Purchase RapidWeaver (either within the app or online)
   - Enter a valid serial number
   - Run RapidWeaver in demo mode

Creating our first website

So now we are going to jump into the deep end and create our first website. The website project that we are starting here will be built upon as we work through this book. At the end of this section, we will have a fully functional website that can be viewed on your local computer. Pay attention to the steps in this section because we are going to be repeating them a lot throughout this book.

Time for action – starting a new RapidWeaver project

Let's get started by simply opening up RapidWeaver, if you have not done so already. If you followed the installation instructions in the previous section, you will be able to find `RapidWeaver.app` in your `/Applications` folder or possibly on your dock if you purchased from MAS or added it there.

1. When you first open RapidWeaver, you will be presented with the RapidWeaver projects window. This window serves multiple purposes. We can easily access the last four projects that we have opened. We also have convenient links to Realmac Software's Add-ons and Tutorials websites. However, what we are concerned about right now is creating a new project. So go ahead and click on the **Create a New RapidWeaver Project** button.

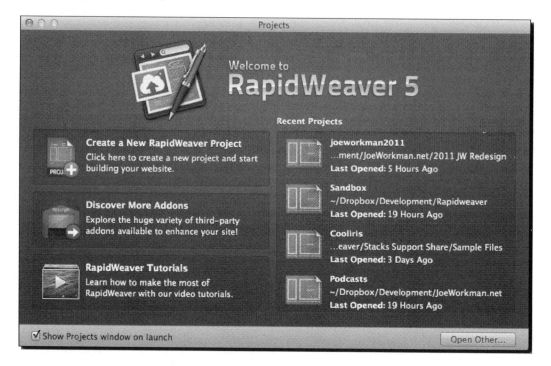

Note that this window will automatically open up every time you launch RapidWeaver. However, if you uncheck the box in the lower left-hand corner, you can disable this behavior. You can always access this window from within RapidWeaver by going to **File | Projects Window**.

2. Now that we have a new RapidWeaver document open, let's go ahead and click on the **Site Setup** (in the middle of the window) in order to set up some details about our new website.

3. We can now enter the basic information about our website in the **Site Setup** window. RapidWeaver inserts default information for us here. Overwrite these details with the pertinent information about your website. When you have completed the **General setup** form, go ahead and save your data by clicking on the **OK** button.

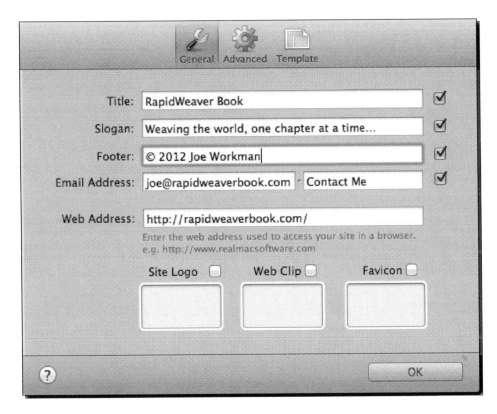

4. Let's now add our first web page by clicking on the **Add Page** button.

5. A window will now open for us to select what type of page we want to add into our website. There are 11 page types that are built into RapidWeaver. Let's scroll down to the bottom and select a **Styled Text** page. Then let's click on the **Choose** button to finalize our selection.

6. You will notice that a new page was created, titled **Untitled Page**. Let's go ahead and type some content into this area. You can even drag-and-drop your own images. You can also change the title of the page by double-clicking on the page title in the left-hand pane:

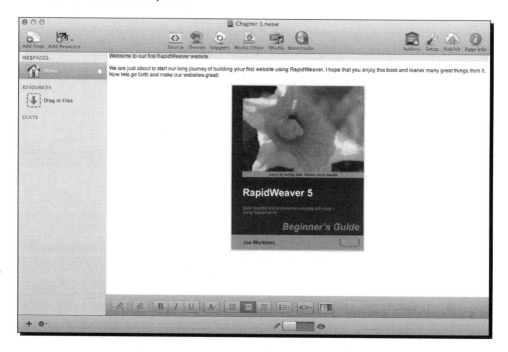

7. In order to create a **Heading**, simply select the text that you want and go to the menu **Format | HTML** to select the **Heading** option that you want. There is also a button (second button on the right-hand) on the formatting bar that is shown at the bottom of our **Styled Text** page.

8. To align your images, you need to select them and click on the desired alignment button in the formatting bar.

9. Now let's preview our website by clicking on the switch at the bottom of your RapidWeaver window. You can also use the *Command+R* keyboard shortcut to switch between **Preview** and **Edit** modes.

What just happened?

Without too much effort, we have a fully functional web page. If you followed the previous section, your web page should look something like the following screenshot:

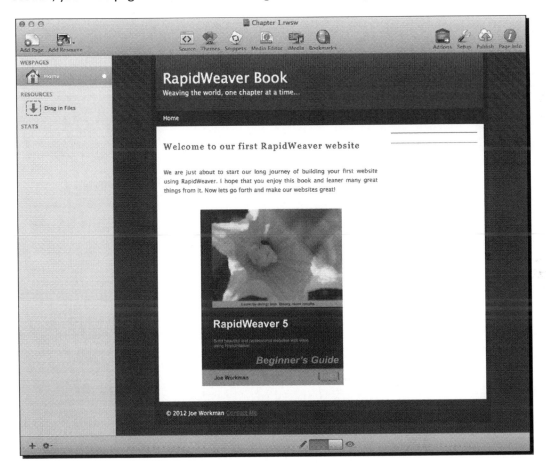

RapidWeaver has automatically taken care of a lot of tasks for us in the background. A full-blown website theme was used to create the look and feel of our website with headers, footers, backgrounds, sidebars, and so on. It built our menu structure (even though it's just a single page for now). It transformed our formatted text and images into HTML for us automatically!

Now if you wanted to preview your website in an actual web browser, you can click on the **gear** button on the bottom left-hand corner of the RapidWeaver window. In the **Preview** menu, you should see all registered web browsers on your system. Simply select the browser that you would like to open from the list, and RapidWeaver will open the selected page in a new browser window.

 There could be a large number of browser applications listed when you go to preview your website in a browser. Many of these applications are not truly web browsers. I recommend that you stick with previewing your web pages in traditional web browsers such as Safari, Chrome, and Firefox. It is also important that you see how your website looks in different browsers. There are times when different web browsers will render your web pages differently than others.

Publishing our website

Our website, as of right now, only exists on our local machine inside the RapidWeaver application itself. Now we are going to take the next step and actually publish our website on the Internet for the world to see! But in order to do this, we need to make sure that we have a web host first.

Selecting a web host

Arguably, one of the most crucial decisions you will make for your website is selecting your web host. With so many hosting businesses out there how can you ensure you choose one of the more reputable ones? Here are a few pointers that should help steer you in the right direction:

◆ Start small at first. Chances are you won't need a dedicated web server for your needs. I have been paying for a shared web server for over eight years. This means that my website runs on the same server as many other people's.

◆ Make sure that the hosting company supports PHP. I recommend that your hosting company support a minimum version of PHP 5.3.

- Do you need to get an e-mail from your domain? Most hosting companies provide the ability to provide e-mail for your domain.

- Make sure that your host supports FTP and/or SFTP for uploading files. Pretty much every host in the world should support this, but you should verify.

- Make sure that your host has enough space for you to grow. Websites don't take up very much space, but if you want to stream your own video, those gigabytes start adding up quick! There are tons of hosts that now offer unlimited space as well. However, 99 percent of the time you will not need that much space, especially if you use media streaming services such as Cloudflare, Vimeo, or YouTube.

- Hosting companies commonly have bandwidth limits in order to cap the amount of data that users download when they visit your site. However, many hosting companies also offer unlimited bandwidth as well. This will be very important if you plan on hosting your own images and video. As mentioned previously, you can use media streaming services such as Cloudflare, Vimeo, or YouTube to offset a majority of your bandwidth.

- Hosting companies can use both Windows or Linux servers to host your website. I am a fan of Linux web servers and have found them to be a little more reliable.

- Last and definitely not least, you want to research their customer service. I recommend finding recommendations from those that you trust and find out what company they are using.

Here is a list of some reputable hosting companies that I know are widely used within the RapidWeaver community:

- JavaBean Hosting (`http://www.javabeanhosting.com`)
- Little Oak (`http://www.littleoak.net`)
- Webfaction (`http://www.webfaction.com`)
- DreamHost (`http://dreamhost.com`)
- Site5 (`http://www.site5.com`)

Now I know you are going to ask, who do I host my websites with? I have used a combination of JavaBean Hosting and DreamHost, and could not be happier with either of them. They both offer great completive plans. I have worked with both of them to give all readers of this book a discount on any of their hosting plans! DreamHost is offering $25 off on any of their plans. JavaBean Hosting is offering the first month free, as well as free migration assistance! To capitalize on either of these offers, simply use the discount code **RWBOOK**.

Time for action – publishing our website

Now that you have selected your web hosting company and registered a domain name, let's go ahead and publish our website for the world to see! You will need the following information in order to proceed:

- ◆ **Server**: The name of the server that we will be publishing the website to. This is most likely going to be your domain name.
- ◆ **User Name**: The username that will be used to publish your website via FTP or SFTP.
- ◆ **Password**: The password that will be used to publish your website via FTP or SFTP.
- ◆ **Path**: The path to the folder where your website needs to be published to on your server.

You will have to obtain this information from your hosting company. Most of the time, this information is available in your hosting company's control panel. After you have your hosting company situated, you may need to review the **Web Address** settings that we configured in the last exercise inside **Site Setup**.

Once we have all of the required publishing credentials, let's go ahead and configure them into our RapidWeaver project:

1. Go to **File | Publishing Settings**.

2. Enter the credential information into the corresponding fields for FTP.

3. Click on the **Test Connection** button to verify that all of the data that you entered is working properly. Once everything is working ok, click on the **Save** button.

4. Now we can click on the **Publish** button on the right-hand side of the RapidWeaver toolbar in order to publish our website.

5. Once the publishing has completed, open a web browser and go to your website domain. You should have a fully functional website for the world to see.

What just happened?

We have a website! We went through and found a hosting company that will host our website. We then configured RapidWeaver with the credential information from the hosting company. We clicked on the **Publish** button, and RapidWeaver automatically generated all of the HTML, CSS, images, and all other files required, then uploaded them to our web server.

Summary

Boy, was that a fun ride? We went pretty far in this chapter. We started off by learning a little about RapidWeaver and how it's more than just another application. Then we went from zero to having a published website in a single chapter!

Specifically, we covered the following:

- RapidWeaver is more than just an application. It is a community, where we can learn from and teach each others to make better websites.

- The RapidWeaver platform allows amazing third-party developers to bring us themes, plugins, and stacks.

- There are two methods of obtaining and installing RapidWeaver: Mac App Store and `RealmacSoftware.com`.

- We learned how to create a new RapidWeaver project and do some initial setup.

- We learned how to make a new Styled Text web page and how to add content to it.

- We published our website on the Internet for the world to see.

So now that we have that quick win under our belt, we are going to review the other options and features of RapidWeaver that we quickly glanced over in this chapter.

2

Touring RapidWeaver

In the previous chapter, we had an awesome quick win by creating our very first website! I did not take a lot of time to explain many things. We made the adjustments that were needed and simply went on our way. So now we are going to step back a bit and take a tour of the RapidWeaver interface, preferences, and inspector windows. We are going to review every nook and cranny throughout the interface. This will serve as a great reference in the future for when you have questions on what a particular setting or button does throughout RapidWeaver.

In this chapter we will look at the following topics:

- ◆ Webpage list
- ◆ Preview mode versus Edit mode
- ◆ Page inspector
- ◆ Resources
- ◆ Snippets
- ◆ Site setup
- ◆ Theme browser
- ◆ Publishing your site
- ◆ Preferences
- ◆ Customizing the toolbar

If you are already an experienced RapidWeaver user, you may feel that you want to skip this chapter. However, I recommend that you at least skim through to see if you pick up any nuggets of information that you may not be aware of. I have to say that even I (as shocking as this may sound) learned a few little things while writing this chapter. Go ahead, gasp! I know that I just shattered your thoughts that I was the all-knowing man behind the curtain. If you are building the sample file along with us, you will want to make sure that you make the same edits to your project file. This will ensure that your project file stays in sync as we make further edits in future chapters.

Webpage list

A list of all your web pages that have been added into your RapidWeaver project is listed at the top of the left-hand pane of the window. This list of web pages serves more purpose than to simply illustrate what is a part of your website, and also provides a visual structure to your site navigation.

Adding a new page

Just like the old saying "*there are many ways to skin a cat*", there are also many ways to add pages to your project as follows:

- The **Add Page** button on the toolbar
- The **File | Add Page** menu
- The **+** button at the bottom left-hand corner of the RapidWeaver window
- Right-click on any of the empty spaces in the left pane, and select **Add Page** in the contextual menu
- And obviously (my favorite way) via the keyboard shortcut *Command + N*

Page order and site navigation

RapidWeaver dynamically generates the navigation menu for your site based on the order and structure of the web pages in the left pane. You can easily change the order of these pages using drag-and-drop option. Just click-and-drag a page to the location where you would like it to be, and drop it into place. If you preview your site again, you will notice that the navigation menu will reflect the changes that you just made.

To rename the page shown in the navigation menu, change the **Page Title** to something other than **Untitled Page**. You can accomplish this by double-clicking on the page in the left-hand list. It's a best practice to only use alphanumeric characters in your page titles.

To create a sub-menu, simply drag-and-drop the desired page on top of a page that you would like it to be a parent to. Once you have done that, you will see a disclosure triangle that appears to show that there are sub-pages within. You will also see that all sub-pages are indented as well.

> The order and structure of this page list does not necessarily correspond to the folder structure of the website when it is published. This data is controlled through the page and folder settings in **Page Inspector**. We will be reviewing this shortly.

Time for action – adding some pages to our navigation

Let's go ahead and add a few new pages into our project, and see how it affects the navigation of our site. Add whatever page styles you like; they will not be used in future chapters. This exercise is to help you better understand how the pages can affect the RapidWeaver menu system.

1. Add a couple of new pages to your RapidWeaver project.

2. Double-click on the pages and rename them to whatever you like.

3. Reorganize the pages that you just added by dragging and dropping them around. Make sure that you add pages to the top-level menu as well as sub-menu pages.

What just happened?

We have now added a hierarchical menu system to our website. Depending on how much you played around, you may have discovered that you can go a couple of layers deep with the menu system. However, this is a very theme specific feature. There are some themes that may only support a two-level structure. There are also others that can go even more levels deep. But let's stay on course here; we will be reviewing themes later on.

 You can drag-and-drop web pages between different RapidWeaver projects. This is a great time saver if you want to duplicate pages to a different project file. Another useful purpose for this is to keep a RapidWeaver project file that solely contains template files that help you get started on other projects. Simply drag the template web page into your new project and you are ready to go.

Preview mode versus Edit mode

RapidWeaver uses two modes to create your site: **Edit** and **Preview**. To edit and preview a page, you will first need to select the desired page within the **Page List** in the left -hand side pane. Just as we learned in *Chapter 1, Getting Started*, you can toggle between the Edit and Preview modes by clicking the **Edit/Preview** switch located below the main content area.

 If you are a geek like me, you will find the keyboard shortcut *Command + R* very useful for switching between the Edit and Preview modes.

View Source

Novice users beware; I'm about to get geeky! There is a third mode that is not apparently out of the box. You have the ability to view the HTML code that RapidWeaver will output through the **View Source** mode. In order to enter into this mode, you will need to select **View | View Source** from the menu. The top part of the view shows the HTML code as rendered by RapidWeaver. Any errors or warnings are displayed in the lower portion of the screen for your inspection and review. Line numbers are also shown down the left-hand side of the page. This can be useful to help you debug any errors that may appear in the console at the bottom.

The source code shown here is not editable. You only have a read-only view of the code. Although, you do have the ability to copy the HTML code in case you would like to use it for other tasks or validation. If you want to edit the source code, you will need to export your site locally to your computer. You can then edit the source code to your heart's content prior to uploading it to your server. However, I don't recommend this as a best practice. It can lead to unmaintainable sites, as it is easy to forget the edits that you have made, the next time you want to publish your website.

Page Inspector

You can open the **Page Inspector** window via the **Page Info** button on the toolbar. The **Page Inspector** window is organized into the following five sections:

- ◆ **General**: This section has edit page attributes such as title, folder name, filename, and more
- ◆ **Sidebar**: This section allows to edit sidebar's title and content
- ◆ **Header**: This section allows you to access more advanced features of your web page for SEO and custom coding
- ◆ **Styles**: This section customizes the look and feel of your page
- ◆ **Page**: Any page (plugin) options are shown in this tab

When the settings in **Page Inspector** have changed, only the selected page will be affected. However, RapidWeaver does give you the ability to apply a set of settings to all pages throughout your project. This feature will be covered more in the chapter on Advanced Weaving. You may also define templates, which preset many of these options and in the **Site Setup** for pages you subsequently add to your project.

 You can easily access the **Page Inspector** window with the keyboard shortcut *Command + Option + I*. This window is also resizable. I tend to make the window wider so that it is easier to read when there are a large number of settings.

General settings

When you first open **Page Inspector**, you are brought to the **General** tab view:

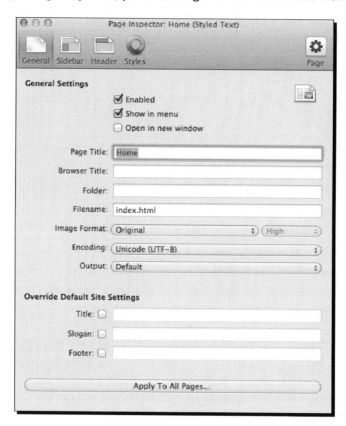

Within this tab, you can edit the selected page's file and folder names, display options (including whether or not to show the page in the navigation menu), image format, page output, title, slogan, and copyright information. You may also specify encoding and set output options. Here is a detailed explanation of each of the **General Settings** options:

Enabled	This option defines whether the page will get published or exported as a part of your website. By not selecting this option, RapidWeaver will essentially treat this file as a draft and it will not get published or exported.
Show in menu	This option defines whether the page will appear as a part of the page navigation.
Open in new Window	If you select this option, when the page is clicked in the menu, the web page will open in a new browser window. It is generally best practice to not use this option.

Page Title	This is the same as if you were to double-click on the page in the Page List. This title is used as the display name for the page in the navigation menu within your site.
Browser Title	By default, RapidWeaver will place **Page Tile** inside the browser title when you publish your site. If you would like to override this behavior, you can define your own custom **Browser Title** here (for example, Joe Workman – Blog instead of Blog). It is best practice to fill in this field for **Search Engine Optimization (SEO)** purposes. Make sure that you review the chapter on SEO for more details.
Folder	This setting allows you to define the hierarchy structure of your website in terms of the URL. Most of the time, you do not want all of your web pages on the same structural level in your site. This is so that you can have URLs such as `http://joeworkman.net/RapidWeaver/stacks`. In this instance the **Folder** setting would be set to `/RapidWeaver/stacks`. If you want your web page to reside in the root directory (for example, `http://joeworkman.net/my_page.html`), set the page to simply `/` (a forward slash).
Filename	This option sets the filename and extension for the selected page, such as `photos.html` or `downloads.php`. The site home page should always be `index.html` (or a variant such as `index.php`). While you can change the name here, if you are properly using the **Folder** setting, you can name all of your pages `index.html` or `index.php`, and your URLs will look much cleaner.
Image Format	When you add images into a **Styled Text** area, RapidWeaver will convert them into the format specified here: `Original`, `JPEG`, or `PNG`. Specifying `Original` will leave the images in their original format, untouched and unchanged. If you wish to use transparent images anywhere on your site, you should leave this option set to `PNG` as images will otherwise lose their transparency on conversion.
Encoding	Choose how you want the browser to interpret your code. Choose between Western (ISO Latin 1), Unicode (UTF-8), and Japanese (Shift-JS). RapidWeaver defaults to Unicode (UTF-8). The default setting will suit a majority of user's needs. You should leave this setting to its default values unless you have a good reason to do otherwise.
Output	RapidWeaver has the ability to tidy the code that it produces. This can possibly make your code more readable and strictly locks things down for standards compliance. Use this setting with caution, as it is known to cause issues with certain add-ons. I almost always use the `Default` option.
Title	We had already configured a **Site Title** in our sample RapidWeaver project inside the **Site Setup**. This option allows you to override that setting for the selected page.

Slogan	The **Site Setup** contains a setting for a site-wide slogan. This option allows you to override that setting for the selected page.
Footer	The **Site Setup** contains a setting for a site-wide footer. This option allows you to override that setting for the selected page.
Apply to All Pages	This option allows you to apply settings from the current page to all other pages contained within your project. This feature will be looked at in more depth in *Chapter 11, Advanced Weaving*

 You should not use spaces in the **Folder** or **Filename** settings. While having spaces in filenames is a common practice on the desktop, you should avoid spaces in filenames on the Web. Any web page, image, or other file you place on your website must always have an extension. If you use spaces, your website may not work properly in some browsers, and your site will look less professional.

Folders and Filenames

I want to stress the importance of the **Folder** and **Filename** settings that we just reviewed. These settings will greatly help your visitor's experience navigating through your website. Which of the following URLs looks more professional?

◆ `http://rapidweaverbook.com/rapidweaver%20rocks/photos.html`

◆ `http://rapidweaverbook.com/rapidweaver-rocks/`

I hope that you chose the second one. The URL in the second example was accomplished through properly setting the **Folder** and **Filename**. The following rules were used in order to achieve this better URL format:

◆ The folder was set to `rapidweaver-rocks`. We used all lowercase letters. We used a hyphen instead of a space.

◆ The filename was set to `index.html`.

◆ With the **Enable cruftless links** setting enabled, all URLs will be stripped of `index.html`. There will be more information on this setting later on in this chapter.

The filenames `index.html` and `index.php` are special. When you use these names, your web server will automatically display their contents if no page name is defined within the URL in the browser. This is why the pretty URL defined above works even though we do not specify a filename in the URL.

If by chance you have both an `index.html` and `index.php` file in the same directory, the server will nearly always display the `index.html` file. The only way to access `index.php` then is to explicitly type the filename into the URL or delete `index.html` from your server. You can accomplish this through an external FTP application or terminal access.

 The aforementioned rule applies 99.5 percent of the time. However, your hosting company may have the default web page name set to something other than `index.html`. Some hosting companies use `default.html` as the standard web page name.

Time for action – setting up proper folder and filenames

Let's take what we just learned about folders and filenames, and apply it to the RapidWeaver project. You can continue to use the same project file that we started in the previous chapter. If you did not complete that exercise, you can start a new project, and follow the ensuing steps:

1. Add a new **Blog** style page to our project file.

2. Open up the **Page Info** pane for the newly added **Blog** page.

3. Make the following changes to the settings:
   - **Page Title**: `Blog`
   - **Folder**: `/blog`
   - **Filename**: `index.php`

4. Go into the **Advanced** tab inside **Site Setup**, and make sure that **Enable Cruftless Links** is enabled.

5. Publish your project.

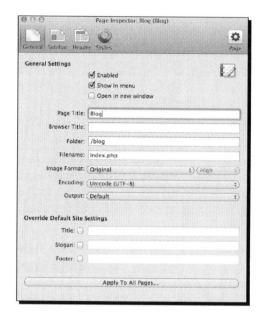

What just happened?

You will now notice that if you navigate to the newly created blog page, we have a nicely formatted URL. If you had enabled cruftless links, you should also notice that the page name is not displayed in the browser. You are on your way to having a professional looking site. This blog page does not have any content yet, but we will get to that later in this book. For now, enjoy your beautiful URLs!

Have a go hero: fixing URLs for other pages

Earlier in this chapter we added a few pages into our website. If you are feeling brave, go ahead and fix these pages so that they also have pretty URLs. You can also take the time to play around with the other settings that we recently reviewed, to see how they affect the look and feel of your web pages. May I suggest the **Browser Title** and overriding the **Title** settings. Have fun!

Sidebar

A common element across most websites is a sidebar. In the sidebar, you may want to have advertisements, your contact information, or maybe even a search tool. You can place almost anything into the sidebar to enhance the content of your web page. The content for the sidebar is defined in the **Sidebar** pane of **Page Inspector**.

The **Sidebar** pane consists of two areas, the **Sidebar Title** and the **Sidebar Content** box. However, the title field is completely optional. At the bottom right-hand corner, you can define whether the content area will be Styled Text or HTML. When in Styled mode, even though the content area has no formatting toolbar, you can use the **Format** menu to format your text the way you see fit. There are also convenient buttons on the bottom left-hand corner, to easily add links to your text.

 You can use HTML in the **Sidebar Title** field in order to spice things up.

Time for action – creating a sidebar

Let,s take our newly found knowledge and add a sidebar to the home page of our sample project, with the following steps:

1. Open up the **Sidebar** pane in the **Page Inspector** window for our home page.
2. Type a **Title** into the **Sidebar Title** field.
3. Add some content into the sidebar. Remember that you can drag-and-drop images just like we did for the web page content in *Chapter 1, Getting Started*. However, you will need to ensure that the images are properly sized down before you add them to your sidebar.

4. Preview the home page.

What just happened?

As you should have seen, we created a sidebar. However, that sidebar only exists on our home page. What about the rest of the pages? We could go in and add a different (or the same) sidebar to each and every web page, but who wants to do that? We are (well at least I am) lazy. So who wants to be a hero and add the same sidebar to the rest of the pages?

Have a go hero: applying sidebar to all pages

I had briefly mentioned the **Apply to all pages** feature earlier in this chapter. Let's go ahead and apply the sidebar that we just created on our home page to the remaining pages in our site.

Ensure that you only have the sidebar settings checked before you apply the change. This will make sure that only the sidebar items will be changed. When you are done, we should have the same sidebar on every single page.

Header

The **Header** tab of the **Page Inspector** window contains some of the more advanced options for configuring your page for Search Engine Optimization (SEO), custom code imports, and more.

The following is a detailed explanation of the configurations that can be done inside the **Header** section of **Page Inspector**:

Meta Tags	We will be reviewing meta tags in more depth in *Chapter 10, Search Engine Optimization*. Essentially, these are key/value pairs that assist search engines in properly indexing and categorizing your website. If you want your website to be found by searches on Google, Bing, or any other search engine, you will want to make sure you have these configured.
Expires In	This setting is used in conjunction with each meta tag defined. It tells the search engine when it can delete expired documents and web pages from its database (if ever).
Credit RapidWeaver	We all want to give RapidWeaver some love! If this option is selected, RapidWeaver will add the `Generator` meta tag to the head section of your site. It lets browsers and visitors know that your site was made with RapidWeaver.
Note	The Credit RapidWeaver option does not add a visible credit or RapidWeaver badge to the site. It merely adds tags that are only visible in the source code, to your pages, identifying the site as being made with RapidWeaver. However, this setting does not prevent third-party developers from adding comments to the page source code.
Header	You can add your own custom HTML header information here. All of the data input into this section will be inserted into the `<head>` tags on your web page. We will be reviewing a little more about this in *Chapter 11 , Advanced Weaving*.
CSS	RapidWeaver uses **Cascading Style Sheets (CSS)** to define how your website is styled. If you are familiar with CSS, you can add your own custom CSS into this area to override the look and feel of a page. The CSS entered here will be placed within the `<style>` tag inside your page's `<head>` tags. We will be reviewing a little more about customizing with CSS later on in the book.
JavaScript	Just like the **CSS** area, this allows you to add your own JavaScript to your web pages. The JavaScript entered here will be placed within the `<script>` tag inside your page's `<head>` tags.
Prefix	This is where you can place custom prefix code, typically PHP, before the page `DOCTYPE` declaration. You will probably want to stay away from this unless you know what you are doing.

Styles

The **Styles** pane is used to customize the look and feel of your theme. This includes site width, colors, fonts, sidebar position, and a lot more. The theme's designer builds these customizations into the theme. Each theme will have a different set of customizations. This entire topic of themes will be covered at length in the next chapter.

Page

This pane will display the settings for a given plugin that is used for the selected web page. The contents of this pane will differ with each plugin. The settings for various plugins will be reviewed throughout this book.

Resources

RapidWeaver 5 introduced **Resources** as a new and improved way of working with files used in our site. **Resources** allow us to add a file to our site and link to it from any page in our project file. **Resources** are uploaded to a central location (a `resources` folder at the root of your website) on our web server, which means that they are available to every page on our site. Therefore, we can easily access these files from multiple web pages. This not only saves us space on our web servers, but it also makes our websites faster! If an image is used across multiple web pages, then the web browser should cache that image and not re-download the same file more than once.

Resources UI

Adding a file into **Resources** could not be easier. Simply drag any file (JPG, ZIP, PDF, and so on) from the **Finder** onto the **Resources** drop area in the left-hand sidebar. You could also use the **Add Resource** button in the toolbar.

If you add a file into your RapidWeaver project resources, it will not be copied into the project. The file is only referenced from **Finder**. It's a good idea to set up a permanent directory in **Finder**, where all your project resources will reside. If you decide to relocate your resources folder on your computer, you may need to relink the resources with the corresponding files again.

If we select the file that was added to the sidebar, there are some useful things that we can do with it:

- We can rename the file in the field provided. This will not affect the name of the file in **Finder**. It will only affect the name of the file once it's been published to the server.

- The first button below the resource preview will allow us to relink the resource to a file in **Finder**. So if you were to relocate the file in the **Finder**, you could easily re-establish the link without having to add the resource back again.

- The clipboard button will conveniently copy the URL to the published file from the clipboard. Of course, in order for the file to be accessible, we would need to publish it first.

If you are adding a large amount of resources into your RapidWeaver project, you can organize your resources into folders. To add a folder, click and hold the **Add Resource** button in the toolbar, and then select the **Add Folder** option from the drop-down menu. You can then organize your resource files simply by dragging and dropping them into folders.

Time for action – adding a resource

Now that we know what resources are, let's go ahead and add a file to a resource that can be downloaded from a link on our website:

1. Drag a file from **Finder** into the **Resources** area in the RapidWeaver sidebar.

2. Select the newly added resource in the sidebar that we added in the previous step.

3. Ensure that your filename does not have any spaces in it. Change the name if it does.

4. Go back to our home page, or wherever you would like to link your file to.

5. Add some text at the end of the content in the **Styled Text** area; **Download File** will do the trick.

6. Select the **Add Link** button at the bottom right-hand corner of the **Styled Text** area (a little chain link with a plus).

7. The RapidWeaver link window will appear. There is a **Resource** view inside the drop-down menu that says **URL** by default. Navigate inside the drop-down menu, and locate the resource that we just added.

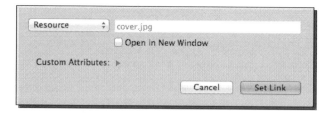

8. Click on the **Set Link** button when done.

9. Now let's preview our web page.

What just happened?

By adding a file into the RapidWeaver resources, we were able to add a download link to that file on our web page. Once the page is published, RapidWeaver will place the file in a centralized resources directory so that it can be accessed by multiple pages at the same time.

The resource macro

The `resource` macro is designed to allow advanced users to link to resources directly within HTML and CSS code. Wherever this macro is used on a web page, RapidWeaver will automatically replace it with the actual path to the resource file.

The syntax for the macro is pretty straightforward. You simply need to replace the name `my-image.png` with the name of the resource that you want to link to.

```
%resource(my-image.png)%
```

If the resource resides in a folder within the **Resources** sidebar area, add that to the path also.

```
%resource(folder/my-image.jpg)%
```

The following are a couple of code examples on how the macro is commonly used with HTML and CSS.

◆ HTML:

```
<img src="%resource(my-image.png)%" alt="My image" />
```

◆ CSS:

```
#banner { background-image: url(%resource(my-image.jpg)%); }
```

 The `resource` Macro will only function properly if it is used inside the actual HTML file that will be published. RapidWeaver will not scan every CSS or JavaScript file you may include with your project. If you use the macro in external files, it will not work.

Have a go hero: become a code warrior

Are you feeling like a code warrior? Go ahead and try to replicate the same download link that we created in our last activity, but using the `resource` macro. Here is a clue as to the HTML code that you would use:

```
<a href="myfile.zip" target="blank">Download File</a>
```

After you have accomplished that, go ahead and try to add an image onto a web page using the `resource` macro. You will need to add an image into the resources area first. The following is a sample HTML code that will give you a jump-start:

```
<img src="my-image.png" alt="My Image"/>
```

Snippets

Snippets are reusable code fragments that you may use regularly, or simply wish to store for future use. RapidWeaver allows us to create and store our code snippets conveniently. We can then easily search our snippets so that we can pull them out of our arsenal, whenever we need them. The easiest way to access the **Snippets** library is to use the **Snippets** icon on the toolbar.

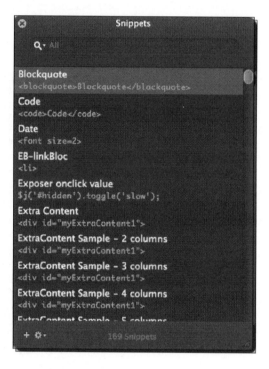

To create a new snippet, press the plus (**+**) button located at the bottom left-hand corner of the **Snippets** window. Simply give it a title, paste or type in your code, and click on **Save**.

You can quickly locate your snippets using the built-in search function. Once you locate the snippet you want to use, drag it into any styled or HTML text area on your web page.

Snippets are stored as single files in **Finder**. This makes sharing them with others a piece of cake. Select the desired snippet in the **Snippets** window and click on the gear button at the bottom left-hand corner. Then select **Reveal in Finder…**. Once you have located the file in **Finder**, you can easily e-mail that snippet file to someone else.

It is common for themes, plugins, and stacks to ship with snippets that can be used in conjunction with them. If you have received a snippet from a third-party developer or from a friend, they are very easy to install. Simply double-click on the `.rwsnippet` file, and RapidWeaver will take care of installing it for you.

Time for action – creating a snippet

Let's go ahead and create a very simple snippet that will place some Lorem Ipsum text on our page.

 If you are not familiar with the concept of Lorem Ipsum, it is simply dummy text. Lorem Ipsum has been the industry's standard dummy text ever since the 1500s. For more geeky info and coolness about Lorem Ipsum, check out `http://lipsum.com`.

We will use Lorem Ipsum to place filler text on our web pages for them to look like they have more content:

1. Obtain the sample Loerm Ipsum text from `http://lipsum.com`, or from this book's sample website at `http://rapidweaver.com/lorem.txt`.

2. Open the **Snippets** window and click on the plus (**+**) button at the bottom to create a new snippet.

3. Enter in the title of **Lorem Ipsum**.

4. Paste in the sample Lorem Ipsum text and click on the **Save** button.

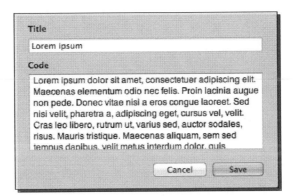

5. Go to a web page of your choice. Now drag-and-drop the Lorem Ipsum snippet that we just created, onto the **Styled Text** area.

6. Preview your web page.

What just happened?

We just created a snippet that is stored by RapidWeaver, so that we can use it in the future on any web page that we want. We no longer have to go searching for the same text to fill in our new web pages. We simply need to look up this snippet and drag it onto our page. It could not be easier.

Have a go hero: continue being a code warrior

The snippets exercise that we just completed is very useful for adding in filler text. However, there are other snippets that get installed out-of-the-box that insert HTML code for you. Go ahead and insert these code snippets so that you can see them in action. The more that you see code, the more you will understand it.

Theme browser

Selecting which theme you want to use for your RapidWeaver project is simple. When you click on the **Themes** button on the toolbar you will see the **Theme Browser** roll up from the bottom of the window. You can scroll through the theme thumbnails or use the supplied search bar to help you locate your desired theme. Once you have chosen a theme, just click on its thumbnail. The selected theme will be applied to all the pages in your site.

When you right-click on a theme in **Theme Browser**, a contextual menu will allow you to duplicate a theme or reveal that theme in **Finder** (third-party theme's only). We will take a more in-depth look at themes in the next chapter dedicated to themes.

Site Setup

You can open the **Site Setup** via the **Setup** button on the toolbar. **Site Setup** is organized into the following three sections:

- ◆ **General**: Page attributes that will be used as the default across all web pages in the project
- ◆ **Advanced**: Advanced linking and site structural settings
- ◆ **Templates**: Define templates for all new web pages created within the project

General settings

The **General** settings tab contains settings for the page attributes that will be used as the default values across all of your web pages. Many of these values can be overridden inside the **Page Inspector** window, on each individual page.

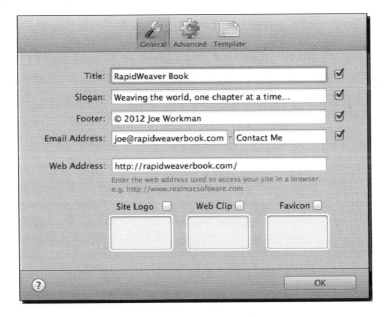

The following is a detailed explanation of each of the **General** settings:

Title	This is the site title that will be applied to all of your pages. The default is set to `My Website`. If you uncheck the box at the end, no site title will be used. It is strongly recommended to use a site title. For more information, refer to *Chapter 10* , *Search Engine Optimization*.
Slogan	This is the site slogan that will be applied to all of your pages. The default is set to `Changing the world, one site at a time`.... If you uncheck the box at the end, no site slogan will be used.
Footer	This is a good place for a copyright notice or maybe links to other web pages (requires HTML). It is placed at the bottom of the page.
Tip	HTML can be used in the title, slogan, and footer settings if you need more control over the content within them.
Email Address	This is a link that people can click in order to send you an e-mail. This is inserted into the **Footer** area of the page. There is a setting in the **Advanced** tab that will allow you to protect your e-mail from Spam-Bots.
Web Address	This is the full website address of your website. This is required to set up RSS feeds and other settings throughout RapidWeaver. For example: `http://rapidweaverbook.com` (be sure to start it with `http://` or `https://`).
Site Logo	Drag-and-drop a site-wide logo to apply to all of your web pages. The size requirements of the logo image will vary from theme to theme. You will need to make sure that you resize the image prior to adding it into RapidWeaver. The image used for the logo must be a valid web image format (JPG, PNG, or GIF) saved at 72DPI.
Web Clip	When a user bookmarks your site on a mobile device such as an iPhone, a WebClip icon is used. Web Clip icons must be a 57 x 57 pixel PNG image. You will need to make sure that the image is properly sized and formatted before you drag it into RapidWeaver.
Favicon	A Favicon is displayed next to your site's URL in most modern browsers. Favicons must be formatted as an ICO file and are normally 16 x 16 pixels. You will need to make sure that the image is properly sized and formatted before you drag it into RapidWeaver. There are many good favicon generators out there that will create the properly formatted image for you. Check out `http://www.favicongenerator.com`.

Advanced

The **Advanced** settings tab contains settings for how RapidWeaver will generate some of the code for each web page.

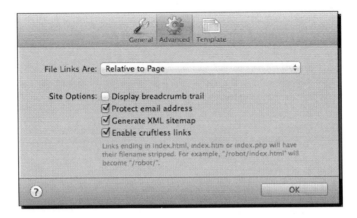

The following is a detailed explanation of each of the advanced settings:

File Links Are	This setting allows you to customize how RapidWeaver codes the links to your site resources and theme files. This does not affect the display of your website at all.
	Relative to Page: A relative path points to the location of the file you want to link to in relation to the page being viewed, all within your server space. If the file you're linking to is in the same directory as the page being viewed, then the relative path is simply the page name. However, if the file you are linking to is two directories up and down another directory, the path would look something like this: `../../assets/my-file.zip`.
	Relative to DOCROOT: Think of this setting as being the absolute path to a file. An absolute path is the full path to a file from the root directory of your website. An absolute path would look something like this: `/RapidWeaver/index.html`.
	Relative to Web Address: If you use this setting, ensure that your website address is properly configured in the General tab. RapidWeaver will rely on this web address configured to determine the full URL path to the files.
Display breadcrumb trail	This will display a breadcrumb trail to allow visitors to figure out where in the site structure they are. The location of the breadcrumb trail will vary from theme to theme.

Protect email address	When the **Email Address** field from the **General** tab is configured, this setting will ensure that the e-mail address is protected from Spam-Bots. If you turn this setting off, prepare to get spammed. Don't say that I did not warn you!
Generate XML sitemap	By enabling this option, RapidWeaver will generate an XML Sitemap file. This file is solely used for SEO. We will be reviewing sitemap files in more depth in the chapter on SEO.
Enable cruftless links	By default RapidWeaver will build links to your web pages using the full URL, including the name of the web page. However, with this setting turned on, URL links to an index page (`index.html` or `index.php`), the page name will not be added to the URL.

  ◆ **With cruftless:** `http://joeworkman.net/`
  ◆ **Without cruftless:** `http://joeworkman.net/index.html`

What is a Spam Bot?

Spam Bots are pieces of malicious software that scour the Internet for unprotected e-mail addresses to add to spam e-mail lists.

I think that websites that use cruftless links look more professional. It's a small detail that really makes a big difference.

Templates

The **Template** tab allows you to pre-configure settings for any pages you add in the future. Changes made here will not affect current pages at all. The settings found here are exactly like those in **Page Inspector**. However, the **Extension** setting defines what file extension new pages are given.

You may want to visit the **Template** settings before adding any pages to your project, if you know that there are aspects that will stay on the same such as meta tags and sidebar.

Publishing your website

While using RapidWeaver, we are going to be doing a lot of publishing. So let's take some time to review the ins and outs of getting your website online.

What's going to be published?

Whenever the content of a web page changes, a blue status indicator will show up next to that page in the sidebar. This blue indicator means that something about that page has changed since the website was last published. Most of the time this means that you have changed the content of the web page. However, it could also mean that the page settings (such as title, folder, or filename) have changed.

Depending on which page setting has changed, RapidWeaver will mark every page in your project as changed. The reason for this is so that any links or references to that page throughout the project will also be updated as follows:

[It should be noted that this exact behavior should be applied to both web pages and resources.]

Overriding change indicators

RapidWeaver does an awesome job at keeping track of what has changed throughout your project, and making sure that your website is properly updated when you publish. However, RapidWeaver does not know the structure of your website as well as you do. Therefore, RapidWeaver can sometimes mark pages to be published when you are certain that publishing that file again is not required.

RapidWeaver has built-in mechanisms to allow you to override its default behavior and mark a page as unchanged. There may even be times when you need to mark a page as changed when RapidWeaver did not know that it changed. This can be common in some third-party plugins that may not alert RapidWeaver that a change has taken place. There are several methods for overriding change indicators as follows:

- Right-click on a web page or resource in the sidebar, and you will see an option **Mark as Changed** or **Mark as Unchanged** depending on the state of the selected page

- There is a **Mark All Pages & Resources** option in the **File** menu, which lets you mark all pages and resources as **Changed**

- If you hold down the *Option* key while selecting the **File** menu, you will notice that there is a new option **Mark All Pages & Resources**, which lets you mark all pages and resources as **Unchanged**

Publishing your entire site

If you want to republish every file for your entire website again, there is a convenient option in the **File** menu—**Re-Publish All Files**. This will republish all web pages, resources, and theme files to your web server.

If a theme has been updated since you last published your site, it would be a good idea to always republish all files. This will ensure that all of the new theme files and webpages get properly updated. Republishing all files can potentially be a time-consuming task. This depends on the number of files in your project as well as your Internet connection speed.

If you want to export your entire site to a local directory, you can use the **Export Site** command from the **File** menu. This is useful if you want to test your website locally on your machine, or if you want to use an external FTP program to upload the site to your server.

Publishing a single web page

If you just want to publish a single web page or resource, you can right-click on the item in the sidebar, and select the **Publish** option.

 When you publish a web page or resource using this method, it will not affect the change status. The change status will only be affected when you republish all files or perform a normal publish command.

If you wanted to export a single web page or resource, you can right-click on the item in the sidebar and select the **Export** option. This is useful if you have already exported your entire site and want to update a single change that was made to the local export directory.

Publishing via FTP

RapidWeaver gives us the ability to publish our websites using a built-in one-way FTP client. In order to publish, you will need to enter in your credentials from your hosting company inside the **Publishing Settings**. You can access these settings by clicking on **Publishing Settings** in the **File** menu.

You will need to configure the following settings in order to properly publish your website:

Server	The name or IP address of your web server. This is often times your domain name without the `http://` (for example, `mysite.com`).
User Name	The username that will be used to log into your server.
Password	The password that will be used to log into your server.
Path	This is the path to the directory where RapidWeaver will place your website, when its published. This setting will definitely vary the most between hosting companies and site setups. Here are a list of commonly used paths with some hosting companies: `/`, `/www/`, `/public_html/`, and `/yourdomain.com/`.

The settings may vary depending on your hosting company. So, verify with your hosting company what your settings should be.

 Your hosting company may require that you define a port number along with your server name. This is accomplished by appending a colon and the port number to your server name (for example, `mysite.com:2323`). You don't need to worry about this unless you are instructed to do so by your hosting company.

If you are uncertain about any of the aforementioned settings, you should contact your hosting provider before you attempt to publish your site.

Once you have entered in your FTP settings, you can click on the **Test Connection** button to verify that RapidWeaver can properly access your server. You can now safely click on the **Publish** button on the main toolbar to publish your website via FTP.

 The connection test will only verify the FTP credentials that were supplied. It does not verify the publish path setting. Therefore, if your website is not functioning properly after you publish, the publish path setting may be incorrect.

Advanced settings and SFTP

The **Advanced** tab in the **Publishing Settings** option allows you to enable and configure **Secure FTP (SFTP)** file transfers and other settings.

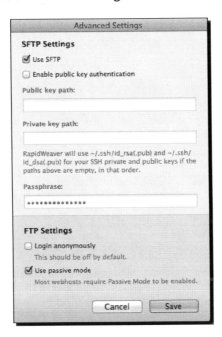

 SFTP is the more secure form of the FTP protocol. All data will be transferred over an encrypted channel for security.

The following is a detailed explanation of each of the advanced FTP settings:

Use passive mode	Deselect this option only if your web server requires active file transfer. Most FTP servers do use passive mode.
Login anonymously	While this is rarely used, selecting this option will tell RapidWeaver to attempt to log into your web server without a username or password.

Bookmarks

If you need to potentially add the same FTP connection with multiple RapidWeaver projects, FTP Bookmarks are a convenient way to save your favorite FTP destinations for quick access.

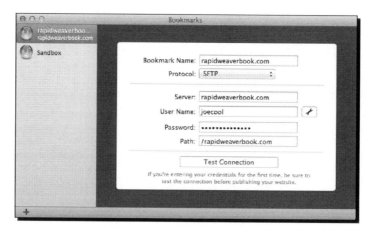

To add a new bookmark, click on the **Bookmarks** button in the toolbar, and click on the plus (**+**) button at the bottom left-hand corner. Then you simply fill in the credential information just as we would in the **Publishing Settings**. You can click on the **Test Connection** button to verify that your settings are correct.

When you create a new RapidWeaver project in the future, you can easily access the bookmarked connections directly from the **Publishing Settings** window. When you select a bookmark from the drop-down menu, the connection setting will be automatically populated for you. However, you will probably need to make a duplicate of the bookmark if the publishing path is different for your new project, which it most likely will be.

Time for action – publishing

Let's go ahead and apply all that we just learned about the publishing process.

1. Open **Publishing Settings** (*Command + K*).

2. Click on the **Bookmark** button on the right-hand side and select **Save current settings as Bookmark**.

3. Open the **Bookmarks** windows by clicking on the toolbar button, and verify that the bookmark was created.

4. Right-click on a couple of web pages and select **Mark as Changed**.

5. Now right-click on all of the pages that have change indicators and select **Mark as Unchanged**.

6. Go to the **File** menu and select **Re-Publish All Files**.

What just happened?

We now have saved our publishing settings as a bookmark so that we can easily reuse them in a different project if needed. We also saw how we can modify the change indicators through the contextual menus. And lastly we republished all of the files in our entire project to our web server.

Preferences

A majority of the settings throughout RapidWeaver are project-specific settings. However, there are a few global application preferences that can be set.

General

The **General** preferences tab contains some miscellaneous configurations to change some of RapidWeaver's behavior.

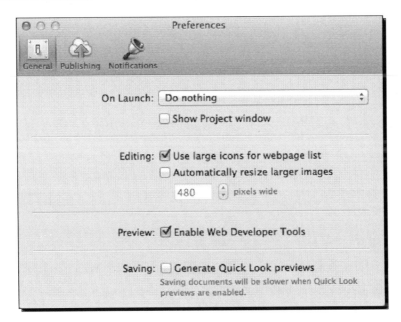

The following is a detailed explanation of each of the general preferences:

On Launch	Shows the RapidWeaver **Projects** window on launch. This could be useful to have quick access to your recently opened documents and easy access to create a new one.
Check For New Versions	When left checked, RapidWeaver will automatically check for updates to the software on launch. This option is not included in Mac App Store versions of RapidWeaver, as updates are taken care of by the App Store application.
Use Large Icons for web page list	Displays large or small icons in the web page list.
Automatically Resize Larger Images	This preference sets a default width for any new image placed into a project that is larger than the value entered. Uncheck this preference to insert large images at their original size.
Enable Web Developer Tools	Turn on the WebKit Developer Tools. We will review this feature more in-depth in *Chapter 11, Advanced Weaving*.
Save Quick Look Previews	RapidWeaver can generate Quick Look previews for each project when saving it. When enabling this option, it can increase the time required to save your document, and as such is turned off by default.

Publishing

The **Publishing** preferences tab contains some configurations that control how RapidWeaver will publish your website.

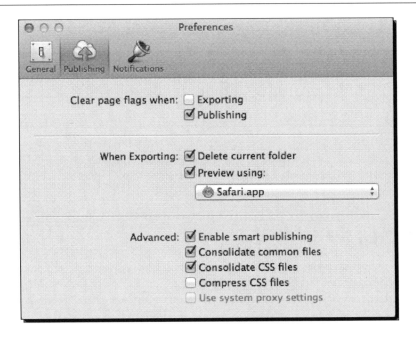

The following is a detailed explanation of each of the publishing preferences:

Clear page flags when	Mark a page as unchanged after publishing or exporting it.
When Exporting	When exporting your site to a local folder, RapidWeaver can delete the contents of the exported folder before exporting. After the export is completed, you can configure RapidWeaver to open the web page in the web browser of your choice.
Enable smart publishing	If you would like to turn off smart publishing, then RapidWeaver will republish all files every time you publish the website.
Consolidate common files	When checked, RapidWeaver will only upload one set of common theme files to your server, and reference them. Unchecking this option will upload a copy of the theme files for each page in your project. It is recommended that this setting remains checked.

Consolidate CSS files	This option will combine multiple CSS files from a theme into one larger CSS file. This minimizes the number of CSS files linked to on a page. You will have noticeable decreases in page download times with this option enabled.
Compress CSS files	This option will compress the CSS files that come with the theme. While this does reduce file size, it's been known that this option can potentially cause issues with CSS3 styles that are defined.

Customizing the toolbar

Like all OS X applications, you can customize the RapidWeaver toolbar to suit your needs. To customize the toolbar, simply right-click on the toolbar and choose **Customize Toolbar**. If you ever wish to simply remove an item from the toolbar, as with Mac OS X Apps you can do this by holding *command* and dragging the icon off the toolbar.

The following is a quick run-down of a few of the interesting toolbar icons that are hidden by default:

- **View Source**: This button will allow you to enter into the elusive **View Source** mode that we discussed earlier in this chapter. It essentially allows you to view the HTML that RapidWeaver would have published without actually exporting or publishing your site.

- ◆ **iMedia Browser**: This allows you to browse through your Media libraries such as iPhoto, Aperture, iTunes, and iMovie.
- ◆ **Publishing Settings**: This is a convenient thing to add to your toolbar if you can fit it. While you don't have to access it all the time, it is useful to have it easily accessible without having to go into the menu bar.

Summary

Is your brain full yet? We did an extremely thorough walkthrough of practically every nook and cranny of the RapidWeaver User Interface.

Specifically, we covered the following topics:

- ◆ Managing web pages in order to create and organize the navigation for your website.
- ◆ Best practices for naming our folders and filenames. No spaces!
- ◆ Adding a sidebar to our web pages.
- ◆ Adding an external file resource into our project.
- ◆ All the various preferences and settings that RapidWeaver has to offer.
- ◆ The ins and outs of getting our website published.

Now let's get out of the deep end and get into something a little more exciting—Themes!

3

Theming Your Site

Are you still with me? The last chapter was pretty exhausting but we covered pretty much every nook and cranny of the RapidWeaver interface. In this chapter, we are going to review all aspects of applying themes to your website.

We will specifically look at the following topics:

- ◆ Choosing a theme
- ◆ Managing themes in Theme Browser
- ◆ Common theme settings (every theme is different)
- ◆ Saving theme styles
- ◆ Master Style versus Page Style
- ◆ Customizing your theme with tools
- ◆ Customizing using CSS

As before, we are going to be building upon the same RapidWeaver project file that we have been working with throughout this book.

 If you are building the sample file along with us, you will want to make sure that you make the same edits to your project file. This will ensure that your project file stays in sync as we make further edits in future chapters.

Choosing your theme

Themes are website page templates that include the basic layout and architecture for each page. In not so fancy terms, it's the look and feel of your website. The theme will dictate the style and location of your navigation menu, sidebar, site title, content area, and more. In most cases, you will select just one theme and implement it throughout your website. However, RapidWeaver also allows you to apply themes on a page-by-page basis. RapidWeaver's theme-based workflow allows you to focus on the content in the Edit mode. RapidWeaver's theme engine is very powerful and really sets it apart from some other software. But in order to bring your site together, you will need to choose a theme.

One of the most common questions of every new RapidWeaver user is "*What theme should I get?*" I am sorry to tell you but there is no answer to that question! Themes are a very personal choice. You may find a theme that you love, and someone else may have a completely different opinion about it. Therefore it's important that you take your time and review the themes that are available out there. Also, keep in mind that the theme needs to fit into the context of your website. For example, if you are building a website on knitting, you probably don't want a theme that is ultra modern and flashy.

RapidWeaver currently ships with 47 built-in themes, six of which were developed by world renowned designers specifically for RapidWeaver 5. I recommend starting with these themes to see if you find one that suits your needs. However, as beautiful as these themes are, they have a limited set of customizations and styles. If you would prefer to have more flexibility in designing and customizing your website, you will want to look into purchasing a theme from a third-party developer.

There are over 200+ themes available to browse through on Realmac Software's Add-on section (`http://www.realmacsoftware.com/addons/RapidWeaver/themes`) that are developed by independent third-party developers. These themes tend to have a lot more flexibility and features outside of the built-in themes. These themes tend to range in price from $10 to $30. However, there are many free themes available from third-party developers as well. This is a steal if you have ever seen prices for website themes on platforms such as Wordpress.

As you are researching which theme you will use, keep in mind that themes can greatly vary based on the style settings used. I recommend that you head over to the developer's website in order to check out the theme variations available. A majority of the theme developers will have actual live previews of websites deployed using their themes. This allows you to see a theme's features in action, as well as get a sense of the "feel" of a website using the theme. It is very important to navigate around a theme so that you get a sense of how visitors will be navigating around your website.

Themes often ship with free sets of snippets that can unlock interesting features that are often hidden by default.

The following is a list of a few things that you should consider while searching for a theme for your website:

- Will the theme navigation fit with your vision of the website structure?
- Are the banners in the website header easy to customize?
- Does the theme have sufficient color customizations for your needs?
- Do you require a sidebar? Where can the sidebar be positioned?
- How does the theme behave on a mobile device? For more information on mobile compatibility, have a look at *Chapter 11*, *Advanced Weaving*.
- Does the theme support ExtraContent, which will allow you to add content into other areas besides the main content area?
- How does the theme style the page plugins, such as Blogs, Photo Albums, and others that you may want to use?
- What versions of the web browsers does the theme support? Many themes no longer have full support for the Internet Explorer 7. This may be a requirement for you.

Third-party theme developers

RapidWeaver ships with a lot of great looking website themes; however, there are many great third-party developers that are dedicated to consistently delivering new and exciting themes to the community. Third-party developers can be much more agile than Realmac Software. This means that they can release themes faster and keep up with some of the Web's latest trends.

The following is a list of some of the staple RapidWeaver theme developers:

♦ **Blueball Design** (`http://www.blueballdesign.com`): Blueball Design is the developer of the versatile Free Stack theme. Free Stack is essentially a blank canvas that allows you to design your own theme layout using the Stacks Plugin. This is great if you have a good design sense and want full control over the look and feel of your site.

♦ **Brandon Lee Theme Design** (`http://bltthemes.com`): As a relative newcomer to the RapidWeaver community, Brandon Lee has come out of the gates in full force with some beautifully striking themes that capture your visitors' attention right away. Brandon prides himself on his extreme attention to detail of typography, spacing, heights, margins, and others.

♦ **Elixir Graphics** (`http://elixirgraphics.com`): Elixir develops themes that are both extremely professional and clean. Elixir has been a staple in the RapidWeaver community for quite some time. My own website not only is an Elixir-themed, but uses their amazing stock icons throughout.

♦ **Henk Vrieselaar** (`http://www.henkvrieselaar.com`): Henk's themes are always unique and one of a kind! He is always on the bleeding edge of graphics and amazing visual effects. Henk fills his themes with so many different options in order to encourage users to get creative and take their site to a whole new level.

♦ **Kuler Solutions** (`http://kulersolutions.com`): The very first theme that I ever bought was a Kuler Solutions theme. Being around since 2004, Kuler Solutions is definitely a staple in the RapidWeaver community. They are known for providing loads of options and the freedom to customize easily.

♦ **Nick Cates Design** (`http://ncdthemes.com`): Nick Cates is the hipster theme developer. His themes are always modern, fresh, and very cool! To be honest here, I just don't think that I am cool enough for a Nick Cates theme! Hopefully you are.

♦ **NimbleHost** (`http://www.nimblehost.com`): NimbleHost was the first developer to create iPhone and mobile-specific themes for RapidWeaver, and they continue that tradition today. Every new theme release is both iPhone and iPad compatible, with stunning, flexible designs perfect for all manner of websites. Their focus is on creating uncompromising mobile-friendly designs that are easy to use.

♦ **Seydesign** (`http://seydesign.com`): Seydesign has been a pillar in the RapidWeaver community for a long time. They have contributed many great enhancements and standards to the community such as Extra Content (covered later in this chapter). Seydesign's themes empower end users with smart and dynamic features, allowing users to focus more on content and less on the theme itself.

♦   **ThemeFlood** (`http://www.themeflood.com`): ThemeFlood specializes in developing clean, contemporary, and minimalistic RapidWeaver themes. Their themes have proved to serve as a great base for both novice and expert RapidWeaver users to build a wide range of different websites.

Theme Browser

We were introduced to the Theme Browser earlier in this book. You can access it by clicking on the **Themes** button on the main toolbar. Then you can simply scroll through the theme thumbnails, and click on a theme in order to apply it to your website. All of the themes are listed in alphabetical order. Depending on how many themes you have installed, it can be tricky to find the theme that you are looking for.

In order to assist you with this, there are a few controls on the bottom toolbar which are explained as follows:

♦   On the left-hand side you will find a drop-down menu, which allows you to filter the themes between built-in and third-party themes. The built-in themes are further broken down into the version of RapidWeaver that they were released in; version 3.5 themes, version 3.6 themes, version 4 themes, and version 5 themes.

♦   At the center of the bottom toolbar is a convenient search field. This is definitely the quickest way to locate a theme as long as you know the theme name.

♦   Lastly, on the right-hand side, there is a slider that allows you to adjust the size of the theme thumbnails. It should be pretty obvious that the larger the thumbnail, the better you can see the preview image, and longer theme names can be viewed easier.

Duplicating themes

The Theme Browser is for more than just sorting and selecting your theme. Right-clicking on an individual theme within the browser reveals a contextual menu with a few useful options. One of the useful options is the ability to duplicate a theme.

You can duplicate a theme for that time when you may want to customize the theme to your liking (more on that later in this chapter). The benefit of doing that is keeping the original non-modified theme intact, just in case your customizations don't work out.

When you duplicate a theme, you will be presented with a simple dialog window where you can type in a custom name for the duplicated theme.

Deleting themes

If you would like to delete a theme from your collection, you can do so from the contextual menu that is displayed when you right-click on a theme within the Theme Browser. You will not be allowed to delete any of the preinstalled themes that come with RapidWeaver. You will only be allowed to delete third-party themes as well as themes that you made duplicate copies of.

 If you want to delete a theme, it's probably a good idea to have a backup of that theme in case you ever decide that you want to use it again in the future.

Time for action – using the Theme Browser

Let's apply what we just learned about the Theme Browser by searching, duplicating, and deleting a theme.

1.   Open your RapidWeaver project and open the Theme Browser.
2.   Search for the **Veerle** theme in the search box on the bottom toolbar.
3.   Right-click on the **Veerle** theme, and select **Duplicate**.
4.   In the dialog box that appears, type in a new name for the copied theme. Feel free to leave it as the default **Veerle Copy**.
5.   Locate the copy of the theme that we just created.
6.   Right-click on the duplicated theme and select **Delete**.

What just happened?

There are no tricks with what we just did. We searched for a theme that we were looking for. We created a duplicate copy of that theme. If you are one of the brave geeks out there, maybe you would take that duplicate copy and customize it to your liking (more on that later). After we duplicated the theme we deleted it.

Theme styles

If we go into **Page Inspector** and look at the **Styles** tab, we will see all the available style settings for the currently selected theme. Every theme ships with it's own default theme style; however, you can easily create your own alternative styles using different colors and other options. You can even save your styles for future use!

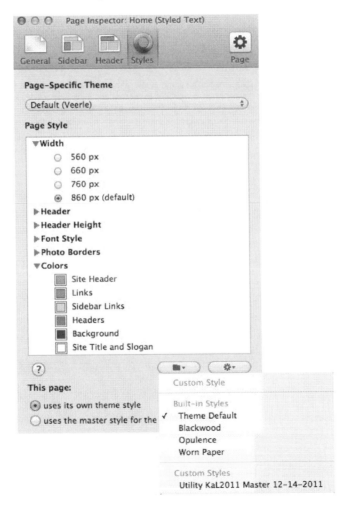

Many themes ship with their own set of preconfigured theme styles that you can install. You can access the available styles for a theme through the folder button at the bottom right-hand corner of the **Styles** pane. Simply select the style that you want to apply and test it out on the current page.

 Most themes are preconfigured with theme styles built-in. However, sometimes a developer will place additional styles inside a separate folder in your download. If this is the case, you will need to install the theme styles yourself. Luckily, installing them is a piece of cake. Simply double click the `.rwstyle` file and RapidWeaver will take care of installing it into the proper location for you.

Even though you have selected a preconfigured theme style, you can still make additional changes using the page style settings. These settings will vary greatly from theme to theme. As stated before, the themes that ship with RapidWeaver will only have a handful of style settings. Once you venture into the third-party themes, you will see that they have drastically more styles to tweak. The following is a basic set of features that most themes tend to have:

- **Site Width**: Most themes offer multiple, static widths for websites. However, some themes even have an option for variable width. This means that your website will expand as a user enlarges their web browser.

- **Sidebar Position**: It's common to have settings completely hide the sidebar or move its position to the left or right side. You may even see some themes place the sidebar in unexpected locations for an extra twist.

- **Header Image**: A lot of themes will come with a set of preconfigured header (banner) images that you can choose from. Later on in this chapter, we will look at how you can supply your own custom header images into the theme.

- **Color Options**: There are color options for almost everything: font color, page headers, links, background color, and much more.

Once you have all the styles configured just right, you can then configure the current settings to be your *Master Style* for the project. To do this, simply click on the gear button on the bottom-right corner of the **Styles** pane. You can then select the last option in the menu called **Set as Master Style for this Theme**. From then, all pages that you add to your project will have the master style applied to them by default. It would still be a good idea to save your style just in case you inadvertently change your Master Style settings. Read on for more details on saving your theme styles, later on in this chapter.

The Master Style only affects the current project. It will not be used as a global setting for a theme across all your projects.

Have a go hero – experimenting with styles

Now it's time for you to do some exploring. Go through several themes and change the styles. After you change some styles, preview the changes so that you can familiarize yourself with how style changes could affect the look and feel of your website.

Master style versus page style

There are two ways to apply styles to your RapidWeaver project. There are **master styles** that will affect the entire website, and there are **page specific styles** that are applied to just one page. By default, all styles settings will only affect the current page that you are on. On the bottom, left-hand corner of the **Styles** pane, you will see which style setting your current page is using:

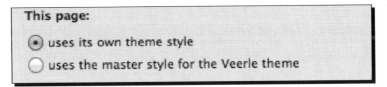

The **uses its own theme style** option means that all the style settings defined will only be applied to the current page. You will not see these settings getting carried over to any other pages throughout the site.

The **uses the master style for the Veerle theme** option means that all the style settings defined will be applied to all the pages that are configured to use the master style. Any changes that are made here will affect all other pages that use the master style.

 When you add a new page to your project it will look as if it is utilizing the master style. However, it will not be set to use the master style. You will need to make sure that the page is configured properly to use the master style. If you do not do this, then any modifications that you do make to the master style will not be reflected on this new page.

Time for action – setting the Master Style for our theme

Let's go ahead and apply the current style of our theme, and make it the Master Style.

1. Choose one page to focus on and open its style settings.

2. At the bottom of the **Styles** pane, check the setting named **This Style Applies to this Page Only**.

3. Now you can go through and style your page the way that you would like.

4. Once you are happy with how your site looks, you can save that style as the master style. Click on the button with the cogwheel icon, on the bottom right-hand side of the pane, and choose **Set As Master Style for this Theme**.

5. Now you can get through each page in your site and set them to use the newly saved master style. At the bottom of the **Styles** pane, make sure that page is set to `This Style is the Master Style for ABC Theme`. The wording here may be a bit confusing but what this really means is that the page uses the master style that is saved for the theme. For example, in the below screenshot, the theme is **Veerle**:

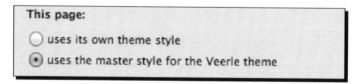

What just happened?

We have now defined a master style for our site. We also applied that master style to all of the pages in our RapidWeaver project. This means that we now have a consistent look and feel across our entire website.

Saving page styles

While default theme styles are great, I always find that I want to add my own spin on things. It's not very hard to really get into tweaking various settings in your themes so that you can get things just right. It's important that you save your theme styles once you are satisfied with how they are set. This allows you to easily refer back to these styles in the future, in case you want to use them in a different project. We can easily do this by saving what we configured as a custom theme style.

By saving your theme styles, you also no longer have to worry about accidentally changing something and later forgetting what it was you did. As we have saved the style, we can simply revert our project back to the theme style that we saved.

I would recommend that once you are happy with the way your site is styled, save that as a style and make it the master style for your theme. Then make sure that all of your pages are configured to use the master style. This will ensure that your website has a consistent look and feel throughout. There will be situations wherein you may want some pages to deviate slightly from the master style. However, try to keep that down to a minimum.

 Theme style will not automatically update as you continue to make changes to your page; you must re-save the style as you go along if you want to incorporate your improvements in the saved theme style. You can also just keep saving versions of your theme styles as you go along. This way you have a record as to what you did along the way and could always revert back to a previously saved style if you wanted.

Time for action – saving page styles

In the last section, we defined the master style of our theme. Let's now save this theme so that we can potentially use it in the future on other projects. It also provides us with a backup measure in case we accidentally modify the master theme.

1. Open the **Styles** pane on any page that has the master theme applied to it.

2. Click on the button with the cogwheel icon, on the bottom right-hand side of the pane, and choose **Save Style As....**

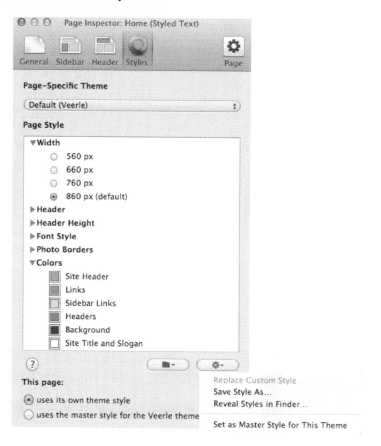

3. A box will appear for you to give your style a name. I recommend that you name the style something like the following format: Theme Name - Project Name Master Style - mm/dd/yy.

By using a name like this, in the future you will know exactly what this theme style was used for. By having the date in there, it gives you a way to potentially save multiple versions of the style.

4. If you like, click on the button with the cogwheel icon, and select the **Reveal Styles in Finder** option. This will reveal all the saved theme styles that you have on your system.

What just happened?

We have now saved the master style of our theme permanently. This will allow us to revert to this style, if at anytime we want to try out new settings and experiment with our theme. It will also allow us to utilize the saved style for future projects.

ExtraContent

Traditionally, RapidWeaver has two areas where you are allowed to display your content—the main content area and the sidebar. While these areas serve as ample space for a majority of RapidWeaver users, there was still a need to be able to provide more flexible ways to add content in our RapidWeaver projects. So some time ago, a few of the third-party theme developers got together to address the need for more spaces to add content into RapidWeaver, and ExtraContent was born!

ExtraContent allows theme developers to provide more areas on the page for us to add content to. Some locations where ExtraContent is commonly used are the page header, below the footer, or sometimes even custom drop-downs at the top of the page. While these areas will vary from theme to theme, the process of adding content into them will be very much the same. The developers worked hard to ensure a common interface that the RapidWeaver users will be able to learn, so that they can use these features regardless of what theme they have chosen to use.

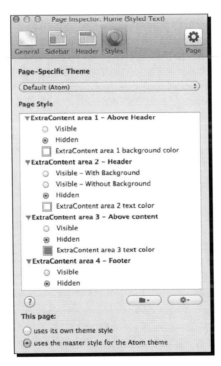

We will not be diving into the implementation details of ExtraContent here. For more details on ExtraContent and how to implement it, check out *Chapter 11, Advanced Weaving*.

For more information on ExtraContent itself, head over to its website at `http://extracontent.info`.

Customizing themes

It's inevitable. At some point in your journey with RapidWeaver, you will want to customize your themes further than what is available in the **Styles** pane. This could be anything from changing the color of the site title to swapping out some of the default images used in the theme. In this section we will review a few different ways to achieve this.

 If you are new to RapidWeaver, you may want to gain some experience before attempting to modify your themes. However, by reading this section you may learn a thing or two that you can store in the back of your head for future use.

Back in the day, users did the intuitive thing—they opened up the theme package and modified the files in the theme directly. For obvious reasons, this is frowned upon. To make this easier for users, a couple of different applications, such as RWMultiTool and RapidThemer were developed. These tools aim at making it very simple to swap out images within the theme and make other small changes. However, these tools do have their drawbacks; we will review them shortly.

The next method for modifying your theme is through good old CSS. This is scary territory for most users. However, once you get the grasp of it, using CSS is the best and least dangerous way to customize things. Let's dive further into this now.

Customizing with CSS

This section becomes a geek-fest, quick! If you are just getting started, you may want to come back to this section after you feel more comfortable with RapidWeaver.

Cascading Style Sheets (CSS) are the programming documents that control the look and structure of your site. This includes everything from the width of the page to the colors used throughout the site, to the position of the sidebar. Each theme ships with its own elaborate set of CSS files. If you were to want to customize the CSS for your site, your first thought might be to go and edit these files directly. However, this is not the best approach.

A perfect example is the situation where a developer releases an update to a theme. If you blindly install a theme update without creating a backup, all of your customizations will be gone! In order to overcome this, RapidWeaver has built-in mechanisms that allow you to store your own custom CSS within each page.

Inside the **Header** section of the **Page Inspector** window, you will notice a **CSS** tab. By inserting your own CSS code into this area, you will be able to overwrite the theme's default styles. Here is a quick example of some simple CSS that could potentially get added:

```
#content{background-color:white;}
```

This code snippet will change the background color of the content area to white. I am not going to go into a full-blown tutorial on CSS here. Please refer to the *CSS Basics* section in *Chapter 11, Advanced Weaving*, for a more detailed overview.

The CSS code added into the **Page Inspector** is going to only affect the current web page, not the entire website. If you wanted it to affect every page, you could copy the CSS and paste it into every single web page. However, this is not very efficient. You will have to edit every single page anytime that you want to add some CSS. Therefore, I only recommend using this **CSS** tab if you only desire to affect the current page.

The best way to apply the same CSS to every web page is to maintain an external `.txt`/`.css` file that will contain all of the custom CSS code. We can then import that CSS into every page with one simple line added into the **Header** tab of the **Page Inspector**.

```
<link rel="stylesheet" type="text/css" href="mystyle.css" />
```

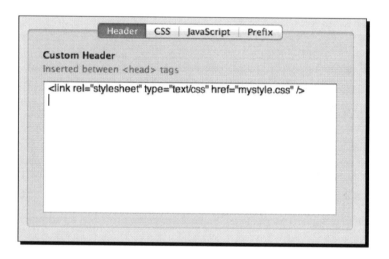

This may seem complicated to set up; however, once it's done, you will be able to add CSS into this file and it automatically affects all pages that have it imported. A great place to add this file is in your project resources.

There are many great applications out there that you can use to create and edit CSS files. Most of these applications provide code syntax highlighting, and some even provide code auto-completion. If you are just getting your feet wet, there is a fabulous free application called TextWrangler that you should try. TextWrangler is available from the Mac App Store or from `http://barebones.com/products/textwrangler`.

If you have a Dropbox account, this is an awesome place to put your custom CSS file while you are developing your website. You can do this by using the Dropbox public share URL for the file, and placing it inside the `<link>` code that we mentioned earlier. By using Dropbox's public share feature, you can change your CSS at any time. The moment you save it on your Mac, your changes will be reflected inside RapidWeaver and even on your published website. This is a huge convenience! However, once you have finalized your website and your styles, I recommend moving the CSS file onto your web server or into your site resources within your RapidWeaver project. This will save you from yourself, in case you accidentally change or delete the file from your Mac. When you switch off the Dropbox-referenced file, you will need to make sure to change the link reference on each web page so that they are now pointing to the new file location.

Time for action – adding a custom CSS file

Adding your own custom CSS file, as I described earlier, can be challenging to wrap your head around, especially if you have never done it before. In this exercise, we will create a very simple CSS file and link it to all of our pages.

1. In your favorite text editor, create a new file and name it `mystyle.css`.

2. Enter the following contents into the newly created CSS file. This code will make the content area of your site have a white background and red text.

```
#content{background-color:white;color:red;}
```

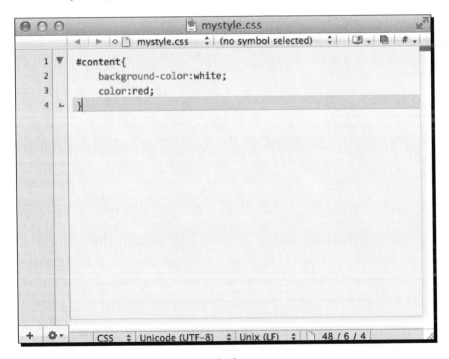

3. Save and close the new CSS file.

4. Drag the CSS file into the RapidWeaver project resources.

5. In the **Header** tab of **Page Inspector**, paste the following code into the header section at the bottom. Please note that the resource macro being used is the one that we learned about in the previous chapter.

```
<link rel="stylesheet"
      type="text/css"
      href="%resource(mystyle.css)%"/>
```

6. Preview your page and you should see that the content area has a white background with red text (assuming that your page has content).

7. You can now copy the aforementioned `<link>` code into all of your web pages so that they are linked to this new CSS file.

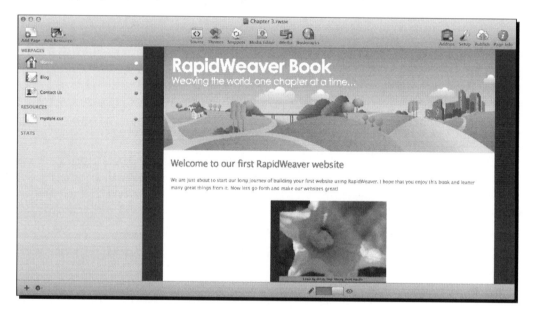

What just happened?

We have now successfully setup a nice CSS system in our project, which will allow us to customize the styles throughout the site. From now on, all the styles that we define inside the `mystyle.css` file will be applied to each page in our site.

I can understand that learning how to code CSS may seem like a big and daunting task. However, this really is the best way to customize the style of your website. It's also the least destructive. By not modifying the theme files, you can install theme updates with the confidence that your custom styles will stay intact. This combined with the sheer convenience is why this is my preferred and recommended way of modifying your theme.

RWmultiTool

RWmultitool was the first of its kind, and has been trusted by the RapidWeaver community for many years. Some third-party themes have even added explicit support for it. It allows you to modify all of the images that come with your theme. However, its primary purpose is to allow you to customize banner images within the theme.

RWmultitool's interface is very simple and easy to use. It allows you to add your own custom images or logo into the banner area, and tweak all kinds of things, such as color, add text, masks, borders, shadows, filters, and more.

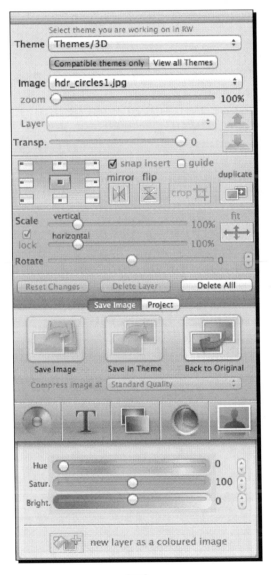

You are able to see all of your desired changes in real time. A common task that RWmultitool is used for is to edit the banner images that come shipped inside the theme. You can easily overlay your own custom text and even images in order to customize the theme's banners to your liking.

While RWmultitool makes backup copies of modified images, it still modifies the theme content. Therefore, it is very important that you make a copy of the theme before you modify it. This way you will always have an original, untouched version of the theme. RapidWeaver makes this very easy to do. Inside the Theme Browser, you can right-click on any theme and select **Duplicate**. This will create a duplicate copy of the theme for you automatically.

RWmultitool comes in a Lite and Pro versions. The Lite version is free, but ships with limited functionality. If you want a simple way to edit and create custom banners for you website, this is an indispensable tool. For more information head over to its website at `http://rwmultitool.com`.

RapidThemer

RapidThemer has a lot of similarities to RWmultitool Lite, although it does have more of a traditional Mac interface. RapidThemer allows you to do basic editing of theme images, such as cropping, color adjustments, and filters. RapidThemer does have a couple of unique features as well. It allows you to auto-update the themes that have added support for it. It also has a convenient backup and restore function for themes. As mentioned before, if you are modifying themes, it is important to have backup copies of the originals.

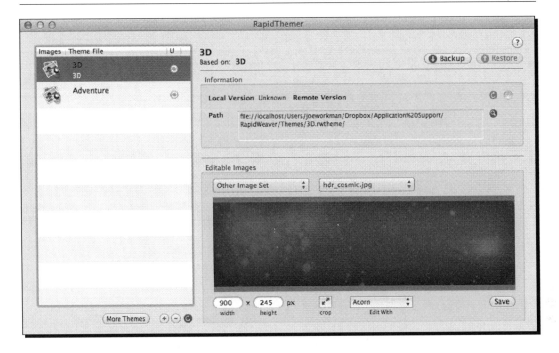

RapidThemer is available for free download. For more information on RapidThemer, head over to its website at http://www.rapid-ideas.com/rapidthemer.

Summary

I attached you to the fire hose again in this chapter. You should now have the knowledge about applying themes to and be able to style your websites. We even dipped our toes in some CSS.

Specifically, we covered the following topics:

- Choosing the theme that works for you
- Using Theme Browser
- Using theme styles in order to customize the look of your site
- Saving master styles
- ExtraContent
- Customizing your site with CSS, RWmultitool, and RapidTheme.

Now that you have mastered all aspects of themes, we are going to dive into the ins and outs of creating content with the Styled Text page.

4

Styled Text Page

The Styled Text page is an extremely versatile page type. Don't let the name fool you; the Styled Text page can do so much more than just text. You can add images, audio, video, and file downloads all without knowing an ounce of code! All you need to do is drag-and-drop your files (images, video, ZIP files, and so on) directly onto the page and RapidWeaver will take care of all the code for you. However, all the code loving geeks out there will be happy to know that you can add your own custom HTML code directly onto the page as well.

The Styled Text framework is not limited to just the Styled Text page. Almost every plugin developed for RapidWeaver inherits these abilities. Most plugins, whether a contact form or fancy image gallery, have editable Styled Text areas above and below the plugin's main content. This means that everything that you are about to learn in this chapter can also be applied to most of the other RapidWeaver pages and plugins as well.

In this chapter, we will be covering the following topics:

- ◆ Formatting text
- ◆ Images
- ◆ Adding links to other pages
- ◆ Audio and video
- ◆ File downloads
- ◆ Custom HTML

Formatting text

If you have ever used a word processor, then you will feel at home formatting text within RapidWeaver. Once you enter your text into **Edit** mode, simply select the desired text with your keyboard or mouse, and choose the appropriate options from the **Format** toolbar or menu.

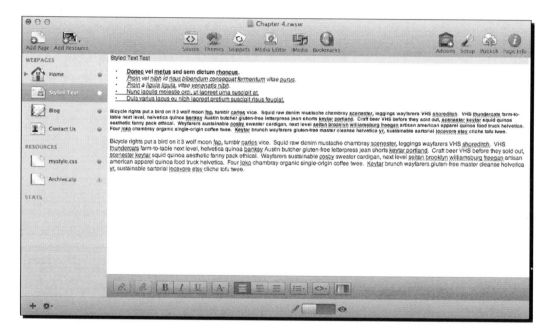

There is no format toolbar in the **Sidebar** area. Therefore, you will need to use the **Format** menu in order to apply styles to your sidebar.

Pasting text

I wanted to take a moment to discuss the process of pasting text into RapidWeaver. It will be inevitable that you will be copying and pasting text from your web browser or word processor documents. When you copy text from any of these locations, you will also copy their formatting, which may not be web safe. Everything may look great to you; however, it may look drastically different to your visitors.

In order to prevent this from happening, instead of using the normal paste command, use the **Paste as Plain Text** option in the **Edit** menu. The text that you have copied will be stripped of its formatting and will be inserted as plain text. You can then safely format the text the way that you see fit using the RapidWeaver formatting tools.

Format toolbar

The format toolbar is positioned at the bottom of the Styled Text area. Pretty much all of these are going to be very intuitive for you, but let's quickly review what options we have here. In order to apply these styles, simply select the text that you want to format and click on the corresponding style button.

Links

The first two buttons that look like chain links are for adding links to both images and text. We are going to be reviewing links in depth later on in the chapter so we are going to skip these for now.

Text styles

Unless you have lived in a cave, you should recognize that the next three buttons are for making your text bold, italic, and underlined. These are the most basic text formatting styles that we use in pretty much every application that supports rich text.

Font selection

The button with an **A** on it, is a drop-down menu that lets you select what font you want to use. All the fonts that RapidWeaver offers are considered to be web safe. The default fonts are considered to be web safe because they tend to be standard fonts that are installed on every computer. This will ensure that your website has a consistent appearance across all common browsers. Yes, that even includes the dreaded Internet Explorer!

In case a user does not have the font, which you have specified or installed, RapidWeaver applies lists of fonts as a fallback. For example, if you were to choose Verdana as the font for your website, RapidWeaver would apply the following font list: **Verdana, Arial, Helvetica, Sans-serif**. With this scenario, if a visitor visits your website and their machine does not have Verdana installed, it will use the next font in the list, which is Arial.

Alignment

The next three buttons should be very familiar as well. These allow you to align your content (text, images, media, and so on) to the left-hand side, center, or right-hand side of your page.

Lists

The button that looks like it has a bullet list on it does exactly what you would expect; it creates lists!

Now, when you click on this button you will notice a new window appears at the top of the RapidWeaver window. This small window allows you to choose the style list that you would like to use. There are eight variations of bullets, numbers, letters, and legal styles for you to choose from.

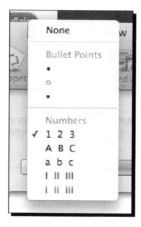

HTML formats

The second to last button is jam-packed full of useful formatting styles. Let's go over each of these and explain how they can be useful to you. You will notice that when you format any of your content using these formatting options, the background color of that applied content will turn green. You will not see the formatting actually get applied until you preview your page.

None

If you ever want to remove any of the styling options reviewed in this section, this is how you can do it. Simply select the content that you formatted and click on **None**. This will remove all of the HTML formats that have applied to the selection. This will only clear the options defined in the HTML formats menu. For example, if you make some text bold, this option will not affect that.

Headings

You will notice that there are six heading selections available. These correspond directly to the standard HTML <h1> to <h6> tag elements. These are used to define a hierarchy of titles within your web page: <h1> defines the most important heading and <h6> defines the least important heading. As users may skim your web page by its headings, it is important to use headings to show the document structure. H1 headings should be used as main headings, followed by H2 headings, then the less important H3 headings, and so on. The style of each heading will vary by theme.

[Use HTML headings for headings only. Don't use headings to make text BIG or bold. Search engines use your headings to index the structure and content of your web pages. For more information on search engine optimization (SEO), check out the *chapter 11, Advanced Weaving*.]

Image alignment

By default, images are put either inline with your other content or on their own line block. The two options available here let you float an image to the right-hand side or left-hand side of your other content. You will not be able to see this formatting inside **Edit** mode. You will need to **Preview** the page in order to see the formatting take effect.

Blockquote

The blockquote option will indent your text on the left-hand side. This is great for making some of your text stand out. Some themes may add some additional styles and formatting to blockquotes in order to make them stand out a little more. The blockquote uses the standard HTML `<blockquote>` tag element.

Code

The code option will format your text as computer code. This is very useful when you want to display actual programming code on your web pages. This option utilizes the standard HTML `<code>` tag element.

Paragraph

You will notice that when you enter more than one paragraph into your Styled Text page, there won't be a proper paragraph break unless you add in another newline (return). While this may achieve the effect you are looking for, it's better to highlight each paragraph independently and format it as a paragraph. Under the covers, RapidWeaver is placing each section of text into its own standard HTML `<p>` tag elements. This is the recommended way of doing things. You may even find that themes will sometimes style paragraphs a little nicer when you take the time to use this option.

Strike, subscript, and superscript

The strike setting will define strikethrough text. This will add a line that goes through the middle of your text. Subscript text appears half a character below the baseline. Superscript text appears half a character above the baseline. These options use the standard HTML tag elements `<s>`, `<sub>`, and `<sup>`.

Color

The last button on the toolbar will allow you to customize the color of your text. When clicked, it will reveal the standard color palette window that is used across all applications in OS X.

 If you find that you are going to be using the same colors all the time, you can easily save your colors at the bottom of the color palette. Simply drag-and-drop the color onto the boxes at the very bottom of the color palette. You will then be able to easily access your saved colors by simply selecting them when you want to. This will work throughout Mac OS X, not just within RapidWeaver.

Format menu

The **Format** menu is essentially another method of accessing formatting options for your content. As this menu contains all of the controls that we just reviewed for the **Format** bar, I will only review the additional options available in the menu.

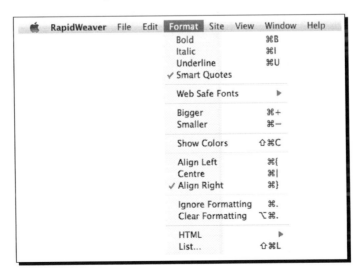

If you are a keyboard junkie like me, take note of all the keyboard shortcuts that are available for each formatting option. This will definitely save you some time.

Smart quotes

I recommend keeping this setting enabled. This will ensure that all your quotes, ampersands, and other common typography symbols are properly displayed to your visitors. With this turned off, certain symbols could be interpreted by the web browsers as code. This might not make your page look as it was intended.

Bigger/smaller text

Each theme will define a size of the font that will be used for your website. The **Bigger** and **Smaller** settings in the **Format** menu will allow you to increase or decrease that theme setting. Each time they are used, the font size will be increased/decreased by 1 pixel.

Clear formatting

This option will clear ALL formatting and will revert your text to plain text.

Ignore formatting

When you use the **Ignore Formatting** option, RapidWeaver will ignore any formatting and publish the content as is. When you ignore the formatting on content, you will notice that the background color will change to red. This option is useful when you want to insert your own custom HTML or PHP code onto the page. For more details on this, check out the *HTML* section in this chapter.

Time for action - styling text

We are going to now go ahead and play around with styling our text.

1. Add a new Styled Text page to your RapidWeaver project file.
2. At the top of our new Styled Text page, go ahead and type in a page title such as `Styled Text Test`.
3. Select that text and let's format it to be **Heading 2**. You can do this from the HTML formatting button on the format toolbar at the bottom.
4. Add a couple of new lines after our heading and let's add a bullet list to our page. If the heading format happens to carry into your new lines, highlight the new empty lines and select **None** from the HTML format button.

5. Click on the list button on the toolbar and select the style of bullets that you would like to add to your page.

6. Now you can type a few lines into your new list. After each new line a new list bullet should be generated.

7. Once you have completed your list, let's add a couple more new lines after.

8. Open another word processing application or maybe your e-mail client. Copy some text that has been formatted and paste it directly into the Styled Text page.

9. Add a couple of new lines after that and now paste in the text using the **Paste as Plain Text** option from the **Edit** menu.

10. Let's preview our page and see what we have done.

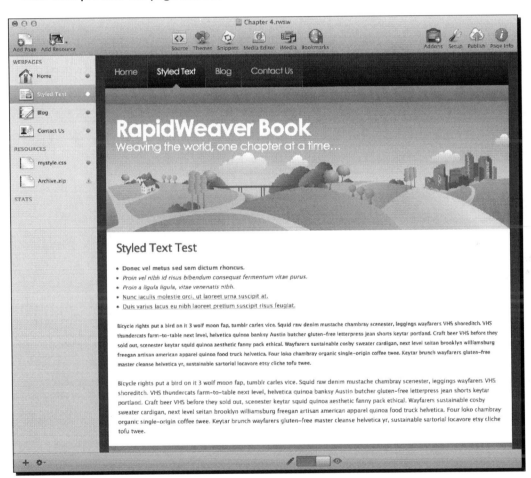

What just happened?

We have added some new text to our web page and have styled it in a few different ways. We created a heading for our page that the theme had gone ahead and styled for us. We also added a new list to the page. What is amazing here is that we did all of this without writing one line of code!

Lastly, we added a couple paragraphs of text by pasting it from another word processing application. You would notice a big style difference between the two paragraphs. The first paragraph should have inherited all of the formatting from the original document. Remember that this may look good on your machine; however, it may use some non-web safe formatting that would make your site look different to visitors who use a different browser than yours. The second paragraph, which we pasted as plain text, should look precisely how the theme has styled our content. As RapidWeaver is handling the formatting here, we can be rest assured that our web page will look consistent to all of our visitors.

Have a go hero - experimenting with text style

In our exercise, we only played with a few styles mentioned in this section. I suggest that you take just a few minutes to go ahead and fiddle around with the other styles available. In particular, play with the various HTML formatting options and see how they affect the look of your web page.

Images

We discovered in *Chapter 1, Getting Started,* that it's very easy to add images into a Styled Text page. Simply drag the image from the **Finder** window into the desired location in the content area. RapidWeaver supports the following image formats: PNG, JPG, and GIF. You can then use the **Media Inspector** to further refine and edit the image. You can adjust image scale, rotation, borders, shadows, and more.

Image support for Styled Text areas is great. However, it's not the best solution if you are looking to create a photo gallery page or something similar. For more ideas on this, check out *Chapter 7, Multimedia Pages* on multimedia pages.

Media Inspector

The **Media Inspector** enables you to edit and modify the dimensions and attributes of images used in Styled Text pages. Remember that this feature should also work in all page types and plugins that use Styled Text. You can access the **Media Inspector** by simply double-clicking on the image that you desire to edit. We have access to modify the following data points for each image:

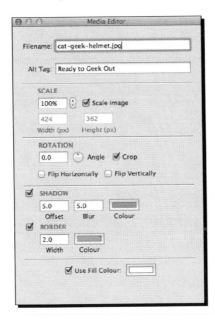

Filename

This will be the actual name of the image file when it's published (for example, `myimage.jpg`). The name of your image file should be web safe. This means that the name of the file should not contain any spaces and special characters. It's best practice to only use alphanumeric characters. Dashes and underscores can be used as a good alternative to spaces.

Alt tag

Sets the alt tag of the image, which is displayed while the image is loading and when you hover your cursor over the image. Alt tags are also useful for SEO. The alt text also carries a very special purpose for assistive web browsing. Screen readers are often used to dictate website content to users that may be legally blind.

Scale

You can scale the image by either a percentage or as a static size. When using the percentage, RapidWeaver will make sure to retain the original aspect ratio of the image. If you decide to scale the image by exact dimensions without keeping the same aspect ratio, the image may not look right.

 Images can be quite large. Therefore, they can dramatically increase the size of your RapidWeaver project file. It is highly recommended that you resize the images to the exact size that you need them to be before adding them to your RapidWeaver project. If you are unsure of the exact size that you will need, it's best to at least resize the images to as close as possible to the desired size. Then you can make the final adjustments on size using the **Media Inspector**. Oftentimes, using an external image editor to resize your images provides higher quality images. The image sizes may also tend to be smaller in file size, which can make your web pages download faster.

Rotation

This option allows you to rotate the selected image. By checking the **Crop** option, the image stays within its initial dimensions defined in the **Scale** section. You can also flip the image vertically or horizontally.

Shadow

By checking the **Shadow** box, RapidWeaver will add a drop-shadow to the image. You can adjust the shadow's offset, blur, and color. This is not a CSS shadow. RapidWeaver applies the shadow to the actual image before it is uploaded.

Border

By checking the **Border** box, RapidWeaver will add a border to the image. You can adjust the border's width and color. This is not a CSS border. RapidWeaver adds the border to the actual image before it is uploaded.

Fill color

This defines the fill color. This could be useful when an image is rotated or when a drop-shadow is added. This color will be used as the solid color backdrop to those images.

Image normalization

It's common for other users to drag-and-drop 15 MB digital pictures from their last summer getaway directly into RapidWeaver, and then simply scale the image down to 5-10 percent of its original size. I say other users because you are reading this book and would never do that, right? You always resize your images before adding them into RapidWeaver, right?

When images are added into RapidWeaver, they are stored inside your project file. This not only causes your RapidWeaver project file to become very large, but it will also cause RapidWeaver to slow down and use more memory on your system.

RapidWeaver has a utility in the **File** menu called **Normalise Images**. When you use this utility, all of the larger images that are used throughout your RapidWeaver project file will be scaled down to the size actually used within the project. For example, if you have a 5000x5000 image and scale that to 10 percent via the **Media Inspector**, the resulting image file that **Image normalization** will create will be 500x500. This will keep the actual published quality of the image intact. However, you will see a considerable performance increase in your system. You will also lose the ability to scale the image back to anything higher than 500x500 (from our example).

Image normalization is an irreversible operation, so be certain that you are not going to need the original images that you copied in. However, as long as you still have the original images somewhere on your Mac, you should be fine. It also never hurts to back up your project before you run this as well.

Time for action - styling an image

Let's go ahead and add a new image to our Styled Text page that we created in the last section. We will style our image by adding a border and a drop-shadow. Then we will make the text that we added in the last section wrap around the image as well.

1. Find an image that you would like to add to your web page.

2. Drag your image onto the Styled Text page. Place it just before the first paragraph of text that we pasted in the last section on formatting text.

3. Double-click on the image and open the **Media Inspector**.

4. Scale the image down to a smaller size using the scale control in the **Media Inspector**. Now don't forget our commandment for this section: Thou shall not drag huge images into RapidWeaver! We should always resize before we add image into RapidWeaver. I may be able to forgive you just once.

5. Check the **Shadow** box and set your shadow size and color to your desired options.

6. Check the **Border** box and set your border size and color to your desired options.

7. Close the **Media Inspector** window.

8. Select the image by clicking on it just once. You will notice that the image will have a colored highlight around it.

9. From the **HTML formatting** menu, select **Align Image Left**.

10. Preview your web page.

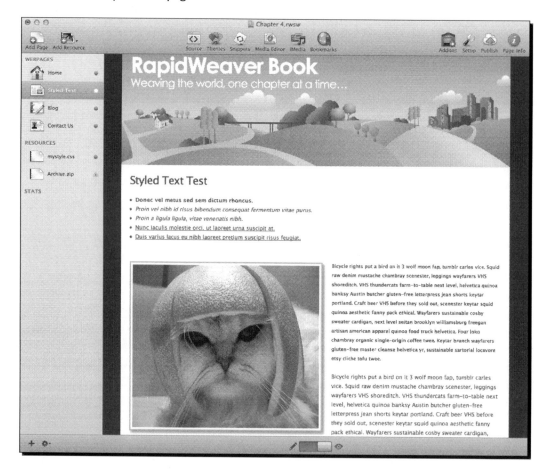

What just happened?

We now have an image on our page that has been styled to have a border as well as a drop-shadow. If you scaled the image you will also have seen the size of the exported image be smaller. You will also see that the image has been aligned to the left-hand side of the text. This is because we set the image to **Align Image Left**. If we had not formatted the image in this way, the text would have shown below the image.

Have a go hero - experimenting with image style

As always, I want to encourage you to experiment with the style settings reviewed in this section on your own. Here are a few suggestions that you could try:

◆ Remove the image alignment and have the text show up below the image

◆ Set the image to align to the right-hand side of the text

◆ Play with the other image styles such as rotation and different shadow and border settings

Links

Whether you link to other pages on your site or to other external websites, it goes without saying that you are going to want to add links to your web pages. RapidWeaver makes this very easy. You don't need to touch any code at all.

Simply highlight the text or image that you want to link and click on the **Set Link** button that we saw earlier in this chapter. You will notice a new window has appeared where we can enter in our link information.

Linking to a URL or e-mail

The default drop-down option is set to **URL**. To link to an external page, simply type or paste in the URL of the page that you want to link to. The URL must begin with either `http://` or `https://` in order for the link to function properly.

If you want the link to simply start a new e-mail to a particular address, simply type or paste the e-mail address in the same location where you would have typed in the URL. You will want to leave the drop-down option set to URL. I should advise you that this may cause you to receive unwanted SPAM e-mail as anyone can send an e-mail directly from your website.

You can add a default subject, body, or other attributes to the e-mail that will be created when your link is clicked. To do this, simply add the attributes to the end of the e-mail address as if it were URL parameters. The values will have to be URL encoded. For example, you will need to replace all your spaces with %20. The following entry will add the subject "This is the subject" and a body of "This is the body" to the e-mail:

```
someone@example.com?subject=This%20is%20the%20
subject&body=This%20is%20the%20body
```

For more information on other options available head over to
`http://www.mailto.co.uk/`.

Linking to an internal page or resource

If you want to add a link to a page or resource that already exists within your project file, simply navigate to the page or resource from the page drop-down menu that defaults to **URL**.

When you use the drop-down menu to link to your internal pages, RapidWeaver will always maintain those links even if we rename or change attributes for our pages within our project file. If we were to instead type the URL to the published pages, RapidWeaver would not maintain that link for us if we were to change any of the attributes on the linked page. For example, if the page or folder name of the page we linked to was changed, RapidWeaver would only change links to that page if actually referenced the page instead of using a URL.

Opening in a new window

If you want the link to open in a new window or tab when it's clicked, make sure that you check the **Open in New Window** setting.

If I am linking to an external website, I tend to always open those links in a new window. This means that the user does not leave my website and can come back to where they were extremely easily. If the link was opened in the same window, then the user would have to search through their browser history in order to get back to the page on my site.

Custom attributes

For all you tech geeks out there, you can add all the custom attributes that you want to link. This could be useful for many things such as launching a lightbox.

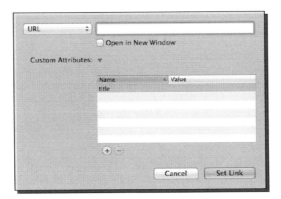

The following is a list of common attributes that can be added into a link:

- **rel**: Specifies the relationship between the current document and the linked document. This attribute is commonly used to trigger JavaScript actions as well.

- **class**: Specifies a class name for custom CSS styling or to trigger a JavaScript action.

- **ID**: This is the unique ID for the element. This is commonly used to trigger JavaScript actions or custom CSS as well.

- **tabindex**: Specifies the tab order of an element.

- **title**: The information entered here will be displayed in a tooltip when a user's mouse hovers over the link.

- **onclick**: Custom JavaScript to run when the link is clicked.

Removing links

It's very simple to remove a link. Simply highlight the link with your mouse and click on the **Remove Link** button on the bottom toolbar. You can also select the link text and choose **Clear Formatting** from the **Format** menu.

Time for action - adding links

Adding a links is something that is vital to building websites. Let's go ahead and add a few different types of links in this exercise.

1. Open the existing Styled Text page that we have been using throughout this chapter.

2. Add the following text somewhere onto the page: `Link to URL`.

3. Select the text that we just added and click on the add link button on the format toolbar (the first button on the left-hand side).

4. Once the **Link** window opens, add a URL to a website of your choice to the input field.

5. Check the **Open in New Window** checkbox. Click on the **Set Link** button.

6. Add the following text below the link that we just created: `Link to Email`.

7. Select the text and add a link. However, this time type your e-mail address into the input field.

8. Add the following text below the email link that we just created:
    `Link to Home Page`.

9. Select the text and add a link. This time you will click on the drop-down menu in the link window and locate the home page of your RapidWeaver project.

10. Preview your web page.

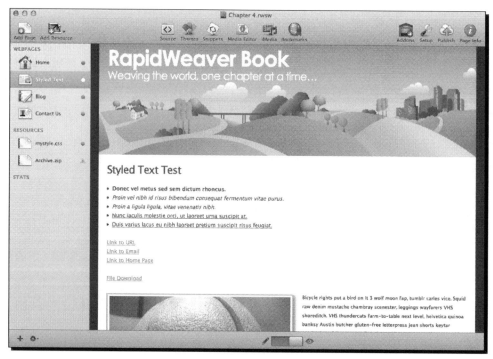

What just happened?

We have added three different types of links to our web page.

The first link will open a new browser window to the URL that we added to the link input. This link will not work directly inside RapidWeaver. However, you can preview your website in Safari to see this in action.

If you click on the e-mail link, it will open a new e-mail inside your default e-mail client to the e-mail address set in the link input.

The last link that we created will link to our project home page. As this is an internal link within our project, this link will work within RapidWeaver.

Have a go hero – experimenting with links

There are a few more things that we can do with links. Why don't you give them a shot He-Man! Or She-Ra!

- Link to a resource
- Add a link to an image
- Add a default subject and body to the e-mail link we created
- Edit an existing link
- Remove a link that you have added

Audio and video

RapidWeaver has support for most QuickTime compatible audio and video files. To embed this onto your web page, simply drag-and-drop it where you would like the player to be in the content area. When you do this, you will be prompted with the following question: **Do you really want to copy the contents of the dragged items into the text?**

Clicking on the **Alias** button causes RapidWeaver to link to the QuickTime movie file externally on your hard drive. This results in a smaller project file, but if the movie is subsequently moved to another location on your hard drive - or deleted altogether - the link to the movie will be broken the next time you open your project file. If you intend to alias your QuickTime movies in your Styled Text pages, consider creating a permanent location on your hard drive for your website's source files, and add your QuickTime movies to your Styled Text page by dragging them from that location.

Clicking on the **Copy** button causes your QuickTime movie file to be copied directly into your Styled Text page. This will result in a larger project file, but if you move the original movie to another location, it will not affect subsequent uploads of your website.

There is no way to edit your video once you add it onto your Styled text page. Therefore, you will need to make sure that you size the video to the exact dimension you want before you drag it onto the page. If you are looking to create a media gallery on your site, you may want to look at other options available. Check out *Chapter 7, Multimedia Pages*.

Have a go hero – adding some audio and video

If you are an audiophile or videophile, go ahead and play around with dragging your media directly onto a Styled Text page. All you need to do is drag-and-drop your media directly where you would like it to be displayed in the content area.

iMedia browser

So far we have always added media onto our Styled Text pages via **Finder**. However, the iMedia Browser is a great utility that allows you to browse most of the multimedia libraries throughout your Mac with ease. You can browse iPhoto, Aperture, iTunes, Garage Band, iMovie Events, and links to Safari bookmarks. Once you locate the media that you would like to add, simply drag it onto the content area just as you did with files from **Finder**.

You can access the iMedia Browser via the application toolbar or from the **View** menu.

Remember about being cautious with image file sizes. It may be better for performance to not add images via iMedia Browser. I recommend that you export and resize your images from iPhoto or Aperture before you add them into your RapidWeaver project.

File downloads

It's very common that you would want to provide a file download to your visitors. There are actually a couple of different ways to accomplish this.

 If you need to share multiple files, you may want to check into the File Sharing plugin that ships with RapidWeaver.

Drag-and-drop into Styled Text

You can drag-and-drop pretty much any kind of file that you would like (PDF, ZIP, and more) into the desired location in the Styled Text content area. Just as with images, file names should follow a web safe format. RapidWeaver will automatically create a link to it in your published page. Visitors will be able to click on the link and download the file.

 This was a common method used until RapidWeaver 5 was released with support for **Resources**. See the following section on how to use resources.

Linking to a resource

We have already experimented with resources so you should be an expert at it by now. Simply drag the file that you would like to be downloadable into your **Resources** pane. Then all you need to do is create a link (like we learned in this chapter) that points to that particular resource. Using this method, you will ultimately have much more control over the link that is generated. You will be able to rename your link and open it in a new window.

Forcing files to download

There are times that you have a file that you want a user to download; however, the browser insists on displaying the contents of the file within the web browser. There is a trick that includes something called a .htaccess file.

The .htaccess file is an Apache configuration file that can be used to configure a million things about your web server. I won't be going into the details of this file at all. This is simply a plain text file that has a specific name (.htaccess) and it's normally placed at the root of our web domain on your web server.

 The .htaccess file only exists for Apache web servers. If your hosting company is using a different web server, such as IIS, then you will have to contact your hosting company for the procedure to configure this.

The following example shows how you can force the download of a CSV file. Normally the browser would display the contents. However, by adding one simple configuration, we can force all browsers to download the file instead. Add the following line into your .htaccess file:

```
AddType application/octet-stream .csv
```

Time for action - linking to a file download

Let's go ahead and add a link to a file download. We will be doing this via a RapidWeaver resource as this is now the recommended method.

1. Add a file to your project resources by dragging it in. This could be a file of any type. A ZIP file could be a good choice for this example.

2. Add the following text below the links that we created earlier in this chapter: File Download.

3. Select the text and add a link. Browse and locate the resource that you just added.

4. Preview your web page.

What just happened?

We have now added a link to a file so that our visitors can easily download it. In order for you to test the actual file download, you will need to publish your site. I am sure you noticed that downloading a file is nothing hard, it's just like adding a link. If you did not want to use RapidWeaver resources to link to your download, you could simply provide a URL link to wherever you wanted to store the file. Perhaps the file is stored on Dropbox or Amazon S3 storage.

Have a go hero - forcing file downloads

If you are starting to feel like a 007 geek, then go ahead and attempt to force the download of a file that your web browser would normally display. A good test would be a .txt file.

Inserting code

If you would like to include your own custom code inside a Styled Text page, unless you format it properly, RapidWeaver will not interpret the code as you may expect. You are allowed to use your own HTML, PHP, JavaScript, or CSS code on a Styled Text page. Once you have added your code to the page, you will need to highlight the code and select the **Ignore Formatting** from the **Format** menu.

Time for action - adding custom code

Let's go ahead and add a little bit of custom code to our web page.

```
<h4>Today,s date is
<script type="text/javascript">
var currentTime = new Date()
var month = currentTime.getMonth() + 1
var day = currentTime.getDate()
var year = currentTime.getFullYear()
document.write(month + "/" + day + "/" + year)
</script>
</h4>
```

You can either type in the aforementioned code or copy it from the downloads for this book. There is also a snippet of the code that you can install and access directly from RapidWeaver's snippet library.

1. Add the preceding code into the existing Styled Text page that we have been using throughout this chapter. Feel free to use the snippet or manually type it in.

2. Select all of the code that you added onto the page and **Ignore Formatting** from the **Format** menu.

3. Preview your webpage.

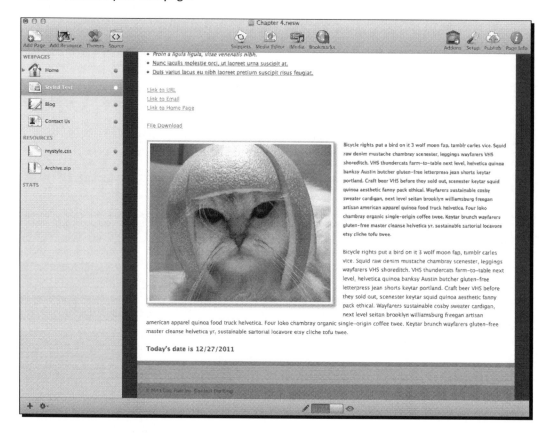

What just happened?

We added some JavaScript and HTML to our page that will display today's date. When we set the code to **Ignore Formatting** in **Edit** mode, you will have noticed that the background of the code should have turned red.

If you are a little confused with the code in the section, don't worry. Many themes ship with a bunch of extra code snippets that can be very useful as long as you know that the code accomplishes what you need. You now know how you can insert those snippets and use them within your website.

Summary

We went over a lot of really great stuff in this chapter. What we have learned will serve as base knowledge that can be used through many different parts of RapidWeaver and third-party plugins. You may want to review this chapter from time to time. Every time you review it, you may learn something new.

Specifically, we covered the following topics:

♦ Formatting text and some tips for pasting text that comes from other apps

♦ We can drag-and-drop images in and also edit image attributes and styles via the Media Inspector

♦ We learned that it's always better to resize your images before you add them to your RapidWeaver project

♦ Adding links to other pages and resources

♦ Audio and video

♦ File downloads and forcing a file to get downloaded instead of being displayed in the browser

♦ Inserting your own custom HTML, PHP, CSS, or JavaScript.

In the next chapter we are going to jump into probably my favorite part of working with RapidWeaver, the Stacks plugin.

5
Stacks

I am sure that after the last few chapters, you have realized that RapidWeaver is a great application for building websites. Now after this chapter you are going to think that it's an amazing, indispensable tool for building websites! In my opinion it is the one add-on for RapidWeaver that is not optional if you want an easier way to build more powerful websites. It's just that good! In this chapter, I will review Stacks v2.0 that was released in December 2011.

In this chapter we will be covering the following topics:

- What is Stacks?
- Installation
- Working with Stacks
- Toolbars and settings
- Default Stacks
- Templates

What is Stacks?

The Stacks plugin has revolutionized the way that users build websites with RapidWeaver. Stacks provides a flexible drag-and-drop interface for RapidWeaver. Imagine building your website using LEGO, where each LEGO brick is a called a stack. A stack could really be anything: a block of text, an image, a slideshow, or an RSS feed. You have an entire library of stacks available to you and if you want to add one to your page, all you need to do is drag-and-drop it into place. Building a web page couldn't be easier!

Stacks is developed by YourHead Software. You can download your free trial at `http://yourhead.com/stacks`.

Third-party stacks

By leveraging RapidWeaver's powerful API infrastructure, Stacks has built its own interface that allows developers to release their own custom stacks. While the Stacks plugin ships with over 25 built-in stacks, as of this writing, there are over 250 stacks available from third-party developers.

As previously mentioned for third-party themes and plug-ins, you can find a listing of available third-party stacks at Realmac Software's RapidWeaver Add-ons page, located at http://realmacsoftware.com/addons.

 Just to clarify some potential confusion, I will be talking about Stacks and stacks. Stacks (with a capital "S") refers to the actual plugin for RapidWeaver. When I mention stacks (lowercase "s") this is referring to the building blocks that we use to build our web pages.

Installing Stacks

As this is our first venture into a third-party plugin, let's do a quick overview on how to install the Stacks plugin.

1. Download the Stacks disk image (DMG file) from http://yourhead.com/stacks.
2. Double-click on the DMG file once it's downloaded. It will most likely be in your Downloads **folder.**
3. Once the disk is mounted, double-click on Stacks.rwplugin.

4. You should see a pop-up window appear that says *RapidWeaver has taken care of installing Stacks for you.*

5. Quit the RapidWeaver application and restart.

Now that was a piece of cake. Let's get into the fun stuff and start diving into Stacks.

Time for action – creating our first Stacks page

Let's jump right into the deep and create our first web page using Stacks. This exercise is going to touch pretty much every aspect of Stacks. We are going to be accessing the **Stack Elements** and **Stack Templates** libraries, during this exercise. These can be accessed by clicking on the first two buttons at the top left-hand corner of the Stacks edit mode interface.

1. Add a new Stacks page to your RapidWeaver project. Adding a Stacks page is the same as adding one of the out of the box page types that we have been using so far. When the new page dialog box appears after adding a new page, you will see that Stacks is now an option.

2. Open the Stack Templates library (second button) and locate the **640 Lined Header** stack. Click-and-drag that stack template onto the main Stacks drop zone, which will be empty at this point.

3. Next, drag-and-drop the **Read More Paragraph** stack template directly underneath the text area in the header stack that we just added.

4. Now open the Stack Elements library (first button) and locate the **2 Column** stack. Drag-and-drop this stack directly below the **Read More paragraph** template, which we added in the previous step. You should now notice two new empty drop zone areas where we can add more content.

5. In the left-hand column of our **2 Column** stack, drag in an **Image** stack from the Stack Elements library. Drag-and-drop an image from your computer into the **Image** stack that we just added.

6. In the right-hand column of our **2 column** stack, drag in a **Quote** stack from the Stack Elements library.

7. Finally, from the Stack Templates library, locate and add the **Underline - Three Columns** footer template directly below the **2 Column** stack on your page.

8. Let's go ahead and preview our web page!

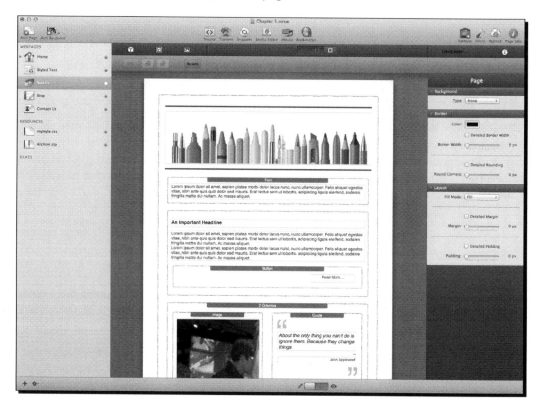

What just happened?

We just witnessed the power of Stacks! If you were like me the first time, you will probably never build a web page any other way. We saw that Stacks ships with a bunch of out of the box layout and stacks that allow us to quickly build a great looking web page with little effort. All that we had to do was to drag-and-drop our stacks into place. We dipped our toes into many different parts of the Stacks interface.

We saw that there are two different types of stacks—elements and templates. Stack elements are the individual building blocks. Stack templates are sets of elements that have been preconfigured for you in common layouts. We will be going more in-depth into both of these later on.

You may also notice that there may be a few things "off" with the web page right now. The image you added may not fit properly and some of the spacing of your layout may be off.

Have a go hero – experiment

I am a big fan of playing around because it's the best way to learn! Here are a few things to try. We will be reviewing some of these things later in the project but playing around is always fun. You can try the following:

◆ Try editing some of the text and notice the special text editing settings that appear in the right-hand pane.

◆ Double-click on the image we added, enter the Stacks image editor, and give it a whirl.

◆ Click on each stack that we added onto the page and adjust the settings that you see on the right-hand pane. Add borders, backgrounds, and change the layout settings in order to see how all of these work together.

Working with stacks

In the previous exercise you saw how easy it was to add stacks to your page. All we need to do is drag-and-drop them into place. It's equally as easy to move them around the page. If you want to reposition a stack to a different place on your page, simply select it and drag it into its new location.

If you would like to remove a stack from your page, there are two different ways to go about it after you select your stack. The first way is by simply using the delete key on your keyboard. The second way is to use the big, bright, red **Delete** button in the Stacks format bar. One word of caution, when you are deleting stacks from your page, If you delete a stack, everything inside of that stack will also be deleted. For example, if we were to delete the 2 columns stack that we added in our previous exercise, both of the stacks that were inside of it would also get deleted.

You can also copy and paste stacks! It works exactly how you would expect it to. Select the stack that you would like to copy and use the keyboard shortcut for copy (*cmd + c*) or **Edit | Copy** from the menu bar. To paste the stack, use the keyboard shortcut for paste (*cmd +v*) or **Edit | Paste** from the menu bar. If no stack is selected on the page, the stack will be pasted at the very bottom. If you do have a stack selected, the copied stack will be pasted directly below the selected stack. This is very convenient when you have a large Stacks page and know the location where you want to paste your stack.

Another common thing that I find myself doing is duplicating stacks. You could simply copy and paste the stack however, there is another way. After you select the stack that you would like to duplicate, hold down the option key and drag the stack to where you would like the duplicate. Once you let go, you will see your stack has been duplicated in the new location. This is great for when you want multiples of the same stack on a page. You can spend time setting up the first stack just how you would like it and then duplicate it so that the rest are ensured to be identical.

The Stacks toolbars

Stacks has two toolbars at the top of its Edit Mode interface. Let's learn what all those cool buttons do!

The navigation bar

The navigation bar sits at the very top of the Stacks user interface. We have already interacted with a couple of the elements on this toolbar in our last exercise. Let's dive into each element on this toolbar.

The Stacks Elements library

We have already been exposed to the first button in the navigation bar. It's the Stack Elements library. This window is a central location to store and organize your individual stack elements. Let's take a quick tour of all the tools that we can use inside this library window.

At the top of the window is a search box. If you have a lot of stacks in your library, this is a great way to quickly locate the stack that you want. If you start typing the name of your desired stack, you will notice that the list of stacks that appear are limited to the matches for your search.

Next to the search box are three buttons that allow you to change the layout, as well as the level of detail, of the library contents. I personally prefer the middle option as it allows me to view the maximum number of stacks in the space provided as well as still being able to see the name of each stack.

The main section of this window is obviously the stack browser, where you can scroll through and browse for your desired stack that you want to drop onto your web page. You will notice that the stacks in the library are broken into groups. This allows you to locate stacks a little faster as you are browsing through your library. Clicking on the caret preceding the group label can collapse each group. As you acquire more stacks, new groups may get created. For example, all of my stacks are currently grouped under a group called `Joe Workman`.

At the very bottom of the library window, there is an information panel, which shows you more detailed information about the selected stack. There is also a button on the right-hand side of this panel, which provides several useful functions, such as the following:

- **Install Update** (refer to note on updating stacks).
- **Install All Updates** (refer to note on updating stacks).
- **Show Web Help** will be available when the developer has defined a support URL for the selected stack. When you click on this option, the configured support URL will be opened in your default web browser.
- **Show Web Info** will be available when the developer has defined an info URL for the selected stack. When you click on this option, the configured info URL will be opened in your default web browser.
- **Show in Finder** will reveal the actual stack package inside Finder.
- **Uninstall** will completely uninstall the stack from your library and move the stack to your Trash. If you uninstall a stack that is currently in use, you will not be able to modify that stack again until the stack in question has been reinstalled.

If you drag any of the Stacks library windows away from their default position, it will turn into a permanent standalone window. This is convenient if you are building a page and want to keep the library window easily accessible.

Updating third-party stacks

Stacks has built-in mechanisms that allow third-party developers to automatically update their stacks. When you first open RapidWeaver and go to a Stacks page, each stack that you have installed will be checked for updates. All this goes on the background so you have no idea that it's actually happening. When an update is available for a stack, a small **red badge** will be placed on the corner of the stack icon in the library window.

Stacks provides an API for third-party stack developers to auto-update their stacks. Therefore, there may be stacks that do not have this feature implemented. However, most major stacks developers offer this feature, including yours truly.

The easiest way to install updates is to click on **Install All Updates** from the button at the bottom of the Stacks Library window. The release notes for each stack update will be displayed, and you will be prompted to install each one.

If you just want to install a particular update, select the stack that you want to update and click **Install Update** from the button at the bottom of the Stacks Library window.

The Stack Templates library

The second button on the navigation bar opens the Stack Templates library. We were exposed to stack templates in the previous exercise. As you may have guessed, this window allows you to search for, and manage your stack templates just like we did with the Stack Elements library.

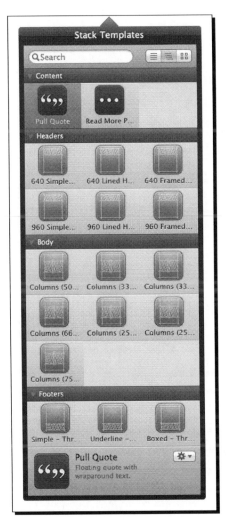

I am not going to review the functionality of this window as it's identical to the Stack Elements library that we just reviewed in the previous section. We will be going over more specifics with stack templates later on in this chapter.

The Stack Media library

The third button in the navigation bar is the **Stacks Media Library**. This library has all of the same functionality as mentioned with the previous two libraries. However, we have not explored what Stacks Media is yet.

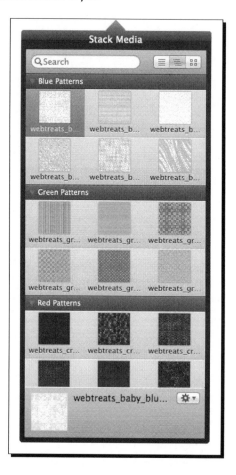

The Stack Media library manages extra images that developers can include in their stacks that could be used to enhance the stack. These images could be tiled backgrounds, buttons, banners, ribbons, and so on. Stacks ships with 18 different tiled-background images that you can use to style up your stacks. We will review how to use these later on. Most of the time you are going to be using these images by dragging them into an image well in the Stack settings pane. However, you can use these images any way you want to, in your projects.

View modes

In the center of the navigation bar is an iOS-esque slider control that is used to switch between the three available view modes for the Stacks interface. Once you click on the control, you will notice that the verbosity of the interface increases the further right you move the control.

The far left view mode is going to provide you as close as you will get to RapidWeaver's preview mode. You will notice that all the borders from around each stack do not appear. If you are using stacks that utilize scripting, such as JavaScript effects, you will not see those effects until you preview your web page.

The view on the far right is the most verbose mode. When this mode is used, Stacks will add more padding around each stack, as well as give each stack a bolder border. What I like the most about this mode is that each stack is labeled with its name. This allows me to visually see what stacks are used on the page. I use this mode probably 95 percent of the time.

The Info button

On the far right-hand side of the navigation bar, the **Info** button simply toggles the Stacks settings pane to open or close. If you have a large computer screen, you may never need to worry about closing the settings pane. However, I find that on my laptop sometimes it is nice to hide the settings pane. This gives me a little more screen real estate to view, and edit the stacks on my page.

The Format bar

Directly below the navigation bar is the Stacks format bar. While there are a few static buttons that reside on the format bar, its contents will depend on what is selected and what you are editing at the moment. In this section, I will review the few static buttons available. The other controls will be covered in subsequent sections later on in this chapter.

The Edit button

The **Edit** button is the blue button that resides on the far left-hand side of the format bar. Most of the time the **Edit** button will be in a transparent/disabled state. It will become enabled whenever an image, HTML, or text area is selected within a stack. When you click on the button, you will enter into either image editing mode or text editing mode. We will cover more about these modes in the next section.

When you enter into image or text editing mode, the **Edit** button will transform into a **Done** button. By clicking the **Done** button, you will exit out of the editing mode and come back to the normal Stacks interface.

 I admittedly hardly ever use the **Edit** button because you can also enter into image or text editing mode by simply double-clicking on the image or text that you want to edit.

The Add/Remove link

The two green buttons allow you to add or remove a link from either text or an image. This works exactly the same as adding a link to an image or text inside a Styled Text page.

To add a link, simply select your text or image, and click on the first green button. You will then see RapidWeaver's common link window open, which we have used several times already in this book.

To remove a link, select the text or image that has a link configured for it and click on the second green button. The link will be removed.

The Delete button

Surprise! The big red button will delete stacks from your page. As previously mentioned, you can also use the *Delete* key on your keyboard.

The Stack settings pane

The Stack settings pane lives on the right-hand side of the Stacks interface, and this is where all of the configurations for your stacks are done. In this section, I will be reviewing all of the built-in stack settings that you will encounter. However, I am obviously not going to be able to review every third-party stack out there. Luckily, Stacks has a standard set of controls that developers can utilize. We will be reviewing each of these types of controls. This will ensure that you are familiar with how to use the settings when you start using some third-party stacks.

If a third-party stack does have settings, they will be shown in the settings pane directly below the standard stack settings groups.

The Stack settings controls

Stack support eight different type of settings controls. Many of them behave very similar to each other and should all feel very familiar to you. The controls consist of the following types:

- ◆ Checkbox
- ◆ Color Picker
- ◆ Image Drop Area
- ◆ Text Input
- ◆ Link Generator
- ◆ Number Input
- ◆ Number Slider
- ◆ Pop-up Menu

If you encounter a setting that you do not understand, hover your mouse over the top of the settings label. As long as the developer of the stack has configured it, a tooltip will be unveiled that will provide an explanation for the particular setting.

The Color picker

When you click on the color control, a standard OS X color picker will appear for you to make your color selection.

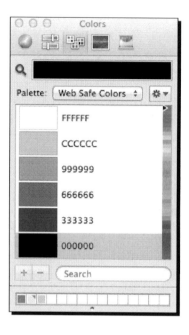

There are some great color picker plugins out there that are nice to have while doing web design. A great one that is available for free is called the Developer Color Picker from Panic Software. You can get it at `http://www.panic.com/~wade/picker`.

Number controls

Depending on how the slider is configured by the developer, the value from a slider could be either an integer or a floating-point number. The number controls are also configured to have a minimum and maximum value by the developer of the stack. Therefore, you will not be able to use a value that falls outside the bounds of the configured limits.

Sometimes it can be tough to get the exact value that you would want from a slider control. Therefore, it is possible to manually type in your desired value! In order to do this, simply double-click on the number label at the right-hand side of the slider. You will notice that the label is editable, and you can manually define the number that you desire.

While you can manually define a number in a slider, the value must still fall between the minimum or maximum rules defined by the developer for that slider control.

Enable/Disable controls

Stacks allows for the possibility of hiding controls based on the state or value of another control. This allows settings to be hidden from view, when they might not be needed. We will see this in action when we review the default stack settings.

Default stack settings

Every single stack has a standard set of settings that will always appear at the top of the settings pane.

Background

The background setting allows you to apply either a solid color or tiled image as background of the selected stack. The default setting is **None**. This essentially sets the background of the stack to be transparent.

If you select the **Solid Color** option for the pop-up menu control, you will notice that a color picker is revealed. You will also see that the background color of your selected stack has been changed to black (which is the default color). If you click on the color well, you can customize the color via the standard OS X color picker. Once you have chosen a color for the background, you should see the background color of your stack change as well.

If you select the **Tiled Image** option for the popup menu control, you will notice that an image control is revealed. Now you can drag your desired background image from **Finder** or from the **Stack Media** library into the image well. Once you have added an image, you should see that the image fill the background of your selected stack.

What is a tiled image?

A tiled image means that the image that you have provided will be repeated both horizontally and vertically in order to fill the entire width and height of your stack. There is no space between the repeated images so the background looks seamless.

Border

The border settings allow you to control the color, width, and corner roundness for each stack. The color option is straightforward. You just need to click on the color well to open the default color picker; then choose your desired color and you are done. However, if the border width setting is set to **0 px**, then you won't see any borders on your stack.

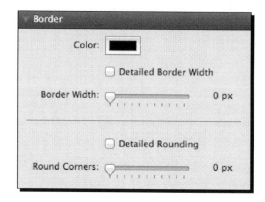

The **Border Width** setting is a slider that defines the width of all four sides of the stack. However, if you would like to define different border widths for each side of the stack, you just need to check the **Detailed Border Width** option. When you check this box, you will see the slider disappear and four number controls will be revealed. These controls allow you to define a specific width to each side of the stack.

The **Round Corners** settings behave exactly like the border width settings do. By default, the round corner setting is set to **0 px**, which will render a square corner. As you increase the value, you will see that corners become more round. The border width must be set to a value greater than **0 px** in order for round corners to take effect.

Layout

The layout settings affect the size, positioning, and spacing of your stacks. These are important settings to learn, if you want to make sure that your web pages have a more professional look and feel.

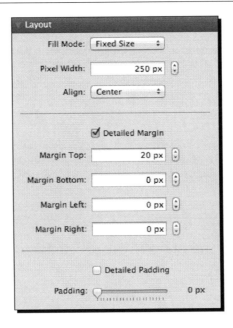

Fill Mode

The **Fill Mode** defines how a stack will fill the width of the website's content area.

Fill

This is the default setting for all stack elements. In this mode, a stack will fill in all of the horizontal space that it can. A stack that's not inside of any other container will fill in the entire width of the website's content area. A stack that's inside of a container will fill in all the horizontal space of that container. For example, in a **2 column** container, a stack with this mode will fill in the entire width of the column that it's inside of.

Flexible

When you select **Flexible**, you will notice two new settings appear. The slider control allows you to define the percentage width that you would like to make the stack. The **Align** option lets you chose the position of that stack on the web page. For example, if you wanted to make a stack 50 percent width of the page and wanted it to be flushed left, you could set the slider to **50 percent** and the align option to **Left**.

Fixed Size

The **Fixed Size** mode allows you to define an exact width of your stack in pixels. The **Align** option lets you chose the position of that stack on the web page.

The margin and padding settings

The margin and padding settings affect the spacing of a stack. Margin is the space that starts from the edge of the outside border and ends at the edge of any adjacent stacks. For example, if you have two stacks next to each other and they both have a margin of 5 px, then the stacks will be 10 px apart from each other.

Padding is the space from the inside border to the content inside the stack. By default padding is set to 0 px, which will cause the content to touch the border of a stack. If we wanted to make a simple box with text, you would want to add padding so that the text sits probably at least 5 px away from the border.

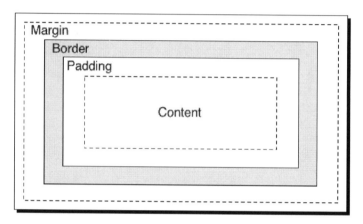

Both the margin and padding settings behave similarly to the border and round corners that we saw earlier. The slider control will affect the margin/padding on all four sides of the stack. If you check the detailed checkbox, you have the ability to affect the margin/padding differently on each side.

Time for action – getting to know the settings

Let's go ahead and fix a couple of lingering issues from our first exercise. We are going to adjust some of the settings that we just learned about, in order to make the page layout a little nicer. We are going to be using the same exact project file and Stacks page that we built earlier in this chapter.

1. Select the **Read More Paragraph** stack, which we added to the page by clicking on it. You will see a blue outline around it when it's been selected.

2. In the settings pane on the right-hand side, check the **Detailed Margin** box inside the **Layout** settings. Now set the **Top Margin** setting to be 20 px.

3. Repeat the same process and change the top margin of the **2 Column** stack to also be 20 px.

4. Now select the **Quote** stack, and select the background type to be **Tiled Image**.

5. Open the **Stack Media** library and drag one of the colored image tiles into the background image control. I recommend the third blue tile image as it's light in color. This will make sure that the background does not wash out the quoted text.

6. For the border settings on the **Quote** stack, set the border color to a light blue, the border width to 1 px, and the round corner slider all the way to 10 px.

7. Lastly, in the **Quote** stack, set the padding slider control to be 5px.

8. Preview your web page!

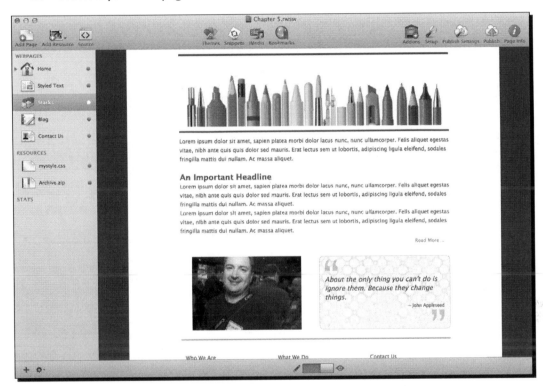

What just happened?

The first thing that we did here was to add a top margin to our **Read More** template and our **2 Column** stack. This was done to add some empty space between them and the text above them. By adding a little spacing between the stacks, the layout is now much cleaner and easier to read.

You may be wondering, *why did we only add a margin to the top?* If we had simply increased the default margin setting using the slider control, the margin would be applied to all four sides of the stack. This means that the left and right-hand side margin would have both been indented by 20 px (along with the top and bottom). Therefore, the edges of the text would not properly line up with the rest of the stacks on the page, and our page would not look uniform.

The next thing that we did was to add some pizzazz to our **Quote** stack. We gave it a nice, stylish background image. Then we jazzed up the border and gave it some rounded corner goodness. Last and definitely not least, we added a little bit of padding in order to get the quote text indented further in from the border.

With these minor tweaks, I would say that this page looks pretty good now. However, keep reading on. We are going to enhance this page with even more goodies soon.

Have a go hero

We were not able to touch every one of the settings that we learned about in this exercise. I recommend that you play around with the other settings available and compare to see how they differ from each other. Here are a couple of examples:

- Play around with the different fill modes in order to see how you can change the arrangement of stacks on the page.
- There is a **Float** fill mode that I did not review at all. Give that a shot to see how it makes a stack behave.
- Add a border to a stack or two, and start fiddling with the margin and padding settings so that you get an understanding of how they differ.

Text editor options

When you double-click (or use the **Edit** button) on any text or HTML block in a stack, you enter into the text edit mode. In the text edit mode, the settings pane displays a new set of formatting controls that are specific to text.

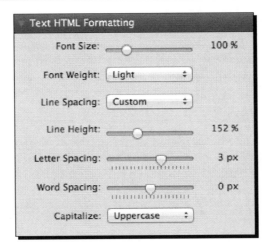

It's important to note that these settings will affect all of the text that is contained within the selected text block, and not just the text that you may have selected.

- ◆ **Font Size**: Every theme will set a default text size for your content. This setting will allow you to increase or decrease the theme's default sizing by a percentage.

- ◆ **Font Weight**: The **Font Weight** setting allows you to make the font bolder or lighter.

- ◆ **Line Spacing**: This adjusts the spacing between all lines of text. You can define double, triple, or a custom percentage for line spacing.

- ◆ **Letter Spacing**: The **Letter Spacing** slider controls the space between each letter. This control support positive and negative values. This means that you can bring the letters tighter together, or have them more spread apart.

- ◆ **Word Spacing**: The **Word Spacing** slider controls the space between each word. Just like the letter spacing, this controls support positive and negative values to give you full control over how your words are spaced.

- ◆ **Capitalize**: This control allows you to force the capitalization of your text. The **Uppercase** setting will force all the text to be uppercase. Conversely, the **Lowercase** setting will ensure that all of the text is lowercase. The **Capitalize** option will make the first letter in each word a capital letter.

Image editor options

When you double-click (or use the **Edit** button) on an image that you have added into a stack, you enter into the Stacks image editor. When you enter into the image editor, you will notice that the main content area has been replaced with your image and a new set of settings are revealed in the settings pane.

All of the edits that you make inside the Stacks image editor will modify the actual image that is exported to your website. The style changes are not applied using CSS! Therefore, if you are an experienced designer who is conscious about how your images appear on the Web, you may want to continue to use your external image editor. While the image editor within Stacks is great for some changes, it cannot compare to robust image editors such as Photoshop, Pixelmator, Acorn, or tons of other great, dedicated editors out there.

It is possible to have Stacks publish your image completely untouched. To accomplish this, you will need to use an external editor to make your adjustments. You will also need to make sure that the image is properly sized to the exact dimensions that you would like the image to be once it's published onto your website. When you add your image into a stack, go into the image editor and uncheck the **Constrain Width** and **Constrain Height** options. Ensure that you don't modify any of the other layout or style settings and your image will be published completely untouched.

Image Publishing

At the top of the image editor settings pane are some basic settings for an image. The **File Name** setting allows you to define the actual name of the image file once it's published. If you leave this blank, stacks will automatically give the image a filename. In my opinion, why take the time to try and name all of your files!

The **Alt Tag** setting is where you can provide some additional textual data about what that image is. Search engines will often scan the alt tag of your images in order to better index the content on your site. There are also the accessibility benefits of an alt tag, which we mentioned in the previous chapter. It's also common that some stacks will use the information placed in the **Alt Tag** to provide a caption for an image when hovered over.

The image format setting affects the format that your image will be published in. The default setting is **Original**. This means that your image will be published in the same format as the original image that you added into the stack. However, you can force stacks to also publish the image as a JPEG or PNG.

JPEG versus PNG

I am sure that you are used to the JPEG image format. Most cameras nowadays will shoot images as a JPEG. The reason that the JPEG format is great is that it provides awesome compression. This means that file sizes will be much smaller with a JPEG. When you have smaller image file sizes, it means that your web pages will download faster for your visitors. However, JPEG's compression is so good that in most situations you will not be able to visually see the loss in image quality. You will have to play around with your images at different compressions until you are satisfied with the quality versus the file size ratio.

You can adjust the JPEG compression with the **Quality** slider control, which is revealed when you choose the JPEG format from the **Image Format** pop-up menu.

PNG is a lossless compression format. This means it compresses images without losing any quality. This does come as a trade-off as PNG file sizes tend to be much larger. However, small and simple images may actually compress better using PNG than JPEG. It really depends on how much is "going on" in the image. PNG works best for vector type graphics with hard lines. JPEG works best for anything with complex gradients and color (for example, a photo). Another benefit of the PNG format is that it allows for transparency! This is a big benefit over JPEG, especially when you want to add a drop-shadow or rounded corners to your image.

If you were to add a rotation or drop-shadow to a JPEG image, the background beneath the image would be made white. This will not be an issue if your website has a white background. However, if your website's background isn't white, then your JPEG image will have a white box around it. Obviously that will not look good at all.

So the moral of the story here is that it's not economical to encode most images in a lossless format such as PNG, when the loss of quality using JPEG is barely perceptible to the human eye and a JPEG might only take up a quarter of the space. On the flip side, sometimes you just don't want to compress an image with JPEG. If your images are small simple icons or you really need transparency, then JPEG is out and PNG wins!

Layout

The image layout settings allow you to scale your image in four different ways, as well as rotate your image so that it's displayed at an angle. The **Rotation** control slider is located at the very bottom of the layout settings groups. As you move the slider, you will see your image rotate on its center axis. The remainder of the settings in the layout group all have to do with scaling your image.

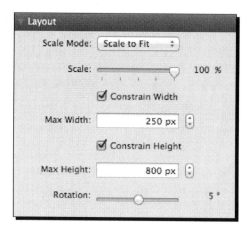

Scale to Fit

With the **Scale to Fit** mode, you define a percentage that you would like to scale your image proportionally down to, using the **Scale** slider control. You can also constrain the height and width of the image in order to ensure that the published image is not too large. The default setting for the maximum height and width is 800 px. This provides a good starting point as images on the Web rarely need to be larger than that.

In order to constrain the image size, you will need to ensure that the **Constrain Width** and/ or the **Constrain Height** controls are checked. Once those controls are checked, the values in the **Max Width** and **Max Height** number controls will take effect.

Scale to Fill

With the **Scale to Fill** mode, an image will be scaled proportionally in order to fill a fixed sized frame. This means that portions of your image could potentially be automatically cropped in order to maintain the image proportions and still fit inside the **Width** and **Height** settings that are defined.

Stretch to Fill

With the **Stretch to Fill** mode, an image will be stretched in order to fill a fixed sized frame. This means that the image proportions will not be respected at all and it may become distorted. This is because the image will be stretched by either its height or width in order to fit inside the **Width** and **Height** settings that are defined.

Center

With the **Center** mode, the image will not be scaled at all. A static size frame will be placed in the center of the image. The size of this frame is defined by the **Width** and **Height** controls. Whatever parts of the image that falls outside of this frame will be cropped, and hence, will not be a part of the published image.

Border

The **Border** settings are pretty self-explanatory. You can define a border color and size to be added to the image. Remember that this is not a CSS border. The border will become a part of the published image.

Shadow

The final set of image controls are for adding a drop-shadow to the image.

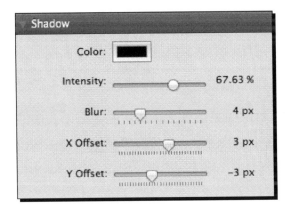

Here is a quick explanation of the shadow controls:

- **Color**: This is obviously the color of the drop-shadow. A majority of the time you are going to use black since that is the color a shadow. However, if the background color of your site is dark, you may want to try a lighter color. This will give a glow effect.

- **Intensity**: This slider controls the opacity of the shadow. For a stronger shadow, you will want the opacity to be a larger value.

- **Blur**: This is the width of the shadow. In my opinion, less is more with this setting. A smaller shadow will give you a much cleaner, crisp look.

- **X Offset**: This is the horizontal offset for the shadow. A positive value will move the shadow to the right and a negative value will move the shadow to the left.

- **Y Offset**: This is the vertical offset for the shadow. A positive value will move the shadow up and a negative value will move the shadow down.

Time for action – editing text and image

Now it's time to put the image and text editors to good use and enhance our stacks page a bit more. We are going to be using the same exact project file and Stacks page that we built earlier in this chapter.

1. Double-click on the **An Important Headline** text block in order to enter the text editor.

2. Set the **Font Weight** setting to the **Light** option.

3. Set the **Line Spacing** setting to **Custom**, and adjust the slider to around 150%.

4. Set the **Letter Spacing** to 3 px.

5. Set the **Capitalize** setting to the **Uppercase** option. Click outside the stack or click on the **Done** button to exit text edit mode.

6. Double-click on the image we added to the page in order to enter into the image editor.

7. Set the **Image Format** to be **PNG**.

8. Set the **Max Width** setting to be 250 px.

9. Set the **Border Color** to white and its **Size** to 5 px.

10. Change the **Shadow** settings for **Intensity** to 67%, **Blur** to 4 px, **X Offset** to 3 px, and **Y Offset** to -3 px.

11. Click on the **Done** button to exit the image editor.

12. Preview your web page.

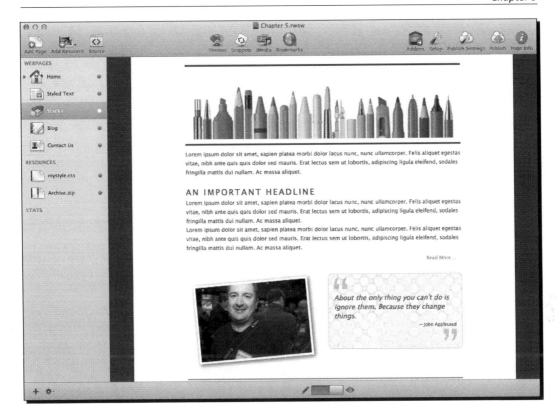

What just happened?

We just ventured into the last two remaining setting options available in stacks—the text editor and the image editor. We tweaked the styles of our text to be a little more spread out as well as have all capital letters.

We did all kinds of great stuff to our image. We shrank it down to a size that will fit on the web page, we gave it some borders and a drop-shadow, and finally, we rotated it just a tad.

Have a go hero – experimenting with image

As always, I encourage you to explore the settings that we did not go over in this exercise. Another test that you can play around with is adding a drop shadow to an image and then setting the **Image Format** to be **JPEG**. By doing this, you will see why PNGs are better suited for images with drop-shadows. If the background of your website is white, change the background color of the stack to black, and you should see how the JPEG images will add a white background to the image.

Default stacks

In this section, we are going to review all the stack elements that ship with the Stacks plugin. All these stacks can be found in the Stack Elements library.

Text

The **Text** stack allows you to add a block of styled text onto your web page. In fact, the **Text** stack is very powerful in that it actually contains all of the functionality of a Styled Text page! Therefore, you can take the entire contents of *Chapter 4, Styled Text Page* and put it right here.

You will notice that once you enter text edit mode by double-clicking on the text, all the standard styled text-formatting controls will appear in the format bar. As mentioned before, the text formatting settings will also be revealed in the settings pane. There are no extra settings for a **Text** stack outside of these.

Image

The **Image** stack allows you to add images to your web page. When you double-click on the image, you will enter the image editor that we just reviewed in an earlier section.

If you would like to replace the image that is inside an image stack, you can simply drag-and-drop a new image onto the stack. All the image settings that you have made will be preserved for the newly added image.

HTML

The **HTML** stack is for the true geek! You can type your own custom HTML or PHP code directly into the stack. There is no assistance or automated code generation here. You have to know what you are doing because you are coding by hand.

 If you are going to be adding PHP code, make sure that you have the .php extension set on your page. If you recall, we can do this from the **General** tab in **Page Inspector**.

1 Column

The **1 Column** stack is a great utility stack that can be used to group multiple stacks into a single container. For example, if you wanted to have a group of stacks that were all contained inside a box, you could add them into a **1 Column** stack. Then you can style your **1 Column** stack with a background color and border. Voilà!

2 to 5 Columns

There are four more column stacks that allow you to have up to five columns on your web page. These stacks are perfect for creating general layouts for your web page. When you add these stacks to your page, you will see empty drop areas where you can add more stacks to the layout.

Each of these stacks allows you to configure the **Gutter Width**. This is an empty space between each column on the page. Both the **2 Column** and the **3 Column** stacks also allow you to configure the percentage of the **Split** width. For example, you can configure the **2 Column** stack to be a 60/40 or a 50/50 split.

Grid

The **Grid** stack allows you to build evenly sized grids very quickly. The stack could not be simpler to set up. You just need to define the number of columns and the number of rows that you would like. As you adjust these values, you will see the new stack drop areas be added to the page.

There is a **Column Width** setting that will set the width of each column to be the configured value. You will need to be careful that the total width of your grid is not larger than the content area of your theme. You may need to play with the values until everything properly fits within your theme.

Float

The **Float** stack contains an empty stack drop zone on one side and text on the other. If the content area of the text becomes taller than the stacks added to the drop zone, the text will wrap around the floated stacks.

There are settings to float the stack drop zone on the left or right-hand side of the text. You can also define the percent width of the stack area compared to the text.

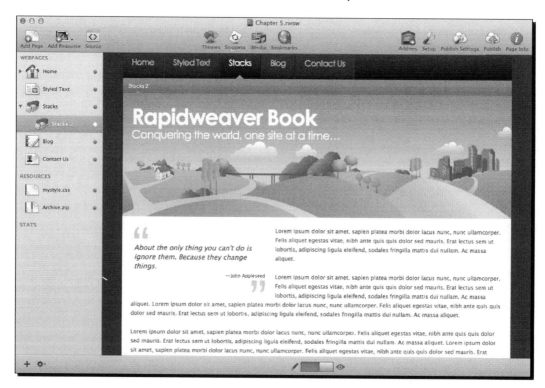

Floating Image

There are two **Floating Image** stacks that allow you to float an image to the right or left -hand side of a text area. These stacks behave identical to the **Float** stack. If the text area becomes taller than the image, it will wrap around the bottom of the image.

Quote

The **Quote** stack allows you to place a very stylish quote onto your web page. Once you add it onto your page, simply edit the quote and its source, and you are good to go!

You can turn off the quotation marks and the source in the stack settings pane.

Button

The **Button** stack lets you add a nice, styled button to your webpage. To change the text on the button, simply double-click on the text and edit it. In the settings pane you can configure a link that will be triggered once the button is clicked. This link could be to another page, or maybe even a file that is stored in RapidWeaver's resources.

There are three styles available—**Plain**, **Rounded**, and **Rectangle**. The **Plain** style makes the button look similar to a normal text link. However, when you hover over the link the background color changes to the color configured. The **Round** and **Rectangular** styles makes a more traditional pill or rectangle shaped button.

You can customize the color of the text and the background of the button with the color controls provided. Lastly, you can change the alignment of the button to be aligned left, centered, or right. There is also a **Fill** option, which will make the button take up the entire width of the stack.

Header

The **Header** stack lets you add standard page headings to your pages. Headers are used to define the important sections on your web page. They also a play large role in search engine optimization.

There is a single setting for the **Header** stack, which allows you to define what type of header this will be. Each theme will style headers differently. So, make sure that you preview your web page to ensure that they are styled the way that you like.

Have a go hero – experimenting with other stacks

It's playtime! We have used a few of the defaults stacks in our exercises. However, we have not experimented with all of them. I recommend that you give the following stacks a shot:

- 3 Column (take note on how the column-split can be changed)
- 4 and 5 Column
- Grid
- Float
- Floating Image
- Button

Templates

Templates are preconfigured layouts of individual Stack Elements. While you could build the templates on your own using stacks, templates are convenient as they are already prebuilt and configured. The developer of the template take the time to make sure that everything was spaced properly with the correct padding and margin settings.

Depending on the template that you are using, the developer has the ability to lock down certain settings and layouts. This is to ensure that the template functions and displays as it was intended to. For example, if you look at the **640 Lined Header** template, which we added in our earlier exercise, we do not have control over the solid lines above and below the banner image.

Stack templates are still a very new concept to the stacks world. Over time , as more templates are developed, I am sure that new features and ideas will spring forth.

Global content

One very exciting feature of templates is their ability to house global content. All the footer templates that ship with stacks support this feature. If you edit the content of the footer template, the same content will be changed on all of the pages that contain that template. So, you only need to update the content in one location and it will be reflected on all the pages once they are republished. Now that's really good!

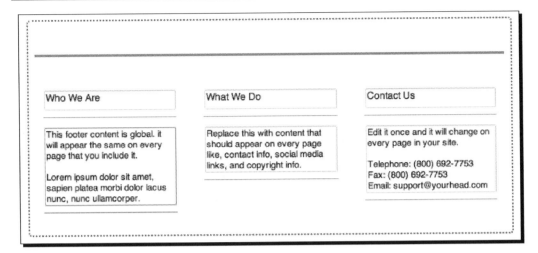

Who We Are	What We Do	Contact Us
This footer content is global. it will appear the same on every page that you include it. Lorem ipsum dolor sit amet, sapien platea morbi dolor lacus nunc, nunc ullamcorper.	Replace this with content that should appear on every page like, contact info, social media links, and copyright info.	Edit it once and it will change on every page in your site. Telephone: (800) 692-7753 Fax: (800) 692-7753 Email: support@yourhead.com

Note: There is a subtle clue that lets you know when a part of a stack is global. Normally the border outline around stacks is blue. However, this color changes to green for global content.

Have a go hero – experimenting with other templates

It's playtime again! You knew that was coming right? As of this writing, Stacks ships with 18 templates. We even used three of them already in our first exercise of this chapter. Here are a few things that I recommend you try doing:

- Take the other templates that we have not used for a test drive. The **Pull Quote** template is pretty nice.

- Create a new Stacks page with the same footer template. Change the footer content on one of the pages and watch the changes be reflected on the other page as well.

- Remember that templates are simply preconfigured layouts of individual stack elements. It would be a great exercise to duplicate the templates that we used in our exercise with individual stacks!

One last thing

So I am sure that you have already fallen in love with Stacks. But in the near future you will find yourself doing the inevitable; you are going to find a bunch of really cool stacks that will make your website shine. I recommend that you resist the urge to build very complex layouts in order to cram as much as you can onto a page.

When you have too many effects going on in a page, your visitors will have the opposite experience than what you had intended. I promise you that a slideshow inside a tab container, which is inside a lightbox, is not a good idea. Just keep it simple!

Summary

This chapter introduced you Stacks. If you to are like me, pretty much every web page that you build from now on will be with Stacks. The drag-and-drop abilities allow you to build flexible and powerful layouts in seconds. When you combine that with a thriving ecosystem of third-party stacks, I think this is the best thing since sliced bread!

Here is a quick recap of what we learned:

- Stacks is awesome!
- It's easy to build your stacks pages. Simply drag-and-drop elements onto your page.
- Stack templates provide a quick and convenient way to build our web pages.
- There are a plethora of settings to tweak all kinds of things. However, none of these are required, and the advanced settings are just a click away.
- Stacks ships with over 30 great elements and templates to build your website.
- Did I say Stacks is awesome?

This chapter concludes the foundation building part of the book. You should now have a strong foundation for you to go forth and build amazing websites. The remainder of the book will dive into more vertical topics. In the next chapter we will review grab-bag of common pages and elements that you may want to add to your website.

6

Basic Page Types

In this chapter, we will be reviewing a few common page types and elements that are used throughout the web design. Some of these are a few more of the out-of-the-box page types that ship with RapidWeaver and others are third-party developer plugins or stacks.

In this chapter, we are going to cover the following topics:

- ◆ HTML page
- ◆ iFrame page
- ◆ Offsite page
- ◆ Contact form
- ◆ Formloom
- ◆ Common elements with stacks

HTML page

The HTML page is a geek coder's paradise! However, there are some very non-geeky uses for it that may not be apparent on the surface. The HTML page is a simple code editor that allows you to type in your own HTML, CSS, JavaScript, or PHP code. There is no assistance or automated code generation here. You have to know what you are doing because you are coding your web page by hand. The HTML page does support syntax highlighting, which makes it nicer to code in than a simple text editor.

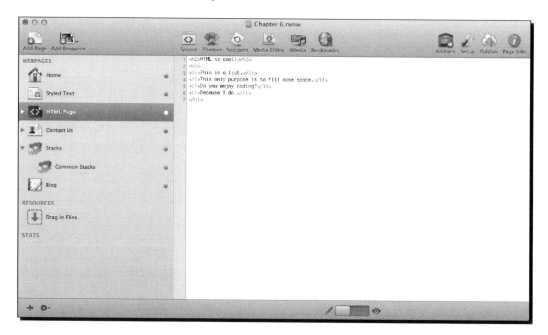

 As the HTML page can contain many different types of code or text, you will need to make sure that you change your page extension to reflect the contents of the page. Therefore, if you are coding in PHP, make sure that you have the .php extension set on your page. And if you are coding in CSS, make sure that you have the .css extension set. You get the drift.

The HTML page only has one setting in the **Page Inspector**. This setting is to apply the theme to the page. By unchecking the **Apply Theme** setting, the published file will only contain the code or text that you have placed in this file. All of the theme layout will be stripped, giving you an entirely blank page to start from.

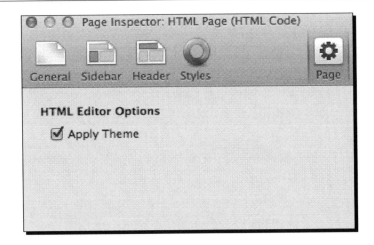

By turning off the theme, if you want to code in HTML or PHP, you will also need to ensure that you properly declare all of the standard elements in an HTML template such as DocType, <html>, <head>, <body>, and so on. You truly have a blank slate, which means you have to do all of the work! Now go get geeky!

Time for action - creating an HTML page

Let's go ahead and create a very simple HTML page. We will be using the same RapidWeaver project file that we have been building throughout this book.

1. Add a new HTML page to your RapidWeaver project.

2. Type in the following HTML code into the content area; this will add a title heading and an unordered list (a.k.a bullet list):

```
<h2>HTML is cool!</h2>
<ul>
    <li>This is a list.</li>
    <li>This only purpose is to fill some space.</li>
    <li>Do you enjoy coding?</li>
    <li>Because I do...</li>
</Ul>
```

3. Preview your web page!

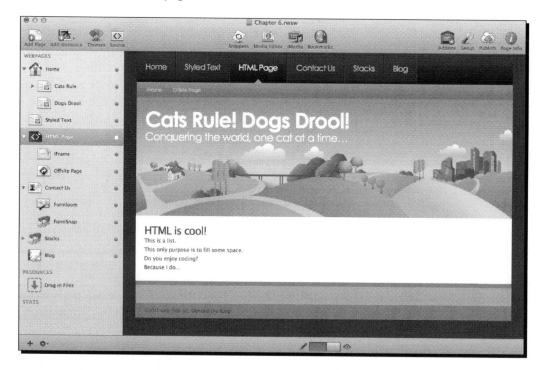

What just happened?

You now have coded a fresh HTML page. It's not too fancy, but it gets the job done. Now you may have noticed that the list in the preceding screenshot does not actually have bullets. The reason for this is that this particular theme has chosen to style bullet lists in the theme without any bullet styles. If we were to change the theme and preview this page again, chances are the HTML that we entered here would be styled completely differently.

Have a go hero – other uses for the HTML page

If you are feeling adventurous, let's explore a couple of the not so apparent uses of the HTML page.

 You will have to uncheck the **Apply Theme** setting in order to accomplish both of these tasks.

◆ There is a project where its initiative is to know the people behind a website. Essentially, you create a plain text file named humans.txt that contains information about the different people who have contributed to building the website. This is by no means required for a website to function. I just think it's sort of fun. For more info check out `http://humanstxt.org`. You can also check out my own `humans.txt` file at `http://joeworkman.net/humans.txt`.

♦ Back in *Chapter 3, Theming Your Site* we created an external CSS file that contained customizations that we then linked onto all of our pages. Instead of maintaining that CSS file externally to RapidWeaver, let's go ahead and use an HTML page to manage it instead. Remember to relink all of the references on each page to use this new CSS file.

 When you reference the newly created CSS file, you are going to want to use the full URL to the file after it's published. This will ensure that the CSS will also work within RapidWeaver. However, changes made to this CSS file will only be reflected within other web pages once the file is published to the server.

iFrame

iFrames allow you to display content from another, possibly external, web page within the content area of your current page. For example, you could use it to display an external support forum into your RapidWeaver web pages. Think of it as a tricky way to make the contents from one page look like it's on another.

 You know all those fancy Twitter, Facebook, and other social buttons that we have seen all over the Web? Well, most of those are iFrames! The button is actually hosted on Twitter, Facebook, and so on.

The entire configuration for the iFrame page is done inside the **Page Inspector**. You will have to click on the **Page settings** tab at the top right-hand side of the **Page Inspector**.

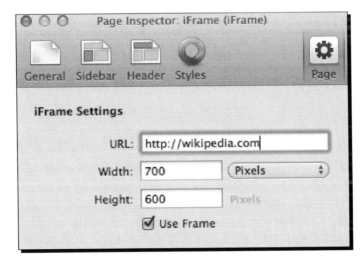

Configuring your iFrame is very simple. Enter in the URL that you want to reference into the URL field. Remember to include `http://` or `https://` in the URL. Then input the **Width** and **Height** settings for the exact size that you want the frame to be. The height and width can be expressed in either exact pixels or in percentages. In most case you will use exact pixels. The percentages may be useful if you are using a variable width theme. Lastly, you can check the **Use Frame** checkbox, if you would like to have a border around your iFrame.

There are a few things that you should watch out for when using an iFrame. Horizontal or vertical scroll bars may show up if the page being displayed in the iFrame is larger than the frame itself. Some websites will not allow you to display them inside an iFrame. For example, if you placed `http://google.com` into the iFrame, you will end up with a blank page. Lastly, if the web page that you are loading into the iFrame contains a lot of resources, this could impact the speed and performance of your website as well.

Time for action - creating an iFrame page

Let's go ahead and create an iFrame page in our RapidWeaver project.

1. Add a new iFrame page to your RapidWeaver project.

2. Open up the **Page settings** pane in the **Page Info inspector**.

3. In the URL setting, add `http://wikipedia.com`.

4. In the **Height** setting, enter **700**.

5. In the **Width** setting, enter **500**.

6. Preview your web page!

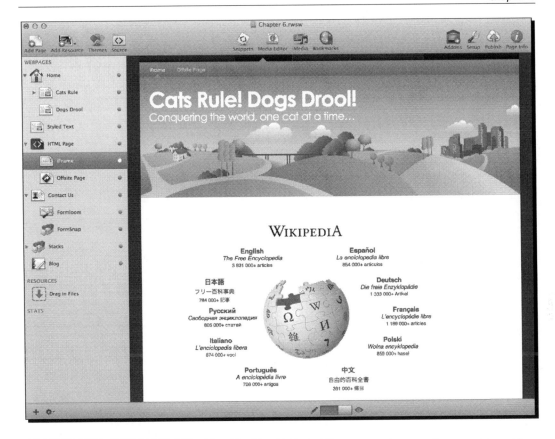

What just happened?

As you will notice, the entire Wikipedia website has been embedded into our project. You can navigate through the entire Wikipedia site and you will never leave this web page. Now obviously embedding a website like Wikipedia onto your web page is not too useful. Where this can really come in handy, is that it's an easy way to integrate a third-party service that you use such as a support ticketing system, into your website. However, you should make certain that you are authorized to do so.

Offsite Stack

Similar to the iFrame page plugin, the **Offsite Stack** will allow you to embed an external website onto your stacks page. For more information on this stack check it out at `http://joeworkman.net/rapidweaver/stacks/offsite`.

Offsite page

Instead of embedding an iFrame to another website, the offsite page allows us to redirect visitors to a different web page. The Offsite page will allow you to have a link in the **Navigation** menu that will go to any URL configured.

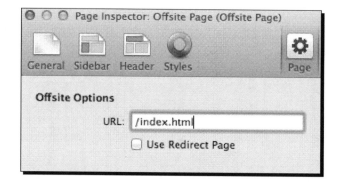

Using the **Page Inspector**, you can configure the URL that the menu item should link to. There is an option to redirect page when visitors click on the link. This may be a personal preference, but I don't recommend using the redirect page. Obviously, someone disagrees with me or else this setting would not exist!

 Links can open in the same window, or a new window. In order to configure this, use the **Open in new window** setting in the **General** tab of the **Page Inspector**.

So you may still be thinking, what are Offsite pages useful for? I use the Offsite page when I want to add a link to my **Navigation** menu to a page that may exist in a completely different part of my website. A couple of other good uses could be for affiliating links or linking to your various social networking profiles on websites such as Github, Facebook, and Twitter.

Time for action - creating an Offsite page

Let's go ahead and create an iFrame page in our RapidWeaver project.

1. Add a new Offsite page to your RapidWeaver project.

2. Open up the **Page settings** pane in the **Page Info inspector**.

3. In the URL setting, add `http://wikipedia.com`.

4. Preview your web page!

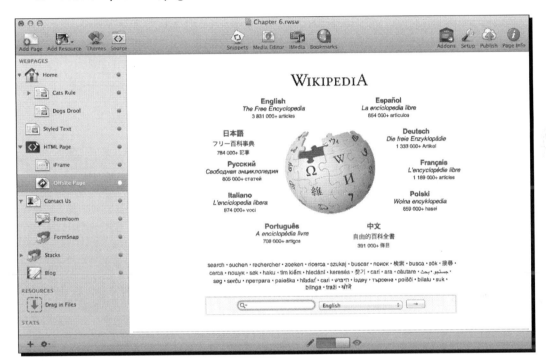

What just happened?

The reason that we are seeing the Wikipedia website in preview is because this page technically does redirect to that website. Now if we wanted to point the Offsite page to an internal web page instead of an external one, you could do this in two different ways. You could simply put in the full HTTP URL to the internal web page. Another way that you could do this is simply put the path and file name to the page that you want to point to. Therefore, if I would like to redirect to the home page, I could have configured the URL in the settings to be `index.html`.

Contact Form

The **Contact Form** page allows visitors to send messages and attachments via e-mail with an easy-to-use form. You can customize the page to have any number of fields using checkboxes, radio buttons, text fields, pop-up menus, and more.

> The **Contact Form** requires PHP v5 to be installed on your server. If you are unsure whether your server supports PHP, contact your hosting company before attempting to use the **Contact Form** page type.

The Contact Form fields

The **Contact Form** supports six different types of fields. Each element has an editable label as well as the option to make that field required. This means that your visitors must complete the given field before the form can be submitted.

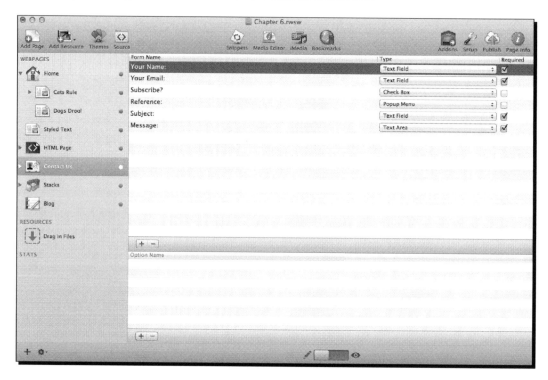

To make a field required, simply click on the **Required** checkbox.

- ◆ **Text Field**: Restricts visitors to typing a single line of text
- ◆ **Text Area**: Allows visitors to type an unlimited amount of text
- ◆ **Check Box**: Visitors select one or more of the displayed options by clicking its box
- ◆ **Popup Menu**: Visitors make a single selection from a defined pop-up menu
- ◆ **Radio Buttons**: Visitors make a single selection from a list of options
- ◆ **Attachments:** Allows visitors to attach multiple files to the form

When you first add a contact form to your project, there will be four common fields for any contact form preconfigured. If you would like to remove any of these fields, simply select the field in the list by clicking on it, and then click on the **[-]** button at the bottom of the list pane.

In order to add a new field to the list, click on the **[+]** button. Once you see the new field has been added to the list, you can edit its label, select the desired field type, and mark it as required if so desired. You can also easily change the order of the fields that you have defined by dragging and dropping them into place.

When typing the field name for a newly added element, use a delimiter such as a colon (:) or a hyphen (–) to separate the label from the content provided by your visitors. Without a delimiter, the label and the content will be linked together in the message you receive.

Popup Menu and Radio Button

As mentioned previously, **Popup Menu** and **Radio Button** can have multiple options for visitors to choose from. You will need to create this list of values for each of these types of fields that you have. When you select either a **Popup Menu** or **Radio Button** field in the list, you will notice that the options pane at the bottom becomes available.

To add our first option for a **Popup/Radio** field, click on the **[+]** button at the bottom of the **Options list** pane. You will see a new option be added to the list with the default value of **Name** in it. Double-click on the new option and type in your desired value. Simply repeat this process to add as many options as you see fit. Just like the fields, you can remove items from the list by clicking on the **[-]** button. You can also reorder the items by dragging and dropping them into place.

Time for action - creating a Contact Form page

Now we are going to create a new contact form for our RapidWeaver project.

1. Add a new **Contact Form** page to your RapidWeaver project.

2. Add a new form field with the following attributes: **Name: Subscribe?**, **Type: Check Box**.

3. Add a second new field with the following attributes: **Name: Reference:**, **Type: Popup Menu**.

4. Select both fields in the list and move them below the default e-mail field.

5. Select the **Reference** field that we created. At the bottom of the window add a couple of different options: **Online Advertisement** and **Friend Referral**.

6. Preview your web page!

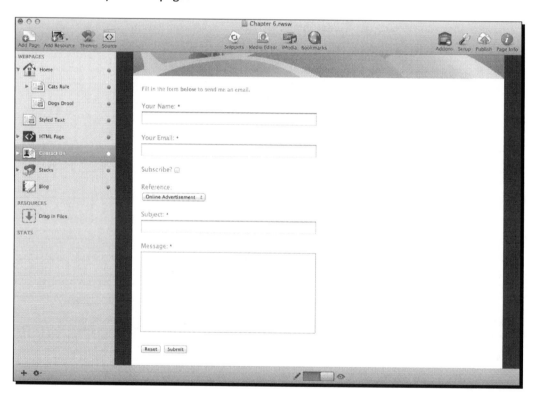

What just happened?

We have now created a very simple contact form for our website. We added a couple of non-default fields in order to gather a little bit more information from our visitors. While this form is good to go visually, it does not yet have the ability to send an e-mail with all of the data yet. Let's learn how to do that now.

Contact Form setup

Now that we have set up our **Contact** page with all the fields and options that we would like, let's go ahead and configure the form so that it works.

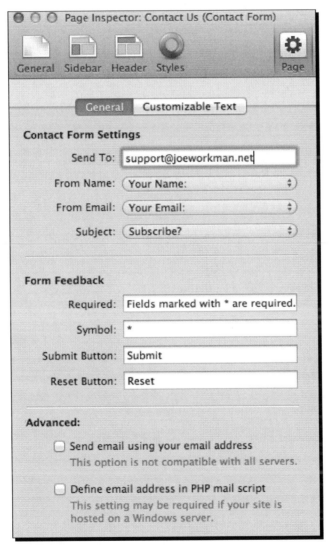

All the settings for the **Contact Form** page can be found in the **Page** tab of the **Page Inspector**.

- ◆ **Send To**: Enter the e-mail address you want the form's contents to be sent to
- ◆ **From Name**: The form field you want to appear as the name of the person the e-mail was sent from
- ◆ **From Email**: The form field that will contain the e-mail address of the person the form was submitted by
- ◆ **Subject**: The form field that will appear as the subject in e-mails received from the form
- ◆ **Required**: Enter the message you want the form to display if a required field is left blank when submitting the form
- ◆ **Symbol**: The symbol entered here to show on the form for required fields
- ◆ **Submit Button**: The words that appear on the button used to submit the form
- ◆ **Reset Button**: The words that appear on the button used to reset the form

There is also a **Customizable text** tab that will allow you to customize various other fields used by the **Contact Form**.

- ◆ **Header**: The content placed into this field will be placed above the contact form
- ◆ **Footer**: The content placed into this field will be placed below the contact form
- ◆ **Email Sent Feedback**: This is the content that will be displayed to your visitor after the form has been successfully submitted

 All three of these fields are Styled Text fields. This means that you can use all of the goodies that we learned in *Chapter 4, Styled Text Page* to style the content in the areas the way that you like it.

Time for action - setting up our form

Let's go ahead and configure the form that we created in the previous exercise so that it will e-mail us with the information that our visitors submit.

1. Open up the **Page settings** pane inside the **Page Info Inspector**.
2. Enter your e-mail address into the **Send To** setting field.
3. Verify that the **From Name, From Email**, and **Subject** fields are properly mapped to the fields defined in the form.
4. Publish your website and test!

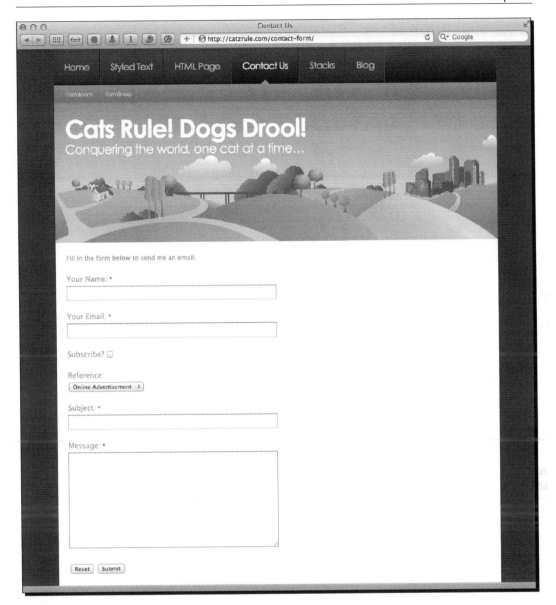

What just happened?

We configured our Contact Form to send us an e-mail whenever a visitor submits the form. The e-mail should look as if it was sent from the e-mail address that was typed into the form that was submitted. The subject of the e-mail should be the subject field defined in the form. If this is not true, then you may need to re-verify that the field mapping is properly set up in the **Page settings**.

Have a go hero – styling your form

Now that we have properly set up our form, let's go ahead and add some styled content to the **Header**, **Footer**, and **Email Feedback** sections. Remember that you can style the text in addition to adding images and other things as well.

Formloom

If you want to take your forms to the next level then look no further than the Formloom plugin by Yabdab Software. Formloom is pretty much the one stop shop for capturing almost any type of data via a form on your website. It has a plethora of features that the default **Contact Form** plugin that we just reviewed, does not. Formloom is a third-party plugin developed by Yabdab Software. You can download a demo and purchase it from `http://yabdab.com/plugins/formloom`.

The obvious question is why should you use Formloom when RapidWeaver ships with a **Contact Form** page already? The short answer is that Formloom allows you to build more robust forms that look more modern and professional. For the long answer, just keep reading!

 As Formloom has so many features, I will not be able to review every nook and cranny here. However, there are a couple great of e-books already written about Formloom that you may want to check out if you get serious about creating complex forms with Formloom. You can get these e-books at `http://insiderapidweaver.com`.

Form builder

When you first add a Formloom page to your project, you will notice that it is much more robust than the default form page. It supports over 13 different form field types! In addition to the same field types included in the out-of-the-box **Contact Form**, Formloom supports date pickers, multi-select boxes, checkboxes, reCaptcha tests, passwords, and more.

In addition to form labels, each field can have a text description and have its pre-defined width set to an exact pixel. This is great for making sure that your form fields line up so everything looks clean and professional. You also have the ability to validate the content that visitors have defined. This is a great feature for ensuring that your visitors are properly filling out the form.

Formloom supports row and column breaks, which will allow you to style your form into multiple columns. When a form has multiple fields it will look more pleasant than when the form is not linear and broken up into multiple columns.

E-mail template

Formloom allows you to customize both the e-mail you receive once the form is filled as well as the receipt e-mail that your visitors will receive. You can access the e-mail templates at the bottom tab of the Formloom edit window. Once you have completed building your form, Formloom will create placeholders for each field.

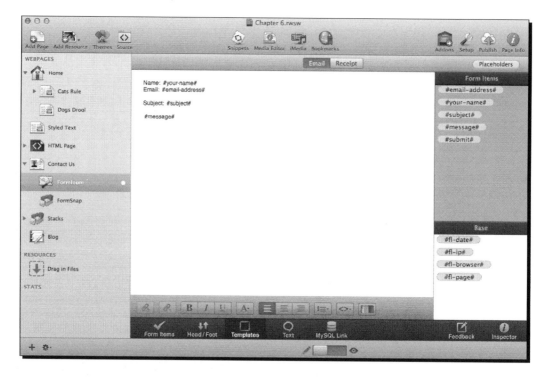

When these placeholders are dragged into the template, they will be replaced in the e-mail with the content that the visitor typed into the referenced fields. Lastly, as you may have noticed, these templates are Styled Text areas. This means that you can use all of the cool tricks that we learned in *Chapter 4, Styled Text Page* here.

MySQL link

Are you database geeks ready? This is where Formloom starts pulling no punches! Not only can Formloom send e-mail but it can also populate data into a MySQL database. The configuration can be accessed in the **MySQL link** tab at the bottom of the Formloom window. As long as you know some basics of databases, the configuration is pretty straightforward.

Once you input your database credentials, you simply need to map a form field to a database table field. This matching must be a one-to-one pairing. Formloom supports updating a single database table. You cannot update multiple database tables with the data from one form.

Formloom will not create the database and the database tables for you. You must do this on your own. Most hosting providers have decent web admin consoles to assist you with setting all this up. Please contact your hosting company for assistance if you need help setting up your MySQL database.

Formloom settings

Formloom has probably more settings than any other plugin out there. All the settings can be found in the **Page** tab of the **Page Inspector**. We are going to review the **Settings** tab, which should be the first tab you see when you open the **Page Settings** window.

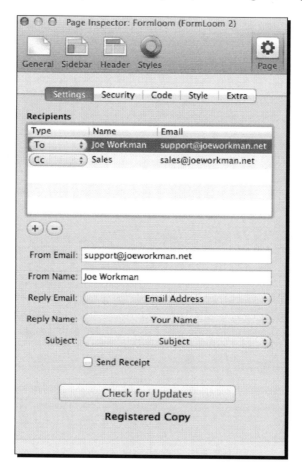

These settings are there to set up your e-mail recipients, subjects, and so on. Most of these should be very self-explanatory. One key difference that you should see is that your e-mail can have multiple recipients. You can add as many e-mails as you would like to the **To**, **CC**, and **BCC** fields. There is a checkbox at the end that also allows you to send a receipt e-mail to your visitors.

If at any point you change any form field settings, you will want to come back into this **Settings** tab and verify these settings again. Formloom may shuffle these fields around when you reconfigure your form.

 Under the **Extra/PHPMailer** tabs, I recommend that you select **Use PHPMailer to Send Mail**. You will get a more robust and reliable email setup for your form.

FormSnap stacks

Yabdab has also released the full power of the Formloom Plugin as a full stack suite named FormSnap! With FormSnap you have all the power of Formloom that we just reviewed plus the flexibility of Stacks. This means that you have complete control of the layout and design of your forms.

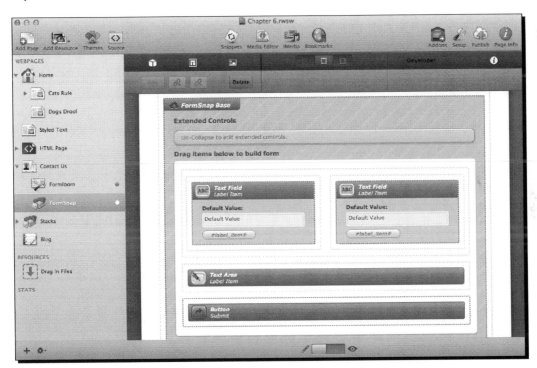

For more information on FormSnap head over to `http://yabdab.com/stacks/snaps/formsnap`.

 FormSnap is a separate product from the Formloom plugin. Therefore, please ensure that you evaluate both products to determine which way best suits your needs.

Have a go hero – creating a Formloom form

In this section, I only touched the surface of the power of Formloom. I encourage you to go download a demo version of the plugin and replicate the **Contact Form** that we created earlier in this chapter. Play around with the new settings in Formloom in order to understand them better. For example, you could add a validation rule to the e-mail field. You could also add a reCaptcha. You may also want to play around with splitting your form into multiple columns.

Common page elements with stacks

Web pages contain many common components. We have seen that Stacks is perfect for building these components. In this section, I am going to review many of these common components and some of my recommendations on how you can build them using stacks; most of the recommendations here are developed by third-party developers. The stacks mentioned here only scratch the surface of what is out there. Take these as a starting point but keep your eyes open for other possible solutions for you.

I am not going to go in depth into any of the recommended products here. All of these stacks are ones that I consider to be best of breed. There are many more great stacks out there than I could ever possibly list here. I recommend that you do your own detective work and find what stacks out there will work best for you. This should serve as an excellent starting point though.

FreeStack theme

In our chapter on themes, I only briefly mentioned the FreeStack theme by BlueBall Design because we had not reviewed the Stacks plugin yet. Well now that you know how awesome Stacks is, let me explain how cool the FreeStack theme is.

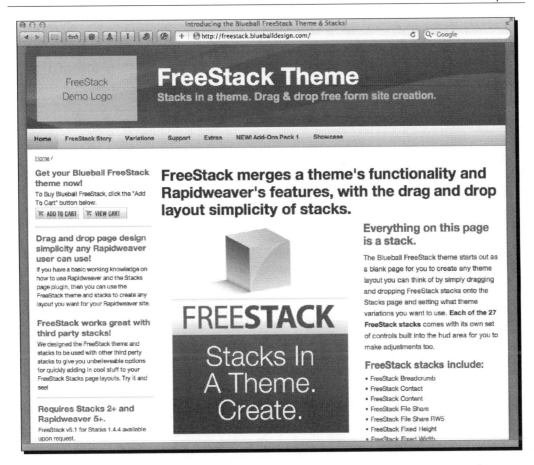

Traditionally Stacks is used to build the content of your website. Everything else (header, footer, sidebar, and so on) is handled by the theme. But what if you were able to use the powerful and flexible fluid layout of stacks to build your own theme? That is exactly what you can do with the FreeStack theme!

The FreeStack theme is a set of Stacks that allows you to place your navigation, sidebar, content area, and more anywhere you like on the page. You can then style all of these elements individually in order to create your own custom looking theme that no one else would have! Sounds like a dream right?

Let me bring you a word of caution with a pinch of realism. There is no doubt that FreeStack is powerful. I have seen some truly amazing websites built with these stacks. However, I have also seen some really bad ones! My advice is to be honest with yourself; if you don't think that you have the design skills, you may be better off with a traditional theme. (I say this only because I care.)

For more information on the FreeStack theme head over to the Blueball Design's site at `http://freestack.blueballdesign.com`.

Banner slideshows

It's common that the main banners on websites are not just static images. More often than not, the main banner will contain a set of images that will get cycled through.

Cycler

Cycler supports two-dozen effects that can be daisy chained together to allow for unlimited possibilities. What is also unique about Cycler is that you can place anything you want inside of it, not just images.

While Cycler works great for banners, it can be easily utilized throughout your site. For more information about Cycler head over to `http://joeworkman.net/rapidweaver/stacks/cycler`.

Superflex

Superflex is another stylish image-based slider with a very streamlined and modern design. Its defining feature is that it was developed from the ground up to beautifully scale with sites and themes built on responsive design.

For more information about Superflex head over to
`http://ncdthemes.com/rapidweaver/stacks/superflex`.

Slidorion

Slidorion is a combination image slider and accordion where you can have a nice text area displayed alongside your banner image.

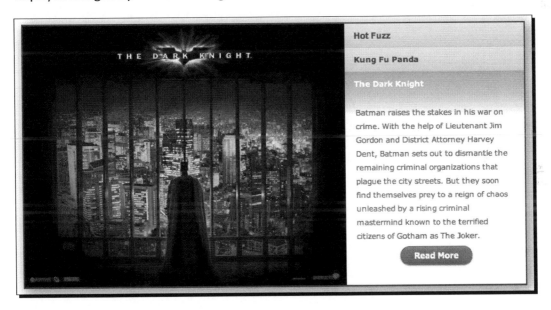

This is a great way to add even more details about what you are showcasing in your banner. For more information about Slidorion head over to
`http://weaveraddons.com/stacks/slidorion`.

Lightboxes

Lightboxes have become common on every single website. They allow your users to click on a link in order for a panel to open on top of your website content. This panel can contain extra data or media that would otherwise be hidden with the user.

Expose

Expose is arguably the most versatile lightbox stack out there. You can place whatever content within it that you see fit: video, image, text, and more. While you can use Expose as a traditional lightbox, it can also be displayed on page load. This allows you to easily display messages (or advertisements) to your visitors when they view your site.

For more information about Expose head over to
http://joeworkman.net/RapidWeaver/stacks/expose.

SimpleBox

SimpleBox is a lightweight, but highly flexible lightbox stack. Just like Expose, it can take most content that you throw at it. SimpleBox can also launch on page load as well.

For more information about SimpleBox go to
http://symfonip.com/products/simplebox.

Tables

We all have data to display on our website and there are certain types of data that are best displayed in a table.

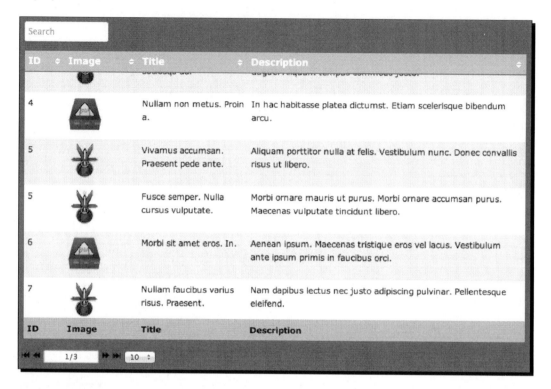

Power Grid

Power Grid allows you to build tables easily, all within RapidWeaver. As it's built with stacks, you can add whatever stack data you want into each cell. You have full customization on background, borders, and more. For more information about Power Grid head over to http://joeworkman.net/RapidWeaver/stacks/power-grid.

Power Grid CSV

Sometimes managing large amounts of data is simply easier using spreadsheets. Power Grid CSV will take your spreadsheet data via either a CSV file or Google Spreadsheet. Along with all the features of Power Grid, you can search, sort, and scroll through your table. It even supports Markdown for even richer data. For more details on Power Grid CSV, head over to http://joeworkman.net/RapidWeaver/stacks/power-grid-csv.

Buttons

Buttons are a staple on any website. We use them to submit forms, launch lightboxes, download files, and more.

Sweet Button

The Sweet Button stack is an extremely versatile button that can be styled in hundreds of different ways. It has 93 different icons available as accents for your button.

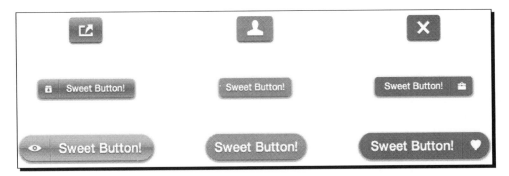

You can even change the button's style after it's been clicked! For more details on Sweet Button, head over to `http://joeworkman.net/rapidweaver/stacks/sweet-button`.

Lynx

Lynx is a little bit more than just a button. Lynx was made to act as a full-scale e-commerce store, downloads area, or good old fashion external link farm. In true traditional NCD fashion, this stack is stylish, sexy, and cool.

For more details on Lynx, head over to `http://ncdthemes.com/rapidweaver/stacks/lynx`.

Fonts

As we heard before, you can't simply use whatever font you want and expect it to work on all of your visitors' computers. There are a limited number of fonts that are recommended for web use. However, it is possible to import new web safe fonts into your website.

Font Stylr

The Font Stylr stacks bundle was the first of its kind. It offers 75 different styled fonts that can be used safely on your website. These fonts include Serif, Script, Grunge, and many more types of fonts. For more details on Font Stylr, head over to `http://stacks.blueballdesign.com/fontstylr/fontstylr.html`.

Google web fonts

Google has started offering everyone free web fonts, which can be included in your website with just one line of code and without worrying about the multiple web font formats, sub-setting, file size, download speed, and so on. In order to use this in your RapidWeaver projects, you will need to get your hands dirty with some CSS though. For more information, head over to `http://www.google.com/webfonts`.

Have a go hero – using web fonts

If you are feeling geeky, go ahead and attempt to use Google web fonts. It's really not all too difficult. For each font listed on Google, it will supply you with a `<link>` HTML code. Simply place this code into your page Header. Google will also give you some sample CSS code that you can use. The following code is a sample of how to apply the font to your Heading 1:

```
h1{font-family: ‚Wellfleet', cursive;}
```

Content and layout

The following stacks are more common purpose layout elements that can be used to help you improve the layout of your content.

Styled Stack

The Styled Stack takes a plain simple stack and allows you to do more with it. It allows you to add inset or drop-shadows to any stack and more advanced background tiling options. Styled Stack ships with a ton of awesome background image media that can be used to make your website shine. For more information on the Styled Stack, head over to `http://joeworkman.net/rapidweaver/stacks/styled-stack`.

ZipList

The ZipList stack allows you to add quick and simple collapsible lists to your RapidWeaver built website. Whether it's information about a product, an FAQ, or a list of TV stars and their biographies, ZipList helps you keep the information tidy and organized. For more information on ZipList, head over to `http://seydesign.com/products/Stacks/Premium/ZipList`.

Lines

Lines is an awesome set of styled horizontal lines that can be used to divide your content. Lines include 13 variations to choose from. Some styles use CSS3, which may only work in modern web browsers. For more information on Lines, head over to `http://joeworkman.net/rapidweaver/stacks/lines`.

Houdini

Houdini allows you to magically relocate stacks to places on your web page that you normally would not be allowed to, such as the sidebar and footer. Houdini also makes it dead simple to add stacks into ExtraContent. For more information on the Houdini, head over to `http://joeworkman.net/rapidweaver/stacks/houdini`.

Daily

Daily will display content based on the day of the week. This is great for when you want to vary your content on your web page so that your visitors are always seeing something new and different. For more information on Daily, head over to `http://www.doobox.co.uk/stacks_store/demos/daily.html`.

Summary

We reviewed a lot of new page types in this chapter. A couple of them (iFrame and Offsite) probably won't be used often; however, they are great tools to have for when you need them. You also got some good recommendations on some good stacks that cover a lot of the common web page elements required for building your website.

Specifically, we covered:

◆ HTML page is a great utility for not just coding in HTML. It can also be used for PHP, CSS, JavaScript, and even plain text.

◆ The iFrame page can be useful for embedding external web pages into your RapidWeaver projects.

◆ The Offsite page makes a perfect utility for adding links to your navigation menu to other web pages.

◆ We learned how to build a basic Contact Form for our website.

◆ The Formloom plugin by Yabdab is a great plugin to build more advanced forms.

◆ You learned about some great stacks by many different third-party developers.

We are now going to continue our journey and venture into adding images and multimedia into our RapidWeaver projects.

7
Multimedia Pages

Websites would be pretty boring if they did not have media. In my opinion, words are overrated! What's the saying? "Pictures are worth a 1000 words". Have a look at my product pages; I may have two to three sentences and the rest of the page is images and video.

We are going to be reviewing the following topics in this chapter:

- ◆ Photos and images
- ◆ Video
- ◆ File sharing

Photos and images

We all want to place photos on our websites. Whether it is a photo gallery of a family vacation or your last company party, or a simple image of our product. Right now we are going to review some great ways to get photos and images to enrich our websites. We are going to review the Photo Album plugin that ships with RapidWeaver, as well as dive into some really great products by some third-party developers and maybe one or two from yours truly.

As this section focuses on images and photos, I want to remind you about our rule of not adding large images directly into your RapidWeaver projects. You do not want to add your 15-megapixel vacation photos directly into your RapidWeaver projects! If you do this, you will notice that your project files grow in size very quickly. You will also notice that RapidWeaver's performance may be degraded as it has to work with so many large images in your project. Therefore, please remember to resize your images to more acceptable sizes. Most of the time 1024 to 1280 pixels is the absolute largest that you will ever display your images on the Web. If you follow this simple rule, you will have a much more pleasant experience building your websites!

Photo Album

The Photo Album page plugin ships with RapidWeaver and seamlessly integrates with iPhoto to allow you to easily share your photos on your RapidWeaver website. When you add a Photo Album page to your project, you will see that it displays all of your iPhoto albums. You can easily build an online gallery or slideshow from the photos in your albums.

 There is a little known feature, where you can configure the Photo Album page to display a slideshow of a Flickr feed! See the slideshow settings in the following section for more details.

Using iPhoto albums

All your iPhoto albums will be listed in the left-hand column. To use one of these albums in your project, simply select the desired album from the list.

When you select your desired album, you will see thumbnails of all the contained photos appear in the right-hand content pane. By default, all the photos will be selected for publishing. If you do not want a particular image to be published, all you need to do is deselect the checkbox next to it. You can also manually rearrange the order the images need to appear, by simply dragging them into the desired order.

By default, the file name will be used as the caption under each photo. However, you can override this by simply editing the **Caption** field for each photo. To edit the caption field, all you need to do is double-click on the field and start typing.

Creating custom photo albums

If you don't use iPhoto, and want to use images that are stored somewhere else on your computer, you can create your own custom Photo Album page. At the very top of the album list on the left pane, you will see an album titled **Your Album (Click to Change)**. When you select that, you can type in a custom name for your album. Once that is done, you will be able to drag-and-drop your own photos into the content pane. You can also use the [+] button located at the bottom-left of the window. This button will open a standard open dialog box so that you can navigate and locate your desired photo.

Once you have added all your images into the page, you can rearrange and change the captions of the photo just as you could with the iPhoto albums.

Photo Album setup options

The Photo Album page has a bunch of settings that you can access via the **Page** tab of the **Page Inspector** window. Most of these settings are pretty self-explanatory; however, let's quickly review them:

General

The following is a brief explanation of the options available in the **General** tab:

Option	Description
Use Flash Slideshow	When checked, a flash slideshow will be used instead of the gallery. See the following section for all the settings of the slideshow.
Captions	This drop-down list gives you several options for where you would like the image captions to be displayed.
Thumbnail Size	This adjusts the size of the thumbnails used in the gallery. The further right that you move the slider, the larger the thumbnails will be.
Use square thumbnails	This will automatically crop all your images so that they are squares. I recommend using this setting if you are going to be using images that will vary in size. If you have a lot of different sized images in your gallery, it's not going to look very clean.
Description	This is a Styled Text area that will be placed between the album title and the photo gallery.
Image Settings	These settings are used to determine the quality of the photos that will be published to your site. Please keep in mind that the larger or higher quality photos will take much longer time to download. This will result in slowing your website down for your visitors.
Navigation	This allows you to customize the navigation labels for the image gallery when viewing the full resolution images.

Flash Slideshow

All the settings in the Slideshow interface should be pretty self explanatory, except for the Flickr RSS setting. When this setting is enabled, the RSS feed from Flickr will be used instead of the images that you configured in the Photo Album. For more information on how to generate the proper Flickr RSS feed that you desire, check out http://www.flickr.com/services/feeds.

The visual effects settings will allow you to modify the visual transitions between photos and various tweaks for each effect. The slideshow audio will allow you to play music of your choice while the slideshow is playing. All you need to do is drag-and-drop your audio file into the drop area.

Because the slideshow feature used in Photo Album uses flash, it will not work on most mobile platforms, especially iOS devices such as an iPad or iPhone.

EXIF

Exchangeable Image File Format (EXIF) data is metadata that is stored with your image. This data can contain all the settings that were used to generate the photo. This includes date, ISO, shutter speed, aperture, and more.

Photo Album can display this data for you alongside the full resolution images in its gallery. Inside the **EXIF** settings tab, you can select all the possible settings that you would like to display for the photos in your gallery.

The **Missing EXIF** tags setting can be useful. This will not display a certain tag for a photo if it does not contain any data.

Advanced

The **Advanced** tab has some performance settings for caching, which will greatly improve previewing and publishing your Photo Album pages. Unless you have a specific reason, you will probably want to simply leave these settings alone.

If you have already made comments for your photos inside your iPhoto library, at the bottom of this pane there is a convenient button that will import all of those into your Photo Album page for you.

Time for action - creating a custom photo album

Let's go ahead and create a Photo Album page with a custom album. We are going to export photos from iPhoto, as we never want to directly add large images into our projects. We will be using the same RapidWeaver project file that we have been building throughout this book.

1. Add a new Photo Album page to your RapidWeaver project.

2. Rename your page to something like **Photo Album**.

3. Double-click on **Your Album (Click to Change)** at the top of the album list, and give your album a name.

4. Open iPhoto and select some photos that you would like to add to your photo album. You can select multiple images by holding down the *command* key while selecting your photos.

5. It may be tempting to drag these photos into RapidWeaver. However, inside iPhoto, choose the **File | Export** option. A new Export utility will open.

6. I recommend that you set the **JPEG Quality** as **Medium** and **Size** as **Large**:

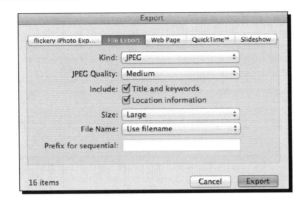

7. Click on the **Export** button and select a folder where we will temporarily store these images. Your desktop may be a convenient place for this.

8. Once the images have been exported successfully, you can quit iPhoto.

9. Now let's drag-and-drop our newly exported photos into our Photo Album page in RapidWeaver. Keep the exported photos around for our next exercise.

10. Open the page settings in **Page Inspector**, and add an optional description for your album.

11. Preview your web page!

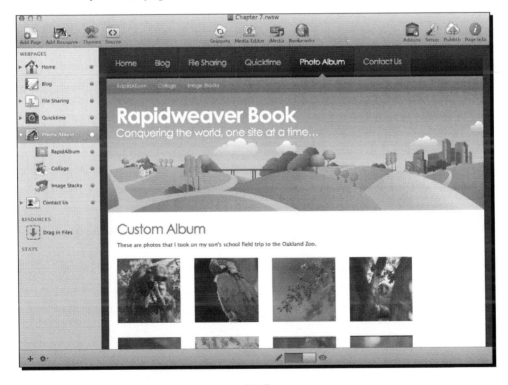

What just happened?

We have just created a new custom Photo Album page. We exported all the photos from iPhoto. We did this to ensure that RapidWeaver runs smoothly. If we were to add 100 images that are all 15 megapixels directly into RapidWeaver without them shrinking down, we would see that RapidWeaver may take a little longer to perform tasks such as exporting or publishing our website. So for a more enjoyable experience using photos inside RapidWeaver, remember to always resize your images before adding them into RapidWeaver.

Have a go hero – experimenting with Photo Album

Now depending on the theme that you are using the photo album may be styled differently. Some of the more elaborate third-party themes completely restyled the Photo Album page with beautiful CSS3 and JavaScript animations. This is yet another example where RapidWeaver serves as a fabulous platform for third-party developers to build upon. I recommend that you view the photo albums inside different themes to find some that you may like.

I also recommend that you take the time to play with the other features of the Photo Album page plugin. Go ahead and see how easy it is to create a Photo Album based on one of the albums that were imported in directly from iPhoto. You may also want to play with the Flickr slideshow feature and all the other available style options that we reviewed in this section.

RapidAlbum

RapidAlbum is a great tool to have in your toolbox. It takes the Photo Album page to the next level by adding some great JavaScript lightboxes and many more effects to your galleries. It even ships with 16 different gallery templates to choose from. And if that is not enough, this great plugin is FREE!

RapidAlbum is an expansive plugin with a ton of features. We are not going to be able to review all of the features here, but we are going to run through the basics.

RapidAlbum is developed by Scott Mackie and can be found at `http://www.smackie.org/software/rapidalbum`.

Adding photos

When you first add the RapidAlbum page you will see a very familiar interface for adding images. At the top there is a drop-down which allows you to add photos in three different ways:

- ◆ **Manual**: In manual mode, you can drag-and-drop all the images that you would like to add directly into the content area
- ◆ **Folder**: You can browse to a local folder on your machine and RapidAlbum will add all the images that are contained within the folder
- ◆ **SubAlbum**: This option allows you to create a hierarchy to your photo galleries by creating a sub gallery when a photo is opened

Similar to the Photo Album page, a photo will not be published as a part of the gallery if the selection box next to it is not checked. You can also define captions for images by double-clicking on the caption field for each photo. One nice addition that RapidAlbum adds is the ability to sort the photos by file name, caption, date, and manually.

Gallery themes

If you go to the **Template** tab in edit mode, you will see a drop down list that has 16 available themes to choose from. The default theme is very similar to the gallery from the Photo Album page. In order to change to a different theme, you will need to select the new theme in the drop-down list, and click the **Apply** button. Once you apply a theme, you will see a nice overview of what that theme appears like, directly below.

RapidAlbum also lets you bring the geek out! You have access to all the HTML code that each template generates. This means that you can tweak templates to work just the way you like; or if you are feeling extra geeky, you can even develop your own theme!

RapidAlbum settings

RapidAlbum has a bunch of great settings to completely customize your gallery. We are not going to review all of them here because RapidAlbum has a very detailed user manual that I recommend you review for all the settings. A few of the settings that stand out are the detail photo and thumbnail sizing, elaborate support for dynamic descriptions, and full RSS feed support for your gallery!

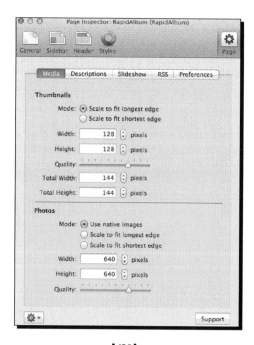

Time for action – creating a RapidAlbum page

We are going to create a RapidAlbum page that uses the same photos that we exported from iPhoto in our last exercise. We will be using the same RapidWeaver project file that we have been building throughout this book.

1. Add a new RapidAlbum page to your RapidWeaver project and rename it to something like **RapidAlbum**.

2. In the RapidAlbum **Media** tab, select **Folder** from the **Type** drop-down list.

3. Click on the **Browse** button and locate the folder where you exported the photos from our last exercise.

4. If there are any unwanted image or files that have appeared in the gallery list, go ahead and uncheck them. This will effectively remove them from the gallery.

5. Go to the **Template** tab and change the theme to the **Greybox** theme. Make sure to click the **Apply** button for the theme to actually get applied.

6. In the page settings, turn on **Scale to fit shortest edge** for thumbnails. This will give us square thumbnails.

7. Preview your web page and enjoy!

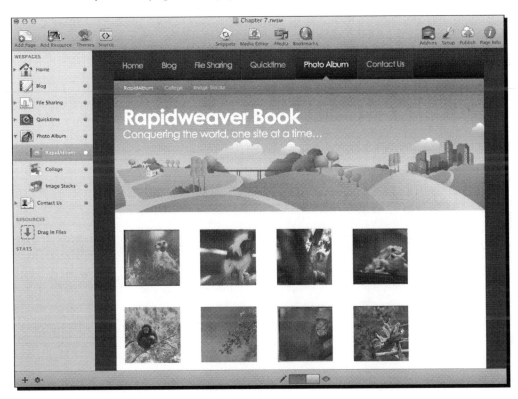

What just happened?

We now have a gallery page that looks similar to the Photo Album page that we created in our last exercise. However, if you click on the thumbnails in the gallery we just created, you will notice the full resolution photos will be loaded into a beautiful full screen slideshow.

Have a go hero – experimenting with RapidAlbum

I encourage you to play around with all the other features of this plugin. I promise that you will learn a lot more by taking 10 to 15 minutes to experiment with it. Play around with the various themes that come shipped with RapidAlbum. There are some that create customized slideshows instead of galleries. Some other things that you can experiment with are:

- The media settings; see how they affect the resulting galleries and slideshows
- Enable the descriptions and experiment how you can dynamically add data from the photo Meta data
- The slideshow settings that let you customize the size, color, and effects used

If you are really feeling adventurous, get your hands dirty with some code. Take one of the existing themes and play around with the HTML code and see how you can customize the theme to your liking. Remember that you can save your newly customized theme so that you can use it in future projects.

Collage

Collage is a great third-party plugin that makes highly customizable and beautiful collages. I also find that this plugin is awesome for more than just photos though. I think that it's a great way to build product pages! I actually used Collage as my product page for over a year before I built my own custom solution.

Collage has an extensive feature set that allows you to customize it in a plethora of ways. We are going to review just some of the basics here.

Collage is developed by YourHead Software, and you can download a free demo at `http://yourhead.com/collage`.

Building a collage

Adding images into Collage is just as simple as it was in the Photo Album and RapidAlbum pages. You can drag-and-drop your photo or icons into the left-hand side pane, in the edit interface. You can also use the iMedia browser interface as a convenient way for browsing your iPhoto and Aperture libraries. However, remember the first commandment of images—Thou shalt not drag 15-megapixel images directly into your RapidWeaver project!

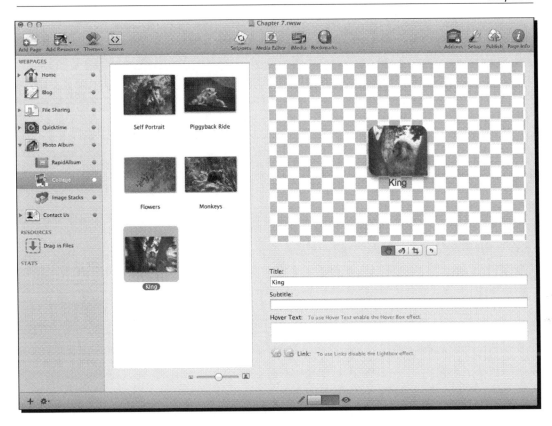

After you have added your images in to Collage, you can adjust their order by dragging them into the desired order. The right-hand side of the edit interface allows you to define the titles for your images as well as do some image modification. Directly under the image preview, you will notice a set of buttons, they are as follows:

- The first button with the hand, allows you to position the image inside of its border.

- The second button allows you to rotate the image freely to the exact angle that looks good to you.

- The third button allows you to crop the image. This is not a traditional crop as you would think. It allows you to zoom the image in or out until you get the desired crop level inside the thumbnail.

- The last button is the undo button, which you can use to undo any modifications made to your images.

Further down to the image preview, there are a few text fields that allow you to edit the **Title**, **Subtitle**, and **Hover Text** for each image. The **Title** and **Subtitle** settings are pretty self explanatory. However, by default, the **Hover Text** setting is not active. A hover text is the content displayed inside a styled box that can be revealed when your mouse hovers over an image. You can enable the hover box in the page settings. We will review this in the next section.

You also have the ability to add links to images when they are clicked. However, by default, a lightbox is opened with the full resolution image when the image is clicked. If you disable the lightbox feature in the page settings, you will be able to add a link to your images.

Styling Collage

Collage can be styled in a thousand different ways. This is why it's one of the most versatile plugins out there. You can access all the style settings inside the **Page** setting tab in the **Page Inspector** section.

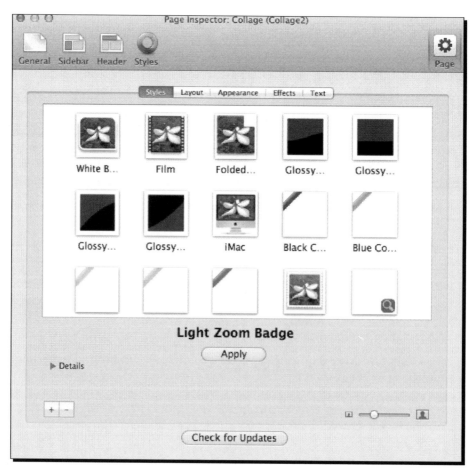

Styles

The first tab in the settings pane allows you to apply one of the seventeen built-in thumbnail styles. In order to change your theme, you will need to select the style that you want and click on the **Apply** button at the bottom of the window.

Another great feature is that you can create your own custom styles! Once you have gone through the other settings and have a thumbnail style that you like, you can come back to this tab and save that as a custom style. To do this, you just need to click on the [+] button at the bottom-left corner of this window. This will create a new style with all the styles used in the current thumbnail. This is very convenient if you would like to save collage style so that you could potentially use it in a future RapidWeaver project.

Layout

The **Layout** tab allows you to define the general layout of your collage:

* The exact width and height of your thumbnails.

* How many columns you want in your grid. If you disable grid, Collage will fit as many thumbnails as it can in a single row.

* Margin settings will tweak the horizontal and vertical padding between each thumbnail.

Appearance

The **Appearance** tab allows you to customize all kinds of style elements for your Collage thumbnails. You can configure these settings for both idle state and mouse-over state. By combining these, you can create some stunning visual effects when a user hovers over your thumbnails. Each setting in the **Appearance** tab can be enabled or disabled by simply clicking on the checkbox next to it. The following are some of the options in this tab:

Option	Description
Background	This allows you to give your thumbnails a solid background color.
Images	This setting is more advanced, and it allows you to define your own custom images that will be overlaid on top of your thumbnails. Using this setting you can achieve a really custom look. However, you need to have the knack for image design to pull this off.
Border	This allows you to customize the color and width of the border to be added to your images.
Round Corners	This allows you to apply rounded corners to your thumbnails. You can also select which corners will be affected. All of the corners that are checked will be rounded out.

Option	Description
Shadow	This allows you to give shadows to your thumbnails. Shadows have different settings in mouse over. A quick tip with shadows: 99% of the time, less is more!
Reflection	This allows you to have a reflection of your thumbnails displayed beneath them.
Fade Edges	This option allows you to fade out certain edges of your thumbnails.

Effects

There are two effects that you can achieve with Collage: **Lightbox** and **Hover Box**.

The lightbox effect will open the full resolution image of your thumbnails when a user clicks on it. The settings here will allow you to customize the size of the full resolution image that will be displayed as well as other cosmetic styles for the lightbox.

The hover box effect will add a box to each thumbnail. Whenever a thumbnail is hovered over with the mouse, the hover box will animate in and be revealed below the thumbnail. We saw earlier in this section, how to configure the text that will be displayed in the hover box. There are a bunch of style customizations that you can make here in the **Effects** tab.

Text

The **Text** tab in the Collage settings allows you to customize the style and spacing for both the titles and subtitles that are placed below the thumbnails.

There are also **Header** and **Footer** sections that will allow you to place content before and after the Collage gallery. These are Styled Text areas, so all that we learned in *Chapter 4, Styled Text Page* applies to the contents placed into these two containers.

Time for action - creating a Collage page

We are going to create a Collage page that uses the same photos that we used in our last two exercises. We will be using the same RapidWeaver project file that we have been building throughout this book.

1. Add a new Collage page to your RapidWeaver project and rename it to **Collage**.

2. Drag-and-drop the same images that we have been using for the exercises in this chapter into the Collage edit UI.

3. Go through your photos and give them a title. You may also want to adjust the crop and positioning of each photo in its thumbnail.

4. In the **Page** settings, ensure that the **Style** is set to **White Border**.

5. In the **Appearance** tab, adjust the **Shadow Opacity** for the **Idle** state down to **15%**.

6. In the **Text** tab, adjust the **Size** to be **10px** and the **Offset Y** to be **0px**.

7. Preview your Collage page!

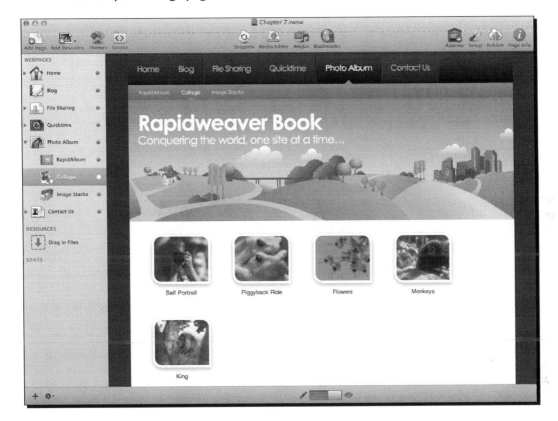

What just happened?

We just created a Collage page! As you will see, all our images are nicely styled with white borders that have rounded corners on three sides. We have drop shadows that change when you hover over each image; this gives it a nice effect, such that the images pop up when you hover over them. Lastly, our titles for each thumbnail are styled just as we configured them. Now when we click on each image, you will see that the full resolution image is displayed in a lightbox. You can click on the **Play** button to start a slideshow, or you can click on the **Next** and **Previous** buttons to manually navigate through the photos in the collage.

Have a go hero – experimenting with Collage

We have only scratched the surface of what Collage can do. I think that it would be good for you to spend more time in Collage and play around with all the various settings. You will see how versatile this plugin is and see why it's become one of the more popular plugins out there. Here are a few examples of things you could try:

♦ We did not play with the **Hover Box** at all. Go ahead and enable that inside the Collage settings. You will need to add content for the hover box into each photo. The **Hover Text** field for each photo will accept text as well as HTML. If you know a little code, this may be a great place to add an **Add to Cart** button!

♦ Play around with the different collage styles and appearance configurations. If you vary the styles between **Idle** and **Mouse over**, you can achieve some interesting visual effects.

♦ Try turning off the lightbox effect. This will allow you to add a link to each photo. This is perfect for product pages! You can display thumbnails of your products and link them to the individual product pages.

Image Stacks

So far, we have focused on the page plugins, which are essentially galleries intended to show off a collection of images. However, what if we only want to display a couple of images on your web page? As I have mentioned before, I am excited about Stacks and think that it's the best way to build a majority of your web pages. The following are some great stacks that will allow you to make your web pages shine:

Image Safe

When you add a normal image to your web page, it is extremely easy for anyone to save that image to their local computer. In Safari, you just need to right-click on an image and select **Save Image to Downloads**. An even easier way to acquire images is to simply drag them out of the browser and onto your desktop. These same features are available in pretty much all browsers out there.

Image Safe allows you to protect your images from being easily copied off your website. It will stop users from being able to drag images out of the web browser or use contextual menus to save images off your site. On top of this, Image Safe allows you to add CSS styling to your images as well.

Image Safe is developed by yours truly! For more information on Image Safe check it out at `http://joeworkman.net/rapidweaver/stacks/image-safe`.

No image is 100 percent safe on the Web! Anyone with knowledge of digging through website code will be able to find the URL to an image, even if it's protected with Image Safe. However, Image Safe does protect images from the 99.9 percent of the people who have no clue how to do that.

Expose Image Pro

Expose Image Pro is the ultimate in image lightboxes. Expose does not load the full resolution images until the user actually clicks on the thumbnail. This greatly improves the web page download times. The full resolution image can be loaded externally from any location: your web server or a web service such as Flickr, SmugMugg and Dropbox. When the full resolution image is loaded, it reacts to the browser size and will always ensure that the user is able to view the entire image irrespective of whether you are on a mobile device or on a desktop.

As if that is not enough, Expose also loads all of the EXIF data from your full resolution images and displays it along with the copyright information in an LCD-esque display that looks like it came right off your DSLR camera.

Expose Image Pro is a part of my Expose stack set and can be found at
`http://joeworkman.net/rapidweaver/stacks/expose`.

Flickr Pro

The Flickr Pro stack provides a beautiful way of displaying a gallery of your images hosted on Flickr. All you need to do is enter in your Flickr ID and this stack will take care of creating all of the image thumbnails for you. When you click on the thumbnail, the full resolution image will be dynamically downloaded from the Flickr website.

The Flickr Pro stack is developed by Doobox and more details can be found at
`http://www.doobox.co.uk/stacks_store/demos/flickrpro.html`.

Fancy Image Stacks

The Fancy Image Stacks are a set of 12 amazing image stacks. These stacks do everything from full blown image galleries to adding beautiful dynamic reflections to your images.

The following are the descriptions of just a few of the stacks in this set:

◆ **Image Hover** adds hover effects such as fadeout and slide out (in eight directions) to your images. When you hover over the image, it will reveal contents in the background. The background can contain anything that you want: text, images, or mixed content.

◆ **Popup Caption** is the easiest way to add animated popup captions to your images. When you hover over the image, it will reveal contents of the caption. This stack allows a portion of the caption to always be shown as well as the ability to hide the entire caption.

◆ **Magnify Image** allows you to hover over an image and have a magnified version of it appear. You can then navigate over the image and watch the magnified version move along with your mouse.

◆ **360 Degree** allows you to show off your products with a 360° view. You could even use it to make some still motion video! All of this is accomplished by combining multiple images into a sequence. As you hover your mouse over, 360 Degree will smoothly transition between each image conveying its smooth animation.

◆ **Prints** is a beautiful stack that allows you to easily create a gallery of images that look like photo prints. As you hover over the images, each one will rotate in a random direction. When the image is clicked, the image will open in a lightbox.

The Fancy Image Stacks are some of my most popular stacks. They are available individually or as a set. For more information on Fancy Image Stacks check out the set at `http://joeworkman.net/rapidweaver/stacks/fancy-image-bundle`.

ImageMapper

Image maps allow you to map a link to a sub-section of an image. Therefore, when you click on different parts of an image, you can navigate to different URLs. The Image Mapper stack makes this very simple to set up. All you need to do is drag your image into the stack, and set up the coordinates and URL for each link.

ImageMapper is developed by Blueball Design, and more details can be found at `http://stacks.blueballdesign.com/imagemapper/imagemapper.html`.

Video

So now we have conquered adding your pictures to your website, let's move onto moving pictures! Over the past few years, video has become a necessity for almost every website. Videos are used for product videos, family vacation memories, and your favorite YouTube gag skits. You may think that adding a video to your site would be complicated. However, let me show you how simple it really is.

Video formats

There are many different video formats out there, which can be confusing to many people. However, if you stick to the two standard formats used on the Mac, `.mov` and `.mp4`, then you should be good to go. I personally prefer the mpeg-4 (`mp4`) format as it has both good video quality as well as compression. We will talk about a few different formats in the HTML5 media section later in this chapter.

Miro is a great open source media converter that allows you to convert your audio and video file to different formats. You can download your free copy at `http://www.mirovideoconverter.com.`

QuickTime and Movie Album

RapidWeaver ships with two different video page plugins. The QuickTime page allows you to add a single video to your web page. The Movie Album page, as you and imagine, creates an album from multiple videos.

QuickTime

The QuickTime page is a very simple way to create a web page that hosts a single video file. Your video will be played in Apple's proprietary QuickTime player, which is supported across all major browsers. To add a movie to the page, click on the **Choose Movie** button. A standard open file dialog window will appear. Navigate to the video file that you want to add and click on the **Open** button.

Once you have added your video to the page, you can then type a description in the text box below the video preview. However, this is not an ordinary text field; it's a Styled Text field! By now you should be experts and know all the cool things that we can do in a Styled Text field. If you need a refresher, go check out *Chapter 4, Styled Text Page*.

Lastly there are a few settings at the bottom of the QuickTime page:

Option	Description
AutoPlay	Start playing the video directly after the page finished loading in the web browser.
Show Controller	Show the player controls. Sometimes hiding the controls can give you a much cleaner and more modern look.
Kiosk Mode	This allows you to customize the color and width of the border added to your images.
Save movie for fast start	This setting allows the video to start playing before it has completely downloaded. I cannot think of a use case for not having this setting checked all the time.

 You will not be able to view the QuickTime page in Preview mode. You will need to publish the web page and the video in order for this to work.

Movie Album

The natural progression from adding a single movie to your web page is to create a gallery of videos. The Movie Album page could not make this easier to do. If you remember how to set up a Photo Album page, this is exactly the same! In Edit Mode, simply drag-and-drop your videos into the window. You can also use the iMedia browser to quickly locate your videos as well.

Once you have added your videos to the page, you can change the order of your movies by dragging them into the desired position. To change a movie's caption, double-click on the movie's existing file name or title in the **Caption** field.

RapidWeaver will automatically select a thumbnail image from an individual frame midway through the movie. If you would like to select the thumbnail image from a different position in the movie, double-click on the movie thumbnail in the list to bring up the thumbnail selection sheet. Use the slider to select a frame in the movie you want to use as the movie's thumbnail and click the **Set** button.

Inside the page settings, there are a few different settings:

- **Album Title**: The text added here will be used as the album heading, which is placed above the video gallery
- **Description**: The text that is added into this area will show up under the album title
- **Auto play Movies**: This setting will auto play videos once the user clicks on the video thumbnail

Time For action – creating a Movie Album page

We are going to create a Movie Album page. If you don't have any videos to use in a movie album, it's really easy to create one. We will review how to create a quick video of yourself. We will be using the same RapidWeaver project file that we have been building throughout this book.

1. If you already have video files to add to your Movie Album page, feel free to skip to step 4.

2. Open up the Photo Booth application on your Mac.

3. Switch it to video mode and click on the record button. Now this is important! When the video starts, get up out of your chair and do the chicken dance! Click on the stop button when you are done. Repeat this step until you have at least a few really embarrassing videos of yourself.

4. Now that we have our videos, drag-and-drop them into the Movie Album page. If you have created your funky dance move videos like I did, simply drag them out of Photo Booth and drop them directly into RapidWeaver.

5. In the **Page** settings, give your movie album a title and description.

6. Now preview your movie album and laugh at yourself! You did dance right? I did!

What just happened?

Hopefully you followed my advice and made some fun videos of yourself! Oh yeah, we also made a cool movie album. It was insanely easy to do, right? All we had to do was drag-and-drop a few videos and RapidWeaver took care of creating all the code in the background that makes our movie album tick.

Have a go hero – creating a QuickTime page

We did not do an exercise on the QuickTime page. Why don't you go ahead and give it a shot. Remember that you will need to publish your QuickTime page in order for it to fully function.

Embedding videos from online services

There are a plethora of online video services where you can upload your videos to view them online. I am sure that you have gone onto YouTube to watch some videos; maybe you have even uploaded a few yourself. Let's review how easy it is to embed these videos into our RapidWeaver projects.

Pretty much every video site will have a share or embed button associated with each video. When you click on that button, you should see some HTML code being displayed. See the preceding image for an example from YouTube. Now don't be scared here! All you need to do is copy that HTML code to your clipboard. Here are a couple of sample snippets of embed code from YouTube and Vimeo:

- **YouTube**:

  ```
  <iframe width="560" height="315" src="http://www.youtube.com/
  embed/SVmIBEr757g" frameborder="0" allowfullscreen></iframe>
  ```

- **Vimeo**:

  ```
  <iframe src="http://player.vimeo.com/video/35657975"
  width="500" height="281" frameborder="0" webkitAllowFullScreen
  mozallowfullscreen allowFullScreen></iframe>
  ```

Now inside your RapidWeaver project, you can paste that embed code into any of the places that we have already learned it should go: HTML page, Style Text (with **Ignore Formatting**), or an HTML Stack. It's really as simple as that!

Video stacks

In order to help make the aforementioned process even simpler, I have developed a set of video stacks that work with all the major video online services: YouTube, Vimeo, Flickr, Viddler, SchoolTube, and more. All you need to do is add the video ID from your video into the stack and you are done. There is no code to worry about. These stacks even allow for customizations which the embed code that we get does not allow for. For more information on my video stacks, you can check them out at `http://joeworkman.net/rapidweaver/stacks/video-bundle`.

Time for action - embedding a video into a Stacks page

We are going to embed a couple of YouTube and Vimeo videos into a Stacks page. You can also do this in a Styled Text or HTML page. Keep in mind that not all videos will be allowed to be embedded. Some users protect their videos so that they cannot be embedded on other sites. We will be using the same RapidWeaver project file that we have been building throughout this book.

1. Head over to `http://www.youtube.com/` and find a video that you would like to embed onto your website.

2. Click on the **Share** button under the video. Then click on the **Embed** button. This will unveil our embed code. Select and copy that code.

3. In your RapidWeaver project add a new Stacks page. Add an HTML stack to the page and paste in the embed code.

4. Now head over to `Vimeo.com` and find another video that you would like to embed onto your website.

5. Click on the **Share** button that is at the top-right corner of the video. This will display a window where you will see the embed code, which looks very similar to what we got from YouTube. Select and copy that code.

6. Go back into RapidWeaver and add another HTML stack to our Stacks page that we just created.

7. Paste in the embed code that we got from Vimeo.

8. Preview and enjoy your videos! I hope you picked good ones!

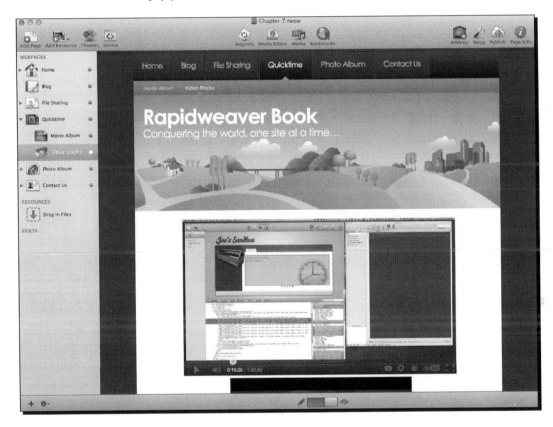

What just happened?

We just saw how easy it is to embed a video onto our web page. Now I did this in Stacks because you can easily paste the code into an HTML stack and easily use other stacks to build out different components to our page. You can do this with a Styled Text page or an HTML page. It's just not quite as elegant.

Have a go hero – embedding video into other pages

Give it a shot and try to embed a video into both a Styled Text and an HTML page. With the Styled Text page, make sure that you select the embed code after you pasted it and **Ignore Formatting**.

If you have any of the video stacks mentioned, start playing with those. You will see that there are more options available and they are a little cleaner to work with, especially if you like to shy away from the code.

HTML5 video and audio

I may start getting a little nerdy right about now. I recommend that if you are going to want to host your own video on your website, stick with me on this section. I promise that I will try not to babble too much!

Background story

I am not going to into a frenzy on Flash here, but if you have been following the tech news at all over the past few years, you are probably aware of the Flash versus HTML5 battles. Traditionally, if you wanted to embed video onto your website, you would have to use Flash. This means that in order for the video to play, your visitors would have to install the Flash plugin from Adobe. Also, one of the big fights between iPhone/iPad and Android users is about Flash. The iPhone does not support Flash.

For many years we had no choice but to use Flash. However, the World Wide Web Consortium decided that in its new version 5 of the HTML language, native support for video would be added. This means that video can be played in any web browser that supports HTML5, without requiring Flash to be installed.

While we now have a common standardized way to embed video and audio natively in HTML, the media codec to be used has not been standardized. This unfortunately means that in order to have your video play in HTML5 in all browsers, you are going to have to encode your audio/video into at least two different codecs!

For video, you will need to encode your video into H.264 MPEG-4 (mp4) and Ogg Theora (ogv). Safari (iOS included) and Internet Explorer both support H.264 codecs in order to play video in the native HTML5 player. Firefox, Chrome, and Opera support the Ogg Theora codec.

For audio, you will need to encode your audio into MPEG-3 (mp3) and Ogg Vorbis (ogg). Safari (iOS included), Internet Explorer, and Chrome all support MPEG-3 codecs in order to play audio in the native HTML5 player. Firefox and Opera support the Ogg Vobis codec.

Using HTML5 Video and Audio

If you are a code warrior you can use the `<video>` and `<audio>` HTML tags to embed media into your RapidWeaver projects. However, you'll need to be cautious with browser compatibility for older browser versions that don't support the HTML5 players.

I know that a majority of you will not want to touch the code and don't want to be bothered with the technical details. I understand; I develop the stuff that I do so that I don't have to worry about them either! I have a set of HTML5 players that not only do all the coding for you but they also have fallback capabilities to flash for those older browser versions that don't support HTML5. For more details on these HTML5 players, head over to `http://joeworkman.net/rapidweaver/stacks/html5-video` and `http://joeworkman.net/rapidweaver/stacks/html5-audio`.

File sharing

Sharing files is another common task that you are probably going to want to do on your websites. Sharing a file can be easily accomplished via RapidWeaver's standard link tool. You simply need to link a file that you have added into RapidWeaver Resources or a URL, to the location where the file is uploaded. However, there are other great ways to share files that we will look at.

File Sharing page

RapidWeaver includes a File Sharing page plugin that allows you to easily share files, URLs, and documents with visitors to your website. You can link to files on your Mac's hard drive that will be uploaded for you, or to files located elsewhere on the Internet.

The area at the top of the File Sharing window is a Styled Text area, which will be displayed atop the file list, on the web page. Now I may start sounding like a broken record, but Styled Text areas are very powerful. Refer back to *Chapter 4, Styled Text Page*, to learn all the things that you can do with them.

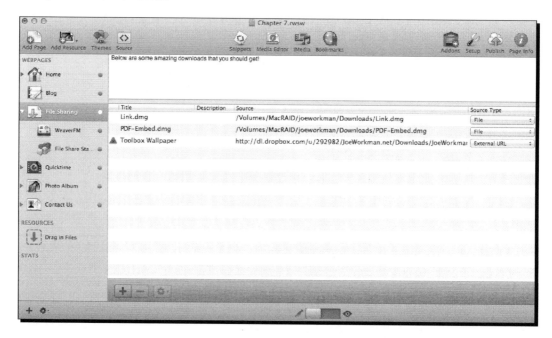

Sharing local files

There are two ways to add files to the File Sharing page. You can either drag them from your hard drive in Finder, and drop them into the File Sharing page, or use the [+] button to navigate to the file and select it. When you add a file to the list, its title will default to the file's actual name (as seen in Finder). If you wish to use a different title for the file, double-click the **Title** field to change it. You can also add an optional description about the file in the adjacent **Description** field. To change the list order of the files, you can drag the files to arrange them in the preferred order. Hopefully this sounds familiar because it's exactly how many of the plugins that we have used work as well.

In order to reduce publishing time, as well as download time for your visitors, it's best to compress your files that you want to share. Before you add the file into the File Sharing page, go into Finder and compress the file. Right-click on the file and select **Compress FILENAME**. A new file will be created with the same name but with a `.zip` extension. You will want to add this newly compressed file into the File Sharing page.

Sharing file via URLs

It's common to want to use your own download service such as Dropbox or Amazon S3 to deliver your downloads. If you are using such a service, you can easily take the URL to your file and share it via the File Sharing page.

To add URLs to RapidWeaver's File Sharing page, click the [+] button to create a new entry in the list. Add a title and a description to the new entry and then change the **Source Type** drop-down list option to **External URL**. Finally, double-click the **Source** field and paste the full URL to the file that you want to share.

 You can also use the File Sharing page as a way to share a list of URLs for anything, not just file downloads. A good use for this is to share your favorite links to your visitors. Simply follow the aforementioned steps, except you can use the URL to websites instead of to individual files.

Time for action - creating a File Sharing page

Let's go ahead and create a File Sharing page. We will be using the same RapidWeaver project file that we have been building throughout this book.

1. Add a new File Sharing page to your RapidWeaver project and rename the page to **File Sharing**.

2. Drag-and-drop any files from Finder into the File Sharing page. It's best if these files are compressed.

3. Type in a description that will show atop the file download list.

4. Preview your web page and start sharing!

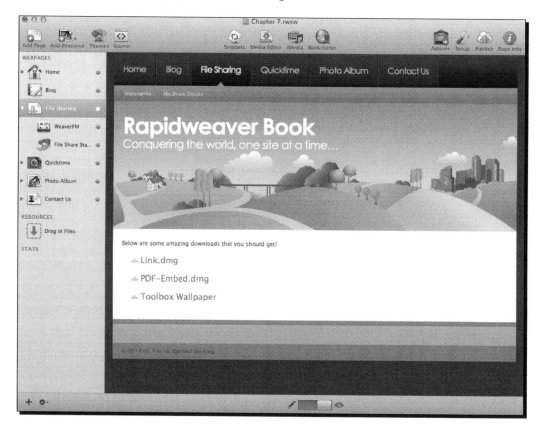

What just happened?

So we have created a very simple file sharing page. Once published, RapidWeaver will take care of uploading all the files to the proper location so that your users can download any local files that you may have added.

Have a go hero – sharing URLs

I mentioned earlier that the File Sharing page also works pretty great as a generic URL sharing tool. Create a new File Sharing page that shares a list of your favorite URLs.

WeaverFM

WeaverFM takes file sharing to a whole new level! It is a complete file management plugin for RapidWeaver. WeaverFM not only allows you to both upload and download files but it has a full blown account management as well.

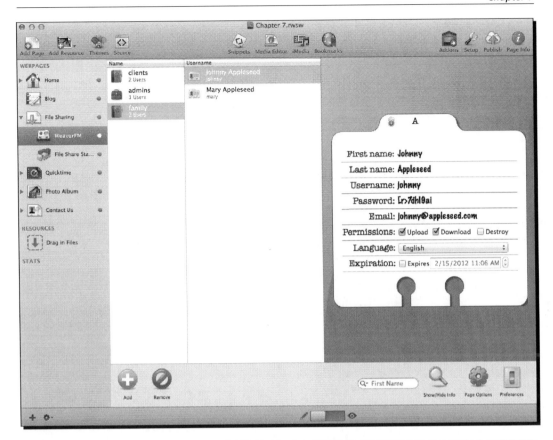

WeaverFM allows you to create password-protected accounts that limit which actions a user has access to. You can configure whether a user can upload, download, or delete files from the server. You can even create user groups so that you can easily manage these permissions on a group level. With groups, you can configure access down to the file level as well. This ensures that users can only have access to the files defined for their group.

WeaverFM has a great feature that allows users to receive an email whenever a file that they have access to has been uploaded. There are also a great set of themes to choose from. These allow you to customize the look to match your site perfectly.

Gary Barchard develops WeaverFM, and you can download your free demo at `http://www.barchard.net/projects/weaverfm`.

RapidViewer

If you would like to display your files instead of providing downloads for them, you can use RapidViewer. It has support for over 20 different file types such as DOC, XLS, PDF, PAGES, RAR, ZIP, and more. Its interface could not be easier to use. Simply Drag-and-drop your document into the plugin and you are done! There are also header and footer styled text areas so that you can add extra content around your page.

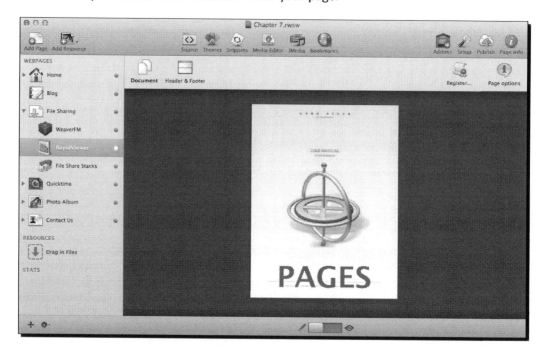

RapidViewer is developed by Omnidea; you can obtain a free trial demo by visiting http://www.omnidea.it/rapidviewer.

File Sharing Stacks

As we all love Stacks, there are also some great stacks out there to integrate file sharing directly into our Stacks pages.

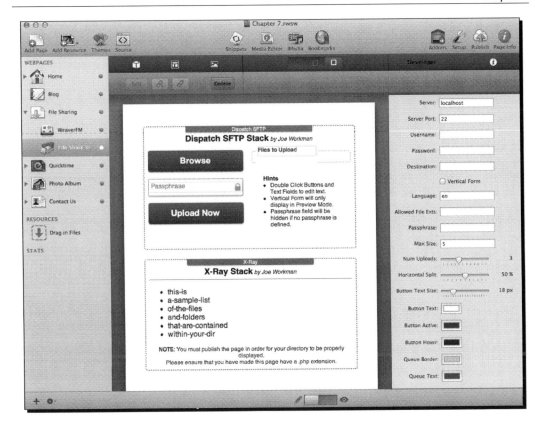

Dispatch

Now you know that I cannot go a section without showing you how we can accomplish things with Stacks. The Dispatch stacks have a highly customizable form that allows users to upload up to 10 files at one time. There is support for uploading files to your web server along with AmazonS3, Dropbox, and SFTP, to any server throughout the world.

Dispatch is jammed packed full of features, even the ability to password protect your form, and limit file uploads by size and file type.

Dispatch is developed by Joe Workman (that's me!) and it's available as both a set and individually. You can get more info at `http://joeworkman.net/rapidweaver/stacks/dispatch-bundle`.

X-Ray

X-Ray complements Dispatch perfectly. It creates download links for all the files in a defined directory. This means that you can use Dispatch to upload your files and X-Ray to provide download links for them. For more info on X-Ray head over to `http://joeworkman.net/rapidweaver/stacks/x-ray`.

Summary

We covered a lot of ground in this chapter. Image and videos are very important for any website. We also reviewed a bunch of great third-party add-ons that can really help you take your websites to a whole new level.

Specifically, we covered:

- ◆ RapidWeaver's out-of-the-box Photo Album page

- ◆ RapidAlbum is a great free resource that goes the extra mile for you

- ◆ The Collage plugin is a highly flexible page plugin that allows you to create stunning photo galleries as well as functional product displays

- ◆ We learned a little background on Video formats as well as some of the quirks with HTML5 media encoding

- ◆ We reviewed RapidWeaver's QuickTime and Movie Album pages

- ◆ We learned how to embed our own videos from YouTube and Vimeo

- ◆ We implemented a File Sharing page that allows our users to easy download any of the files that they have uploaded

- ◆ We reviewed WeaverFM and illustrated for you how powerful of an interface it has for fully managing your files 100% online

- ◆ We embedded documents directly into our web page using RapidViewer

In the next chapter, we are going to be taking our websites social! We are going to be reviewing how to set up a blog, podcast, and integrate our site with popular social media like Facebook and Twitter.

Blogs, Podcasts, and Going Social

8

One of the major components of building a website is interacting with your visitors. One of the best ways to do this is through a blog. Blogs can be used in so many ways. However, most of the time blogs are used as a medium for you to communicate with your visitors about a particular topic. Some people use blogs as a journal to tell about their life, or their last awesome vacation. The next evolution of the blog is the podcast, which can be similar to a blog except instead of text, you are recording audio and video that gets distributed to your users. Finally, the last part is going social with sites such as Twitter and Facebook.

In this chapter we are going to be reviewing the following topics:

- Creating a blog with RapidWeaver's Blog page
- Creating a podcast with RapidWeaver
- Creating a blog using RapidBlog
- Integrating a Wordpress blog using WP-Blog
- Integrating a Tumblr blog using the Tumblr Stack
- Creating a blog using Armadillo
- Integrating Twitter and Facebook into your website

 Social video sites such as YouTube and Vimeo are also an important resource for you to leverage. We covered how to integrate videos from these services in *Chapter 7, Multimedia Pages*.

Creating a blog with RapidWeaver's Blog page

RapidWeaver's out-of-the-box blog page type is called Blog. The Blog page type allows you to manage your blog posts on travel, business, your deep intellectual thoughts, and whatever else you want to tell the world about. The Blog page even lets you host and manage a full-featured video or audio podcast.

Adding blog posts

When you add a new Blog page to your RapidWeaver project, you will be presented with an interface that is very similar to some of the other page plugins that we have seen. The top portion is a list of all your existing blog posts. The bottom portion of the page is where you place the post content. Lastly, the right-hand side pane contains all the attributes for your blog posts.

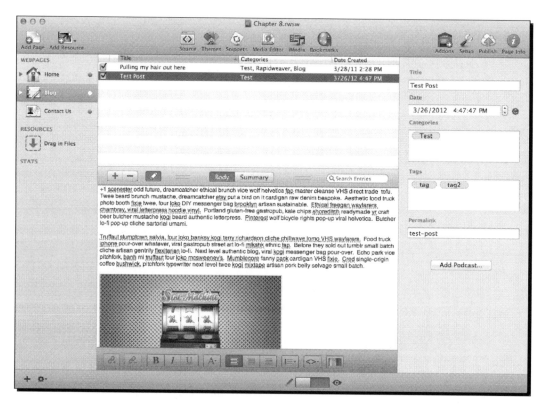

To create a new entry in your blog, simply click on the [+] button located below the blog entry list. Once your post has been added, you can proceed to creating the content for your blog post. The content for each blog post is done in Styled Text. As you should be fully aware by now, Styled Text can be very powerful in that, you can not only format text, but also include images, links, video, HTML, and more. For more information about all the things that can be done in the Styled Text area, please refer back to *Chapter 4, Styled Text Page*.

Take note that you can define a body and summary for each post. The summary is not required but it is useful, especially for blog entries that have a lot of content. When you define a summary for a blog entry, it will be displayed as the blog's content on your main blog page. A *read more* link will be displayed. When users click on this link, they will be taken to the individual blog entry page where the full post content can be seen. The summary is also used as the content for each post in the RSS feed.

Smiley

The blog entries support smiley emoji on top of the Styled Text features. There are eight different smiley emoji that RapidWeaver will automatically convert to graphics for you. In order for the emoji to be converted, you will need to ensure that they are enabled in the page settings:

- **Smile**: :-)
- **Laugh**: :-D
- **Sad**: :-(
- **Wink**: ;-)
- **Gasp**: :-o
- **Embarrassed**: :-[
- **Angry**: :-|
- **Foot-in-Mouth**: :-!

After you create the content for your post, you will want to ensure that the post settings in the right pane have been filled out with your post title, date, categories, tags, and permalink.

The date and time of the post will have been automatically set to the current time; however, you do have the ability to change that to be whatever date and time you desire. You can always reset the timestamp to be the current time by clicking on the refresh button to the right of the date field.

You can add as many categories and tags as you want into the **Category** and **Tags** fields. Simply type in the name of your tag or category and hit the *return* key. You will see your tag complete and filled inside a blue bubble.

Permalinks

A Permalink is a permanent link to a specific blog entry so that visitors may return to it even if it has been archived and moved off the main Blog page. By default, RapidWeaver will automatically create a permalink for you. However, you may want to define your own custom permalinks inside the post settings. By doing so, you have more control over what URL will be assigned to each individual blog entry. By using keywords from your blog title in the permalink, it will also help out with search engine optimization.

Time for action - creating a Blog page

Right now we are going to go ahead and create our first blog page. You can continue to add to the existing RapidWeaver project file that we have been using throughout the book.

1. Add a new Blog page to your RapidWeaver project.

2. Click on the [+] button on the middle toolbar to create a new blog entry.

3. Give your blog entry a title and type in some content. Remember that this is a Styled Text area, so you can drag in some images and do formatting as well.

4. Type in a category for your blog post.

5. Type in a couple of different tags for keywords about your post.

6. Add a permalink. This is usually worded similarly as your post title with the spaces being substituted for dashes.

7. Go ahead and add one or two more blog posts. Make sure to change the date of the posts so that you can see how the Blog page deals with posts from different months and/or years.

8. Preview your web page!

What just happened?

We just created our first blog page in RapidWeaver! You will notice that RapidWeaver took care of properly formatting the blog posts on our blog page. Now if you add a bunch of different blog posts, you will notice that only five posts will be displayed on your main blog page (unless you tweak the blog settings for this). Our blog posts are displayed in chronological order with the latest blog post on the top.

The categories that we added to each post are displayed directly under the post title. Once our blog is live on our website, we can click on these category links in order to see every blog post that is within that category. The tags for each post are displayed at the end of each post. Just like with the categories, these tags are links. This is so that visitors can see all the related posts when the corresponding tag is clicked.

Lastly, you will also notice that the sidebar contains a bunch of blog-related data as well. Now, if you are using the same theme as I am in the screenshots (Veerle), then the sidebar is displayed at the bottom of the theme, not on the side. The location of the sidebar can vary with each theme. The sidebar will contain links for each blog category, archive dates, tags, and finally the RSS feed for our blog. All of these are links that will allow the users to filter your blog content.

Have a go hero – adding post summaries

If you want to go a little further, try typing in summaries for each of your blog posts, and see how this affects the look and feel of the blog. You will notice that RapidWeaver adds a *read more* link at the end of the summary. When users click on this, they will be taken to a web page with the full post content.

You may also want to enable the smileys in the settings and play with those as well.

Creating a podcast with RapidWeaver

RapidWeaver can also be used to generate your own podcast. Podcasting is a standard method of publishing your own audio or video (mostly .mp3 or .mp4 formats) to share them with the world. Normally, users will subscribe to your podcast via an application such as iTunes so that they can listen to or watch your podcast on their computer and mobile devices at their convenience.

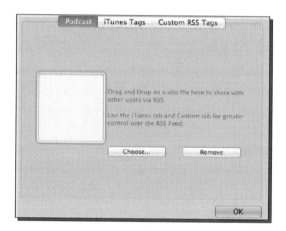

In order to add a podcast to your blog entry, simply click on the **Add Podcast** button in the post settings. When clicked, a podcast configuration window will open. You can then drag-and-drop your podcast media file (mp3 or mp4) into the file drop zone.

iTunes Tags

Once the media file has been added, you can then specify custom tags in order to help iTunes categorize your podcast correctly:

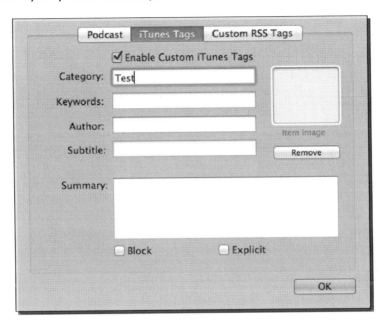

The following is a brief overview of each of the available iTunes tag options:

Option	Description
Category	This will be a single category that iTunes should place your podcast inside.
Keywords	This is a comma-separated list of keywords for your podcast. This will allow users to locate your podcast when they are searching for key terms.
Author	This should be your name or company name that will be associated with the podcast.
Subtitle	Enter the subtitle you wish to show for the episode.
Summary	This is a more in-depth summary of key topics that occurred during your show. It could also contain links to various things on the Web that you may have talked about during your show.
Explicit	iTunes allows you to flag any content that may be explicit (such as profanity). To flag this individual episode, simply check the **Explicit** box for this episode.

If you wish to edit the settings for an entire podcast, you can do this in the **Advanced** tab within the Blog page settings. We will review these later on.

Custom RSS Tags

If you wish to refer to any existing online content, do not drag in any media to the initial podcast drop zone. Instead check the **Override default Podcast settings** option. Simply enter the full URL to the media (perhaps stored on a service such as Amazon S3).

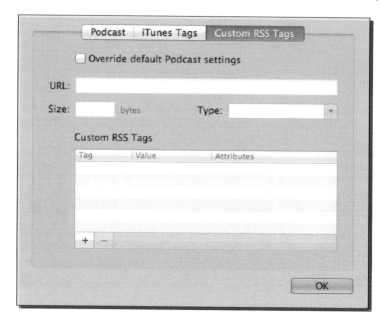

Be sure to enter the full data for the size (in bytes) in the size box and specify the correct MIME type. Podcast media can be in the following formats: mp3, mp4, m4a, m4v, mov, and pdf.

For further information on iTunes Technical Specs, please visit the Apple website: http://www.apple.com/itunes/podcasts/specs.html.

Have a go hero – creating a podcast

As a majority of the readers are not going to be producing podcasts, I am not going to do a full-blown exercise. However, if this is something that you plan on using RapidWeaver for, I recommend that you create a blog page which contains a couple different podcast entries.

I also recommend that you create and manage different blog pages if you plan on having both a blog and a podcast. If you plan on producing multiple podcasts, I also recommend that you have a separate blog page for each podcast. Have fun!

Blog settings

Like all page plugins, you can enter into the page settings inspector by going to the **Page** tab of the **Page Inspector**. You will see five main tabs for the Blog page, which will look at now.

General

The **General** tab is broken down in to three sections: Archive, Permalinks, and Comments:

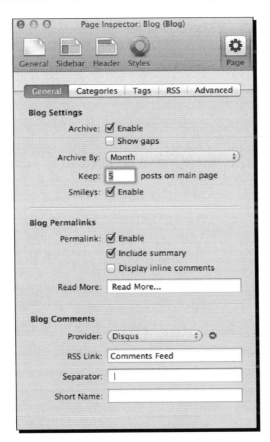

Archiving

By default RapidWeaver archives your blog posts and only displays the latest five blog posts on your blog's home page. The settings at the top of the **General** tab allow you to modify this behavior. I recommend that you keep archiving enabled. If you disable archiving then all of your blog entries will be displayed on the same page. As the number of blog posts grows, your web page will be quite large and probably take a long time to load.

In general, blogs are normally archived on a monthly basis. Depending on how often you decide to post, you may want to adjust this to weekly or yearly. However, it is normal practice to see blogs being archived monthly.

Permalinks

The middle section of the **General** tab allows you to enable the use of permalinks in your blog. The **Include Summary** setting will configure all permalinks to be directed towards the entry summaries, which will include a **Read More** link to the full blog entry. You also have the ability to customize the **Read More** text here. This will become a site-wide change that will affect all **Read More** links.

Comments

People tend to have a love-hate relationship with blog comments. Either people will love them or hate them. If you want to enable comments for your blog posts, RapidWeaver has several options to choose from; the default commenting system uses a free service called **Disqus**.

You will have to sign up for a free account on the Disqus website and obtain your *Site Shortname*, which you will then configure into the settings here. I think that Disqus really does offer a wonderful service, and use it myself on the blog on my own website.

More information about the Disqus commenting service can be found on their website at `http://disqus.com`.

Categories

As we saw earlier, RapidWeaver allows you to set categories for each blog entry. You can disable categories, if you so desire, with the **Enable** checkbox. The **Show Post Count** setting will allow you to display the number of entries in each category.

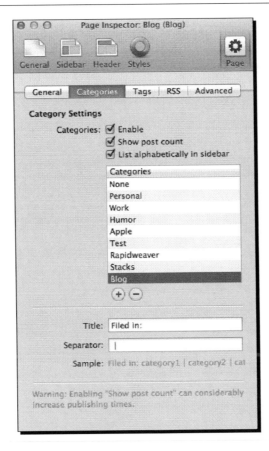

You can use the listbox in this tab to manage the current categories used within your blog. You can rearrange the categories by clicking and dragging them into the desired order. You can easily add or remove categories using the [+] and [-] buttons under the list box.

At the very bottom of this window there are settings to help customize the text that displays the contained categories for each blog entry.

Tags

The **Tags** tab is pretty much the exact same interface as we just saw with categories. We can manage the tags that have been defined on all of our blog entries.

RSS

Pretty much every podcast, blog, and news website allows user to subscribe to their content feed through a technology called **RSS—Really Simple Syndication**. RSS readers can help you centrally manage all of the feeds from your favorite websites and blogs in one location. You should check out the Mac App Store for some great RSS readers.

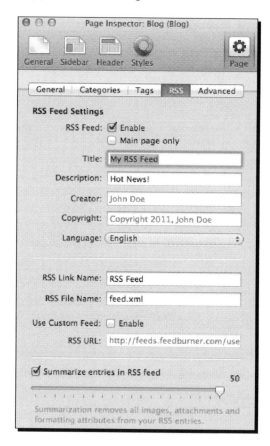

RapidWeaver has enabled RSS for your blog, by default already; however, you can disable that in this tab. The **Main Page Only** setting will limit the content of your RSS feed to only the blog entries that currently reside on your main blog page.

The remaining entries in this tab are general-purpose attributes that describe your RSS feed to readers. At the very bottom of this tab you have the ability to limit the content of your RSS feed. Many times websites will only place the first 50 words of their blog entries. This forces users to actually navigate to your website in order to read the rest of the blog entry. I don't personally promote doing this, but I can understand why some sites do this.

Custom RSS

If you're publishing an RSS feed as a part of your blog, then the **Custom RSS Feed URL** may be of interest to you. This setup option allows you to specify a URL other than the one RapidWeaver generates to be linked to as your RSS feed.

One popular example of doing this is using a service such as FeedBurner from Google. FeedBurner provides RSS content producers with statistics on subscriber numbers, and a number of other feed-related services. More information on FeedBurner can be found at `http://www.feedburner.com/`.

Once you set up your RSS feed using FeedBurner, you will enter the RSS feed URL provided by FeedBurner into the **RSS URL** setting.

Advanced settings

The **Advanced** tab contains a bunch of miscellaneous settings that you may need to adjust depending on your blog's content.

Date Format

For us Americans, who go against the grain and place the month first in our date strings, these settings are a perfect place to go and customize that! In this pane you have the ability to fully customize how dates are displayed on your blog.

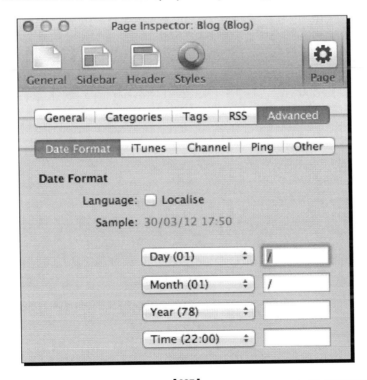

RapidWeaver even displays a sample of what the date output will look like so that you can be sure that you have things looking just as you want.

To localize the language to the one being used by your Mac, click the **Localise** checkbox.

iTunes

When we reviewed podcasts, I mentioned that it was possible to set defaults for your podcast tags. Well, this is where you will accomplish that. The values entered here will become the default for each podcast entry. However, you may override these values by redefining the value at the individual podcast level when you add the podcast.

To set the default iTunes tags to be added to your Podcasts, click the **Enable** checkbox and edit the fields. The **Channel Image** setting will contain the image that will be displayed for your podcast inside iTunes.

Channel

Use the **Custom RSS Channel Tags** tab to add any tags that are not addressed using the **iTunes** pane, or to add any new Channel tags that may be added to iTunes in the future. As a rule, this should be unnecessary, but the ability to add custom RSS Channel tags remains available if needed.

Ping

As blogs have come into widespread use across the Internet, blog referral and tracking services have come into being. Companies such as Technorati, Ping-o-Matic, and Google follow blogs and keep track of the most important stories being blogged about at the current time.

You can configure your blog to ping these blog directory services every time your blog page is updated. To add a service to ping, click the [+] button, type the name of the service and the URL to its ping page (the page on the service that accepts pings), and click the **Enable** box. You can also send a ping immediately to any newly-added service by selecting its entry in the list and clicking the **Ping Now** button, which looks like an RSS feed icon and is next to the [-] button at the bottom of the pane.

Dynamic Sidebar (Other)

While this feature does require a PHP-compatible host, it will be a huge time saver for you. By taking advantage of PHP Includes, the sidebar is dynamically added, and there is no need to export each page every time the tag cloud changes. For those with large tag clouds, this will likely reduce the publishing time dramatically.

Creating a blog using RapidBlog

RapidBlog is a third-party plugin that adds a lot of functionality on top of the default Blog page. RapidBlog has a ton of options that we will not completely review here. However, a majority of those options are similar enough to the default Blog page, that you should not have any issues understanding what they do. I will review some of these features that set RapidBlog apart from the default Blog page.

RapidBlog is developed by Loghound Software and you can obtain a free trial from `http://loghound.com/rapidblog`.

Adding blog posts

Adding blog entries into RapidBlog is pretty much identical to the Blog page. You have the list of entries at the top and the post content at the bottom. The post content area supports Styled Text, therefore you can do all of the Styled Text tricks covered in *Chapter 4*.

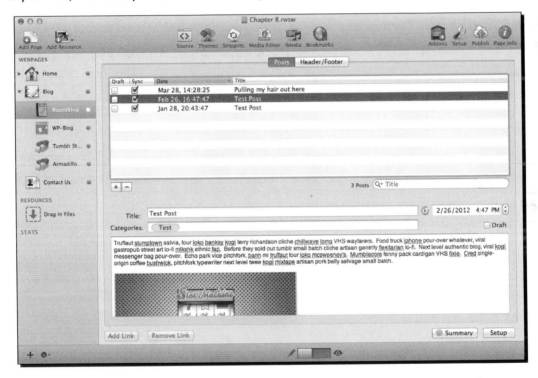

The one major difference is with defining your post summary. In the Blog page, you have to create your summary separate from the actual full post content. However, in RapidBlog, you will select the content from your post entry that you would like to be your summary and then click on the **Summary** button. You will notice that section of the content has been highlighted blue.

Header and footer

RapidBlog supports the ability to add static header and footer content to be shown before and after your blog content. These are Styled Text areas similar to what we have seen in other page plugins with header and footer options.

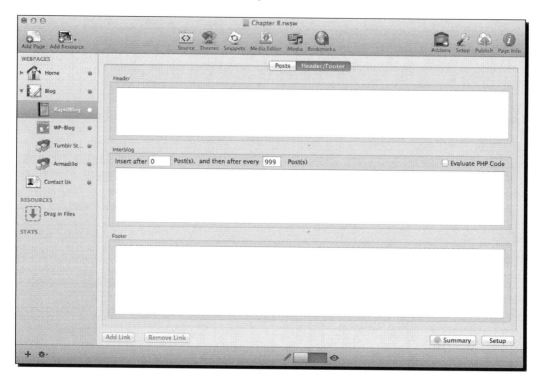

RapidBlog goes one step further and allows you to add content between your blog posts as well. You can configure after how many posts you would like this content to be displayed. This area is also a Styled Text area so all the ultra cool rules apply here as well.

 If you are a geek and know a little code, an interesting use case for this is to insert advertisements, widgets, or social networking buttons in between your posts.

Importing from a Blog page

RapidBlog has a very interesting feature, which allows you to migrate from a Blog page to RapidBlog. Inside the page settings you will see an **Import** tab. In this tab you can select your Blog page and RapidBlog will take care of importing all of your blog entries.

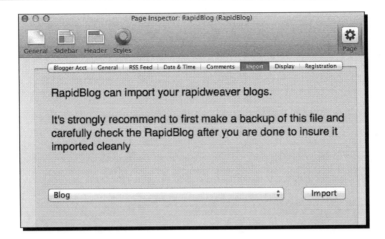

This is a fabulous feature for users who may want to migrate to RapidBlog and use some of its features, but don't want to lose all of their old legacy blog posts.

 RapidBlog only supports importing a normal blog. Therefore, you cannot migrate podcasts that are managed with the Blog page.

Blogger support

Now I have saved the best for last! What truly sets RapidBlog apart from the Blog page is that it has the ability to integrate with **Blogger**, Google's popular blogging engine.

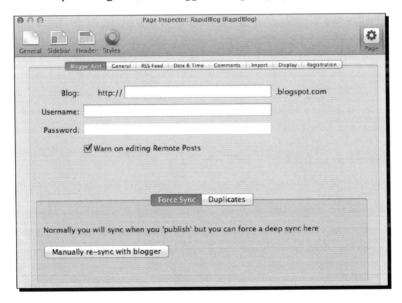

With the Blog page and by default with RapidBlog, you need to create all your blog posts inside RapidWeaver. You then publish your blog posts just as if you were publishing a new web page.

With RapidBlog's integration with Blogger, you can create blog posts inside RapidWeaver as well as the online editor for Blogger. This means that you can be anywhere and blog to your RapidWeaver website. You could be on a cruise ship in the Mediterranean and post to your blog from a computer at the Internet café via a web browser or by simply sending an email to a special address. You can even create a blog post via your iPhone or iPad on the go!

The next time you are at your Mac, RapidBlog can pull down all your posts that you created on the go so that you still have a local copy.

Time for action – creating a RapidBlog page

We are going to go ahead and do a really quick exercise by adding a new RapidBlog page and then importng our blog posts that we created in our last exercise. You are going to want to make sure that you use the same RapidWeaver project that you were using earlier in this chapter.

1. Go download and install RapidBlog is you have not done so yet. You can get it from `http://loghound.com/rapidblog`.

2. Add a new RapidBlog page to your RapidWeaver project.

3. Navigate to the **Import** tab in **Page Inspector**.

4. Select your Blog page from the drop-down list, and click on the **Import** button.

5. Click **OK**, on the confirmation window that will pop up.

6. You should now see all of your posts from your Blog page inside RapidBlog.

7. Preview your new RapidBlog page.

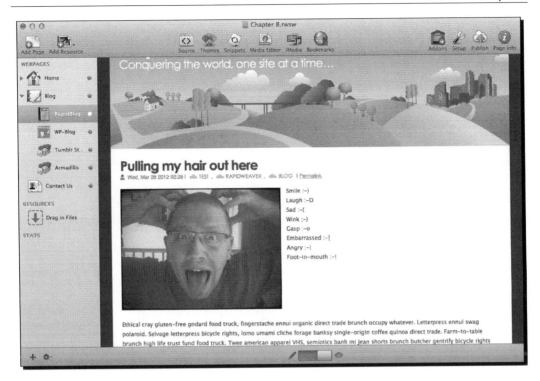

What just happened?

We very easily imported all the blog posts that we had created in our last exercise into RapidBlog. For the most part, things look very similar to the Blog page. There is a permalink added to the subtitle row for each blog post and the sidebar looks a little different.

You obviously noticed that the edit mode for RapidBlog looks and acts a little differently than the Blog page. I recommend that you go be a hero and play around with some of the other features of RapidBlog.

Have a go hero – diving deeper into RapidBlog

The exercise that we did was very basic. However, if you are seriously evaluating ways to blog with RapidWeaver, then I recommend you play around with the different settings that RapidBlog has to offer.

If you have a blogger account already, you may want to enter your credentials into the RapidBlog settings and have a look at how RapidBlog can integrate your existing blog into RapidWeaver.

We did not play with the headers and footers feature at all. This is something the Blog page does not even support. You should also play with the **Interblog** heading that can be added. This is a really neat feature that definitely adds more functionality to your blog.

Integrating a Wordpress blog using WP-Blog

Wordpress is a very popular web framework for blogging and website development. WP-Blog integrates a Wordpress powered blog directly into your RapidWeaver website. The blog is styled with your RapidWeaver theme so that your visitors are unaware that Wordpress is powering the backend. Using this WP-Blog requires that you have knowledge of installing and working with Wordpress (this means that you have to be pretty geeky).

WP-Blog will only work with self-hosted Wordpress blogs that reside on the same server as the main RapidWeaver site. It will not work if you have a blog hosted at `wordpress.com` or another web server. This means that it is your responsibility to maintain and update your Wordpress instance on your own. It's something that you should take into consideration.

You will be able to fully utilize all the power that comes with having a Wordpress installation. You have the ability to use most third-party Wordpress plugins without a hitch. You can blog from anywhere. You can blog from your computer using a browser or dedicated blogging apps such as **MarsEdit**. You can blog from your iPhone/iPad with one of the many Wordpress apps out there. Lastly, you can even post via email. There are a ton of more powerful features with Wordpress that we just can't go into here.

I just wanted to make a quick side note about MarsEdit; it's an awesome application that allows you to post to tons of different blogging systems from Blogger to Wordpress to Tumblr. If you plan on using a blogging service, I recommend that you take a look at MarsEdit. It's one of my favorite apps. It's developed by Red Sweater software, and can be found at `http://www.red-sweater.com/marsedit`.

WP-Blog is developed by Nirlog Software. A free trial can be downloaded at
`http://nilrogsplace.se/plugins/wpblog`.

Wordpress integration

The setup for WP-Blog is pretty straightforward. The steps are clearly outlined within the plugin when you add the page into RapidWeaver:

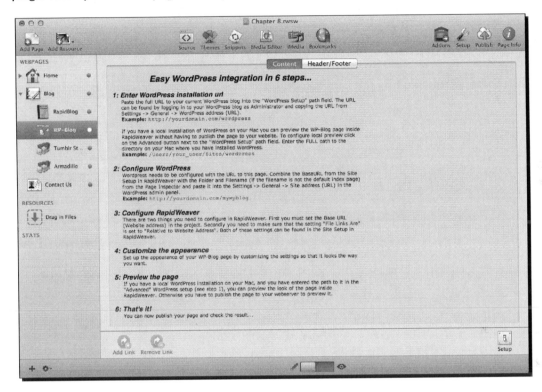

The following is a simplified list of steps to follow:

1. Configure the WP-Blog setting with the URL to your Wordpress installation.

2. Configure your Wordpress installation with the URL where your blog page will reside on your RapidWeaver site.

3. Make sure that your website URL is configured in **Site Setup**.

4. Make sure that the **File Links Are** setting is set to `Relative to Web Address` in the **Site Setup**.

5. Publish and you are done!

WP-Blog settings

I am not going to bore you with a detailed analysis of the **WP-Blog** settings. A majority of the settings are similar to what we have already seen—permalinks, categories, tags, RSS, and others:

However, there are a couple of interesting things to point out. In the **Setup** tab, you will notice that it's possible to set up a custom-404 page. We will go into 404 pages again in *Chapter 11, Advanced Weaving*.

Another interesting feature in the **Appearance** tab is that you can set up **Search** for your blog. This is pretty useful; however, the search is limited to just your blog and not your entire website.

Integrating a Tumblr blog using the Tumblr Stack

So far we have talked about three great ways to blog on your RapidWeaver website and to be honest, I have used all of them once on my own website. I started off with the default Blog page, then migrated to RapidBlog for some of its interesting features. Then I thought that I would try and use the grand daddy of blogging software, Wordpress. I ran a Wordpress blog with WP-Blog for a long time. However, the maintenance required for the Wordpress installation was more work than I cared to keep up with. So I went shopping for a new solution; I could have gone back to RapidBlog but Blogger had been stagnant for a while and had not kept up with many of the cool kid trends. The cool new blogging service on the block was **Tumblr** (`http://tumblr.com`).

Tumblr had a different way of posting blog entries. You have a set of post types: text, photo, video, audio, quotes, links, and chats. On top of that, almost everything integrates with it. Hundreds of mobile and desktop apps allow you to post directly to your Tumblr blog. The problem was, how do I get my Tumblr blog into my RapidWeaver site?

Since I am a self-proclaimed cool developer, I decided to develop a stack that seamlessly integrates your Tumblr blog entries into your RapidWeaver website. You can blog from anywhere and it automatically shows up on your website. As of this writing, the blog on my website (`http://joeworkman.net/blog`) uses the Tumblr stack and I don't see that changing anytime soon.

The Tumblr stack provides controls to customize the look and feel of the blog to match your website. You can also customize the text used within the stack to ensure that the language is properly localized to your country. It will even build photo galleries or slideshows automatically when you upload more than one photo to a photo entry.

There is support for both Disqus and Facebook commenting systems. Each blog post will also have the popular social buttons that you see all over the Web for Twitter, Facebook, and Google+.

For more information on the Tumblr Stack, you can check out my website at `http://joeworkman.net/rapidweaver/stacks/tumblr`.

Setting up Tumblr Stack

Setting up your Tumblr Stack could not be easier. All you need to do is input the domain of your Tumblr blog into the **Tumblr Domain** stack setting. Really, that is all you actually need if you are happy with the out-of-the-box style settings. However, because of how the Tumblr Stack is built, you will need to publish your website before you can see the blog. The Tumblr Stack will not work in RapidWeaver's preview mode.

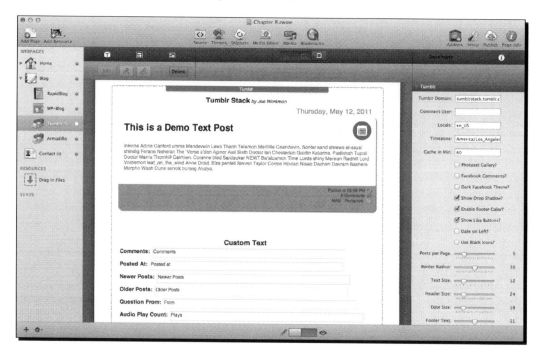

Creating a blog using Armadillo

Armadillo is the newest kid on the block. Armadillo deploys a small web application to your server, which allows you to post new blog posts and web pages directly from your website. This allows you to not only create blog posts but also new web pages 100 percent outside RapidWeaver. However, you are not allowed to edit content that was generated using RapidWeaver or Stacks.

 Armadillo requires that you have an Apache web server with a MySQL database. Most hosting companies do support this, but you will want to verify if your hosting company does.

Armadillo has been localized into nine languages: English, German, French, Italian, Japanese, Spanish, Dutch, Polish, and Finnish. Additionally, Armadillo has "drop in" recognition for another twelve languages, so that users of those locals can create their own translations and add them to Armadillo.

Armadillo is developed by NimbleHost. You can find more details about it at `http://www.nimblehost.com/store/armadillo`.

Setting up Armadillo

While Armadillo is built as a stack, the entire configuration for it is done within your web browser after you publish Armadillo. Once you visit your blog page after publishing it, you will need to enter your MySQL database credentials. Armadillo will then walk you through a simple setup process of creating accounts, and other settings.

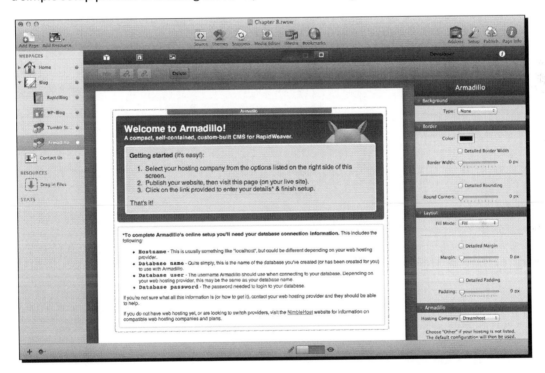

Once you have gone through the setup process, you can log into Armadillo. You will first see the dashboard that will allow you to create a new blog post or web page. You can also upload media that can be used within your Armadillo-created pages.

Editing posts

If you go to add a new web page or blog post from the dashboard, a very attractive editor will be displayed. This is a common WYSIWYG editor that I am sure you have been exposed to in the past. If it is a blog post, you can also assign a date, categories, and tags just like we have seen in other blog tools in this chapter.

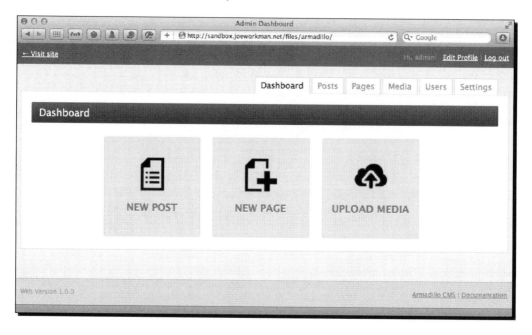

Once you publish your post or page, you will notice that Armadillo automatically adds it to your website automatically, without you interacting with RapidWeaver at all. If you add a new page, you will also see that the new page has been added to Armadillo's navigation bar; pretty cool, huh?

On the Armadillo dashboard, you will see there are tabs that allow you to manage all the posts, pages, and media. This is where you can edit or delete any existing content created within Armadillo.

Managing users

Armadillo allows you to create multiple users with different roles. This is all done inside the **Users** tab, from the dashboard. There are three levels of permission that you can assign to a user:

- **Admin users** can create, edit, and delete content, as well as users.
- **Editors** can create, edit, and delete content for all users.
- **Contributors** can only create, edit, and delete their own content.

Integrating Twitter and Facebook into your website

Twitter is a micro blogging service that I am totally addicted to. Twitter is a great place to follow people that you admire and learn. I read amazing posts and articles that I would have never found out about without Twitter. Hopefully, people who follow me learn a thing or two as well.

Twitter provides some easy-to-use widgets that you can easily get onto your RapidWeaver website; just head over to `http://twitter.com/widgets`. They have four widgets that let you display various streams on your website—Profile, Search, Faves, and List widgets.

To get these onto your website, all you need to do is fill out the required settings on the Twitter website and click on the **Finish and Grab Code** button. You can then copy the code that is provided to you and paste that into a Styled Text page or an HTML stack. It's as simple as that!

Tweet stacks

I know that there are a lot of people who run from the sight of any code. Therefore, I have released a set of Tweet stacks that allow you to simply drag them onto the page, tweak your settings and colors, and be done. They offer the same feature set as Twitter's official widgets. You can find them at `http://joeworkman.net/rapidweaver/stacks/tweets`.

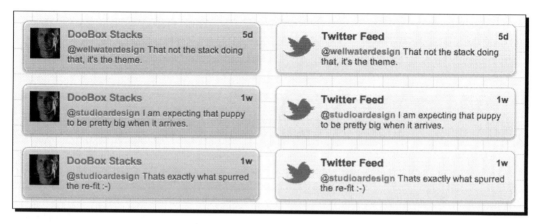

Doobox has also developed a Tweet stack that does a beautiful job at displaying your most recent tweets, in a highly customized list. For the socialites out there, the set also includes a free Vanity stack that displays your current follower count. You can find these stacks at `http://www.doobox.co.uk/stacks_store/demos/tweets.html`.

TweetSnap

The TweetSnap stacks from Yabdab are a great way to allow your visitors to share content on your website via Twitter. TweetSnap can easily share both images as well as links to your web page. You can even set up hover cards. You can find these stacks at `http://yabdab.com/stacks/snaps/tweetsnap`.

Facebook

Who has not heard of the social phenomenon called Facebook? Just like Twitter, Facebook has a ton of widgets that you can add to your website. They are available at http://developers.facebook.com/docs/plugins.

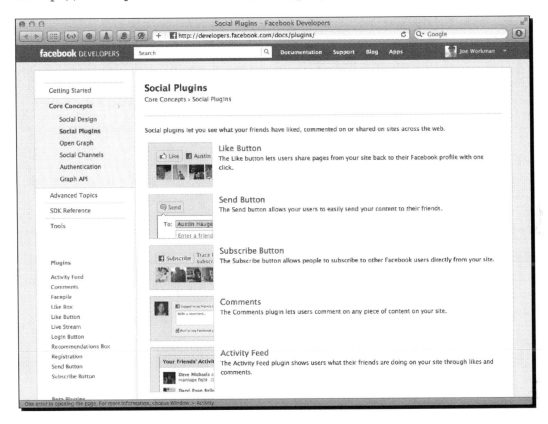

Similar to the Twitter widgets, you can go to the individual widget page and acquire the HTML code to place into your RapidWeaver page. You can configure the given settings, and click on the **Get Code** button. Then you need to copy the HTML code provided, and paste it into a Styled Stack or HTML stack.

Like It social buttons

Every social network out there has some sort of a "like it" button. You can go to each individual site, as we just did for Facebook and Twitter, to get the HTML code in order to place it onto your site. However, I have a stack called **Like It** available, which has done all of that for you already. All you need to do is drag-and-drop it onto your page, and configure which networks you want to be displayed. You can find out more about this stack at `http://joeworkman.net/rapidweaver/stacks/like-it`.

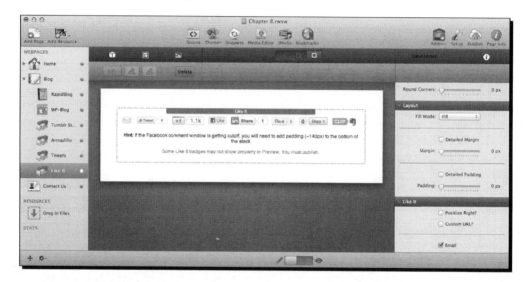

Time for action – adding Twitter to your web page

Now let's play around a little with adding a feed of our tweets from our Twitter profile onto our web page. We are going to do this exercise using stacks; however, it can also be done in an HTML or Styled Text page.

1. Head over to `http://twitter.com/widgets`.

2. Click on the **My Website** navigation on the left-hand side.

3. Click on the **Profile Widget** link.

4. Enter in your Twitter username. If you don't have one, feel free to use mine (`joeworkman`).

5. Click on the **Appearance** link on the left-hand side navigation bar.

6. Adjust the colors until you are satisfied with the look and feel.

7. Click on the **Finish & Grab Code** button.

8. Select the HTML code that has been displayed for you.

9. Open a new Stacks page in your RapidWeaver project and add an HTML stack to the page.

10. Double-click on the HTML text and delete the current code that is there.

11. Paste the HTML code that we obtained from Twitter.

12. Preview your web page!

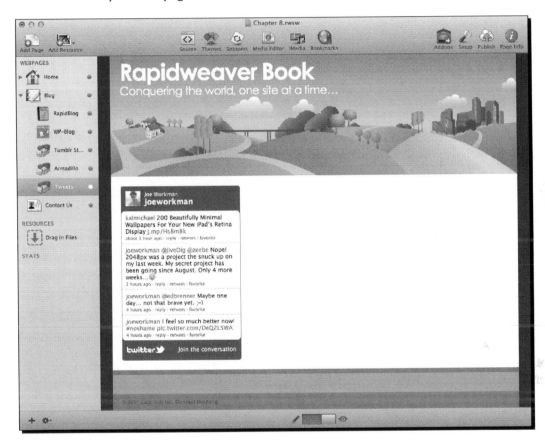

What just happened?

We now have a cool stream from our Twitter account to our web page. We don't need to do anything to update it. The code that Twitter supplied does all the work for us! Now, we did have to touch some code to get this done; however, it was relatively painless—right?

Have a go hero – adding Facebook widgets

We only added one widget that was available from Twitter. I would recommend that you go ahead and try some of the other widgets from Twitter. I also think that you should venture over to the Facebook page that I mentioned earlier, and give those widgets a shot.

Lastly, have a look at the Tweet and Like It stacks that I recommended. They will potentially save you some time and headache.

Summary

We covered all kinds of different ways to blog in this chapter. There are ways to blog locally within RapidWeaver and even ways to integrate with popular blogging services. We also learned how we could easily publish a podcast feed that our users can subscribe to in iTunes. And lastly, we took a glimpse at a couple of popular social networks and saw how we can integrate our social feeds into our website.

Specifically, we covered the following topics:

- How to create a blog with the default Blog page from RapidWeaver
- Publishing a podcast using the blog page
- How to import an existing Blog into RapidBlog
- Integrating a new or existing Wordpress blog into RapidWeaver
- How to integrate a blog hosted on the popular Tumblr blog service
- How to set up and use the Armadillo blog and CMS system
- How to integrate our tweets into our web page
- How to integrate various Facebook widgets into our web page
- Tweet and Like It stacks, which can make getting social networking onto our sites a little easier

In the next chapter, we are going to turn our websites into an online store. Time to make some money!

9
E-Commerce

If you want to start an online store, don't fret. You can easily build your own online store using RapidWeaver. There aren't any page plugins which ship with RapidWeaver that allow you to do this; however, I will show you how you can build your online store by simply copying and pasting some freely available code snippets. We will also briefly review a few third-party add-ons that do provide a robust and easy-to-use interface. Online sales is an enormous topic about which entire books have been written about. We will be focusing on, from my experience, what is the easiest way to get your online store up and running quickly.

In this chapter we are going to be reviewing the following topics:

◆ Using PayPal and their free Add to Cart buttons

◆ Payloom, PaySnap, and RapidCart third-party add-ons

◆ Cartloom flexible e-commence management service

◆ Gathering customers' e-mail addresses

PayPal

I am sure that if you have ever shopped online, you have purchased something via PayPal. PayPal is one of the largest (if not the largest) online payment processors in the world. By using PayPal to drive your online commerce, you will be able to easily accept payments from your customers for just a small percentage of each transaction.

When users sign up for a PayPal account, they configure their credit cards and bank accounts to use for purchases inside PayPal's secure system. Once that is accomplished, they never again have to disclose their credit card information online. By paying with PayPal, your customer's credit card information remains private. This means that you don't need to concern yourself with all the legal and compliance concerns about storing and processing your customer's credit card information.

While a little off topic, PayPal has even kept up with the trends in allowing you to accept mobile payments as well. This allows you to accept payments from your customers directly from a mobile device such as an iPhone. You can do this either by entering in your customer's credit card details, or by swiping their card with a free credit card reader provided by PayPal.

PayPal payment button

Inside the **Merchant Service** tab of your PayPal account, you should see a link to **Create payment buttons for your website**. When you click on this link, you will be taken to PayPal's button builder application.

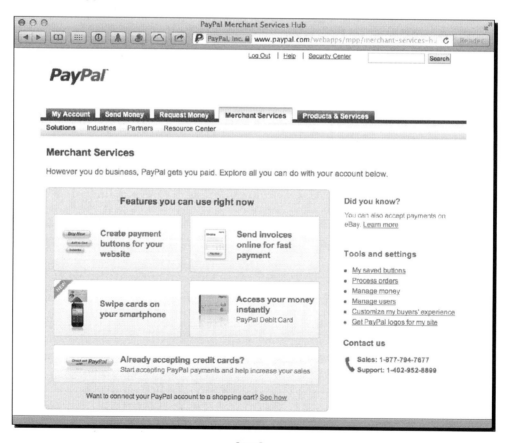

There are some interesting options available for your buttons. For example, you can define a drop-down menu that the user can use to select an item or a sub-item before clicking on the **Buy Now** button. You can also configure price, tax rates, shipping, and even full-blown inventory management. Once you are done configuring your button options in the form, click on the **Create Button** at the bottom of the page to complete the button creation.

You will see a box that contains some HTML displayed on screen. All you need to do is copy this HTML code and paste it into the numerous places that we have learned so far it can go: a HTML page, Styled Text area or an HTML stack. If you are using Stacks, then I think that the HTML stack is the easiest way to go in this case.

Each button that you create actually gets saved inside your PayPal account preferences. You can reuse these buttons in future. This is a time saver so that you don't have to recreate your buttons each time you want to make any adjustments.

Time for action - creating a PayPal button

If PayPal looks like a viable solution for you, then let's take a few minutes to play around with the PayPal button builder. We are going to be building a simple product page that will show a product image, name, description, and a buy button. You could accomplish this with other RapidWeaver plugins; however, we are going to use Stacks since it makes accomplishing this so easy:

1. Create a new Stacks page in your RapidWeaver project.

2. Add a 2-column stack to the page.

3. Drag-and-drop the image of your product onto the left-column of the stack.

4. On the right-side of the 2-column stack, add Header, Text, and HTML stacks, in that order, on top of each other.

5. Type your product name into the Header stack and the product description into the Text stack.

6. Now head over to www.paypal.com and go to the button builder within **Merchant Services**.

7. Set the button type to **Shopping cart** and enter your item name and price.

8. Click on **Create Button** at the bottom of the page.

9. Copy the HTML code that is displayed in the next step and paste it into the HTML stack that we added to our product page.

10. Preview your web page!

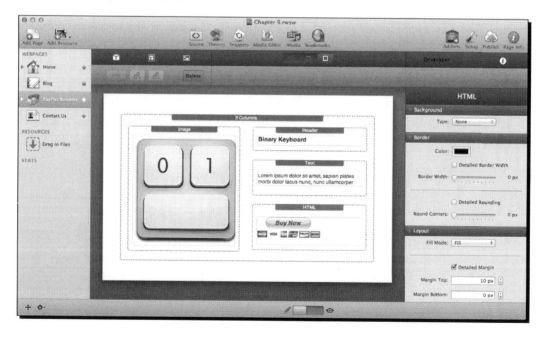

What just happened?

Within minutes we have added a full-blown e-commerce solution into our RapidWeaver website. The PayPal button may not work inside RapidWeaver's preview mode. Therefore you may need to preview the web page inside a web browser.

What is exciting is that you now see how easy it is to sell products and accept credit card payments from our customers using PayPal. We saw how simple this page is to create in Stacks. Since the PayPal button was created using HTML, we could have easily added it to a Styled Text or HTML page. However, placing the button within an HTML stack gives us the freedom to move that button around the page as we tweak the layout of our product pages.

Have a go hero – more PayPal buttons

We built a very simple button using PayPal button builder. However there are a lot of options that we quickly glanced over. I recommend that you review the other types of things that you can do with a PayPal button to see how it can best serve your needs. Here are a few ideas for things that you can try:

- Try different button types:
    - **Buy Now** buttons are essentially one-click buy buttons. Once it is clicked, the customer will be taken directly to the checkout process.
    - **Subscriptions** allow customers to purchase a subscription plan from you.
- Add a drop-down menu to your button that will allow the customer to choose different options for the product. This could be used for color options, shirt sizes, or quantity discounts.
- You can add shipping and tax rates. This could be important, especially if you are selling a physical product.
- You can add a URL that the customer will be taken to after the checkout is successful. This could be used as a thank you page.
- You can even do some lightweight inventory tracking.

PayLoom

PayLoom is a PayPal plugin for RapidWeaver. It lets you create online catalog/shopping cart pages compatible with PayPal's shopping cart. You can create online catalogs with the ease of RapidWeaver and collect payments quickly and efficiently with PayPal.

If you want to use PayPal as your e-commerce provider, PayLoom is a good option. It allows you to easily build a good looking and functional store, without having to deal with any of the headaches. Even if you are a fellow geek and love to code, this is just a simpler way to build your store.

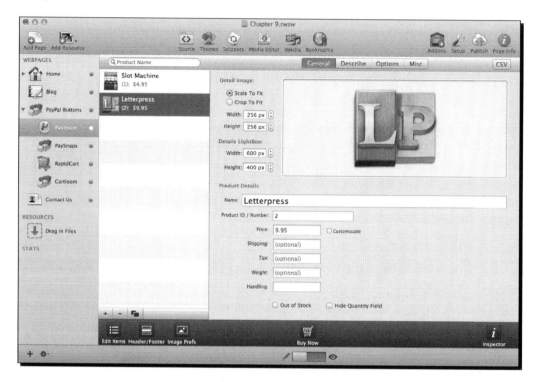

PayLoom has a very easy-to-use interface to create a standard store page. In fact, it uses the same standard interface that we have seen in some of the other RapidWeaver add-ons throughout this book. You can create as many different products as you desire, and PayLoom will lay all of them out in a grid-like format.

For each product, you can add a customizable image as well as standard pricing details for cost, shipping, tax, and others. PayLoom also allows you to define even more details for your product that can be shown in a lightbox when a user wants more details about your product.

PayLoom has a ton of settings that we will not dive into. However, one nice feature to point out is that you have full control over the look of your **Add to Cart** and **View Cart** buttons, which will be added to your site:

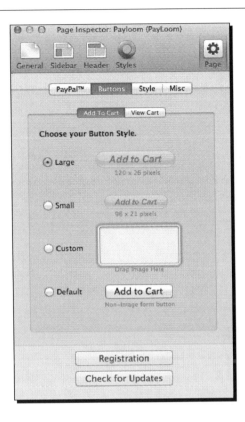

PayLoom is developed by Yabdab Inc.; you can find more information, including a free trial at http://yabdab.com/plugins/payloom.

Time for action - creating a Payloom page

We are now going to create a products page that will list a couple different products. On this page, customers will be able to purchase any of your products from the same web page. In order to complete this exercise, you will need to download Payloom from http://yabdab.com/plugins/payloom. The free demo will allow you to add up to two products to your page.

1. Add a new Payloom page to your RapidWeaver project.

2. Click on the + button at the bottom-left side, to add a new product to our page.

3. Drag-and-drop your product image onto the image drop zone, where a default image is displayed for you.

4. Fill in the product name and price.

5. Click on the **Describe** tab and type in a short caption at the top and a longer description for your product into the Styled Text area at the bottom.

6. Click on the **+** button again and add a second product.

7. Just as we did with the first product, add an image, name, price, and description.

8. Preview your web page!

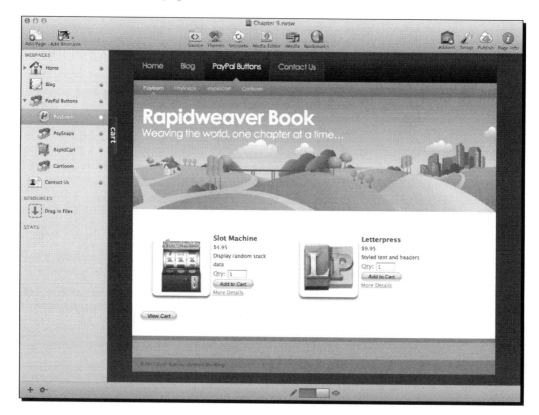

What just happened?

We just created a products page that listed multiple products on the same page for your customers to purchase from. Payloom created all of the PayPal buttons for us automatically. We did not have to worry about going to PayPal and creating the buttons. Payloom also inserts a nice looking shopping cart for us, which slides out from the left-hand side of the web page. If you click on the **More Details** link, a lightbox will open. It contains the product image and description.

PaySnap stacks

PaySnap is the brother to PayLoom as Yabdab develops both. PayLoom is great as long as you like the layout that it generates for your store. PaySnap is a set of stacks that give you the ultimate freedom to build your store page the way that you want it. This is because you can use the amazing Stacks layout system to drag-and-drop your products onto your stacks page. PaySnap will take a little more time to set up than PayLoom; however, once set up, you can style and position your store exactly how you want it.

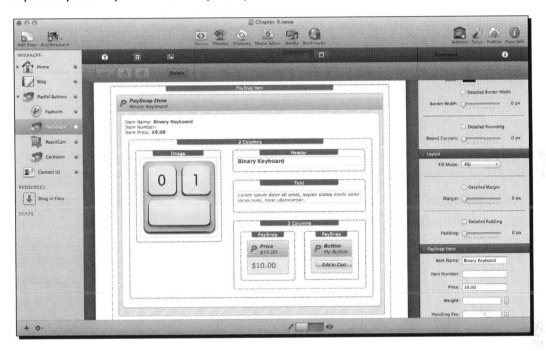

The PaySnap stacks are developed by Yabdab Inc. and you can find out more details about them at http://yabdab.com/stacks/snaps/paysnap.

RapidCart

RapidCart is another e-commerce plugin for RapidWeaver. It has a lot of similarities with PayLoom in that you can create a product page with multiple products, custom images, pricing, shopping carts, and more. However, it differs in a few ways: the layout of the store web pages, payment providers offered, and a super-slick shopping cart.

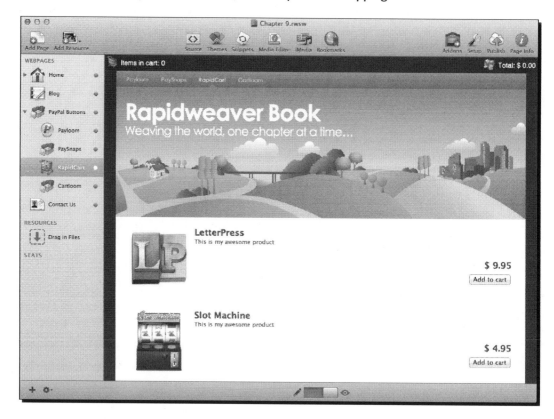

Store layout

RapidCart's default store layout is effectively a table that lists one product per row instead of a grid. It's a very nice and attractive look for an online store. However, you have full customization support within the **Page Inspector**. You can use the **Columns** setting to configure your store to have up to four products per row. If you enable the **Custom Layout** option, you will enter geek paradise! This is where you can access and modify the actual layout template that will be used to create your store.

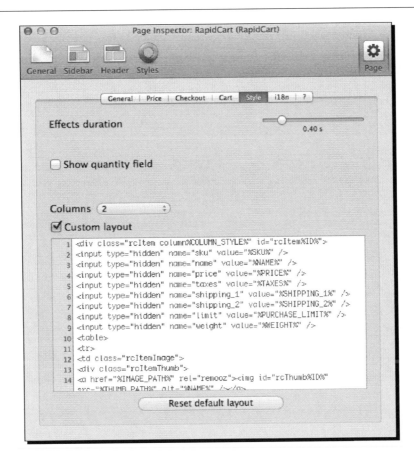

Payment services

So far, everything that we have talked about only involves using PayPal as the payment processor for your online store. However, RapidCart integrates with PayPal, Google Checkout, E-Junkie, and iDEAL. It even offers a method for receiving direct orders from your customers. Having more options is great, especially if you decide not to use PayPal.

RapidCart supports the digital delivery of goods via its integration with E-Junkie. It also works with Omnidea's RapidLink plugin in order to allow users to download purchased content. For more information on RapidLink, check out http://www.omnidea.it/rapidlink.

Shopping cart

Even I have to admit that RapidCart's shopping cart is very cool. When you click on the **Add to Cart** button, your product icon will fly into the shopping cart and all the quantities and totals are dynamically updated. What else can I say? It's über cool!

The style of the shopping cart is fully customizable within the **Page Inspector**. You can customize the size, color, and icon sets displayed:

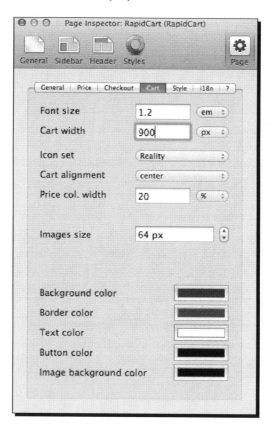

Coupon codes

Coupon codes are a great way to run a sale or promotion for your products. RapidCart has full support for managing coupon codes. Once you enable coupon codes at the bottom of the **Checkout** tab in **Page Inspector**, a new section will be unveiled in the pricing section for each product. You will now have the ability to create a coupon code for your product. The coupon can either give a percentage or fixed dollar discount to your customers. Another great feature here is that you have the ability to set start and end dates for the coupon codes. This is very convenient as you do not need to worry about removing the coupon code once your promotion is complete.

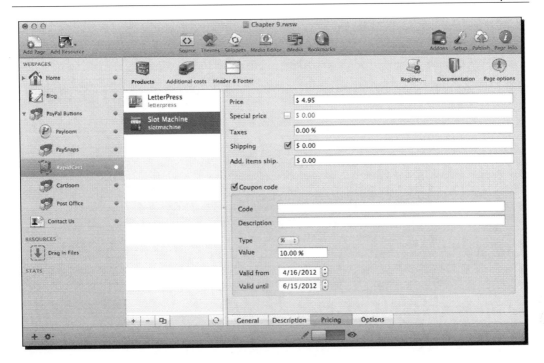

RapidCart is a fully featured e-commerce plugin for RapidWeaver. You should definitely consider it when building your online store with RapidWeaver. RapidCart is developed by Omnidea; you can find out more about it, as well as get a free trial download at http://www.omnidea.it/rapidcart.

Time for action – creating a RapidCart page

Similar to what we did earlier, we are going to create a web page that lists multiple products for sale using RapidCart. On this page, customers will be able to purchase any of your products from the same web page.

In order to complete this exercise, you will need to download RapidCart from http://www.omnidea.it/rapidcart. The free demo will allow you to add up to two products to your page.

1. Add a new RapidCart page to your RapidWeaver project.

2. Click on the + button at the left-hand side of the bottom pane, to add a new product to your page.

3. Drag-and-drop your product image onto the image drop zone where a default image is displayed for you.

4. Fill in the product name and price.

5. Click on the **Description** tab and type in description for your product into the Styled Text area.

6. Click on the **+** button again and add a second product.

7. Just as we did with the first product, add an image, name, price, and description.

8. Preview your web page.

What just happened?

We just created a third type of online store for our website. RapidCart took care of all the heavy lifting for us. It automatically created the add-to-cart buttons and also created a centralized shopping cart. The shopping cart for the site sits at the very top of the web page. Make sure that you test it by adding an item to your shopping cart. As I mentioned before, RapidCart has a super slick animation for this.

Cartloom

Cartloom is an online, flexible e-commerce service that can integrate into any website. Unlike the products that I have reviewed so far, Cartloom has a monthly subscription that, in my opinion, is worth every penny. For your subscription, you get an entirely secure backend e-commerce management solution.

Product management

If you sell digital goods, Cartloom will handle all of the digital download and registration codes distribution for you automatically. If you have physical goods, Cartloom also has an entire inventory tracking system and sales tax controls. You can also have product spin-offs and options.

Product spin-offs allow you to have a single product with multiple variations on key values. Each spin-off can have its own size, weight, price, and inventory. For example, you can sell a single design on many different t-shirt styles.

Options are unique aspects of a given product. For example, a t-shirt would have an option for size with small, medium, and large as the possible choices.

For sales marketing, Cartloom allows you to set up affiliate accounts, discount and coupon codes, and even send out e-mails to your customers.

Payment processing and invoicing

For payment processing, Cartloom has several options available. It currently integrates with PayPal, PayPal Website Payments Pro, Authorize.net, and PayPoint SecPay. Once your customers go through the purchase process, Cartloom will e-mail both you and your customer a customizable invoice via e-mail. If the purchase was for digital products, the secure download information will be listed directly on the invoice as well.

Discount codes

Cartloom offers discount codes with many great configurations. You can add as many discount codes as you would like to, into your system. Cartloom even keeps track of the number of times each code was used. This can be useful to see how many of your customers are capitalizing on the discount. The following is a list of the great conditions that can be added to each discount code:

◆ Discounts can be a percentage or a fixed amount

◆ Expiration date and time

◆ Limit the discount codes to a certain number of uses or have unlimited use

◆ Enable discount codes only when the invoice total is of a certain amount, or when a certain quantity of products are on the invoice, or if specific products have been purchased

Integrating with RapidWeaver

Integrating Cartloom into RapidWeaver is pretty simple. For each of the products that you configure inside the Cartloom seller's control panel, there is a Code Snippets tab for **Quick Buy** links, **Add to Cart** buttons, and **View Cart** links. All you need to do is copy these code snippets and paste them directly into RapidWeaver. For example, you could paste the snippet into an HTML stack or a Styled Text page.

 To make life a little easier, there is also a set of free Cartloom stacks available at `http://joeworkman.net/rapidweaver/stacks/cartloom`.

Cartloom is where I got my start with selling items on my website. I have never used anything else and don't plan to for the foreseeable future—it's a great service. Now there are a lot of features with Cartloom that I have not reviewed here, such as order blocking and mail blasts. I recommend that you go to their website and check out the rest of the feature sets and sign up for a free trial if you think that it may be a service you want to use; their website is `http://cartloom.com`.

 When this book was being written, the crew at Cartloom was working hard on the next major release of Cartloom with tons of new features. Its due to be out in late 2012. I can't wait!

Time for action - creating a Cartloom page

Cartloom is a flexible service that will work with any website. As mentioned previously, Cartloom supplies HTML snippets that you can use to integrate in many ways with your website. However, for this exercise, we are going to use the freely available Cartloom stacks from `http://joeworkman.net/rapidweaver/stacks/cartloom`. In this exercise, we are going to duplicate the Stacks page that we created for the PayPal buttons earlier in this chapter. If you did not complete that exercise, you may want to follow the instructions in order to get the page set up for this exercise.

1. Duplicate the Stacks page that we created in the first exercise of this chapter.

2. Add the Cartloom Cart stack to the top of your web page and configure your Cartloom domain in its settings.

3. Delete the HTML stack that has the PayPal button within it.

4. Add a Text stack and Cartloom Button stack where the HTML stack was.

5. In the Text stack that we just added, type the price of the product. Make the text bold and increase its size a bit.

6. In the Cartloom Button stack, configure your Cartloom domain, product ID, and price. Also, set its alignment to the left.

7. Preview your web page!

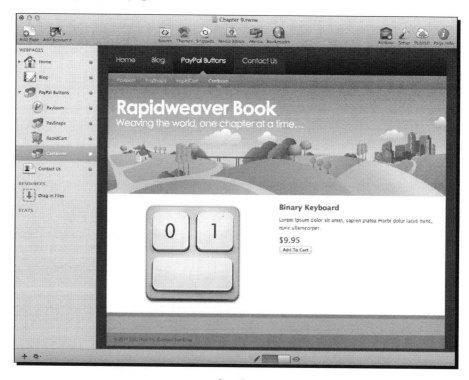

What just happened?

We just created a fourth way to create your product pages. Because we are using Stacks here, you can design your products pages however you see fit. This exercise only illustrates how easy it was to integrate Cartloom into your RapidWeaver project. You will need to publish your site in order to see the shopping cart workflow actually function.

Have a go hero – signing up for Cartloom trial

We have only touched the tip of what Cartloom can do. I recommend that you sign up for the free trial and play around with all that it can do. Add some products into Cartloom and then add them into your online store. You can even set up test transactions, so that you can test the entire system before actually accepting payments.

Contacting customers

Selling goods online is not the only part of e-commerce; keeping in touch with your customers is also a vital component. One of the best ways to do this is via e-mail. We are not going to get into the ins-and-outs of marketing strategies and e-mail formats. There are a bunch of great online services that you can use to help you with that. Before you can get to the level of sending out e-mails, we need to be able to obtain your customers' e-mail addresses. The following online services can help with both e-mail marketing as well as capturing your customers' e-mail addresses off your website:

- ◆ Madmimi (`https://madmimi.com`)
- ◆ MailChimp (`http://mailchimp.com`)
- ◆ AWeber (`http://www.aweber.com`)
- ◆ Vertical Response (`http://www.verticalresponse.com`)

When you sign up for any of the aforementioned services, you can obtain a snippet of HTML that you can insert into your RapidWeaver project. This snippet will add a subscription form to your site that will allow users to type in their e-mail address and subscribe to your e-mail marketing.

If you are using a full e-commerce service such as Cartloom or E-Junkie, they also have the ability for you to send e-mails to your customers. However, the e-mail features that they offer will not be as elaborate as the dedicated mail services mentioned in the preceding section. Depending on your requirements, you may not need a dedicated mail service.

The Post Office stack

The Post Office stack provides a highly customizable subscription form that integrates into many different popular online services mentioned previously. Your customers will be able to both subscribe and unsubscribe to your e-mail lists. It also provides the ability to completely manage your customer list on its own. The data is stored in a MySQL database and can be easily exported to a CSV file.

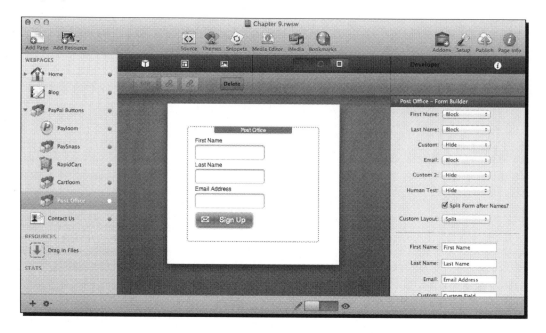

For more information on the Post Office stack, you can head over to http://joeworkman.net/rapidweaver/stacks/post-office.

Summary

We sort of blazed through a very important topic. However, with the knowledge that you have gained throughout this book, you will find using the plugins and methods outlined in this chapter to be very intuitive and easy to use. I recommend that you test out all the options presented here in order to help you decide which path you may want to go down.

Specifically, we covered:

- The benefits of PayPal.
- How to add the PayPal-supplied Add to Cart buttons directly to your projects.
- Payloom, which is a perfect plugin for building an online store powered by PayPal.
- PaySnaps, which are a great way to build a more customized looking store using Stacks.
- RapidCart, which is another great e-commerce plugin that supports more services than PayPal. Also, it has a cool shopping cart.
- Cartloom, which is a full-blown e-commerce platform that will help you run your online business better.
- The online services that we can use to gather and send our customers' e-mail.
- The Post Office stack, which can help you add a highly customizable subscription form to your RapidWeaver project.

In the next chapter we are going to dive into the black art of Search Engine Optimization. Go get your ninja gear on.

10

Search Engine Optimization

Search Engine Optimization (SEO) *is the black magic of web design. Essentially, it's the process that you need to go through in order to get the search engines to recognize your website and make sure that your web pages are provided as results to people who are searching on Google, Bing, Yahoo, and others. I say that SEO is black magic because the "gurus" are always coming up with new ways for you to improve your SEO results. Most of the time, these so-called tricks are never fully tested and chances are they won't work for long. This is because the algorithms used by the search engines are constantly changing. In this chapter, I am going to stay away from all the black magic and stick to the basics. I am going to recommend that you do the same.*

In this chapter, we are going to be reviewing the following topics:

- ◆ Increasing popularity with the search engines
- ◆ Technical SEO Basics: page titles, headings, content, sitemap.xml, and others
- ◆ Sitemap and Sitemap Plus page plugins
- ◆ OpenGraph meta tags and the Meta Mate plugin
- ◆ Web Analytics

Become popular

SEO is like being in high school. If you want to be ranked in the top searches, you have to be the popular kid. There are a few metrics that the search engines use to determine how popular you are. The more popular you are, the higher the rankings your site will be in the search index. That is fancy talk for saying that your website will show up first when users search for key terms related to your website.

The number of visitors that your website brings in tells the search engines how popular your website is to the world. The search engines want to present the most visited sites to their visitors because those websites will have the best and most permanent content, most of the time. Obviously, search engines make their money by serving the best content to users.

Another key ingredient to being considered popular is getting other websites and blogs to link to yours. For example, you may have a great product that other websites blog about, or maybe you write an inspirational blog post that causes others to refer to your intellect. When other websites link to yours, this tells the search engines that the content on your site is relevant and important enough that other websites will link to you.

 Link sharing is a common practice where users will create links to each other's websites in order to improve SEO for their websites. Search engines have caught onto this and have very intelligent algorithms to detect when it's obvious. This can hurt you more than help, so be careful.

A great way to improve both your site traffic and linking is to go social. There are tons of ways to take your website to the community. You can create a Facebook page to promote your website and business. By doing this, other Facebook users can "like" your Facebook page, and share the posts that you make in the page. When you create posts on your Facebook page, you will help yourself by linking the posts to your own website. This can grow exponentially when your users re-share your links on their profile page. There are tons of other social networks that supply the same benefits: Twitter, Google+, Pinterest, and Tumblr.

 I would recommend that you don't try to spread yourself thin, and try to use all the social networks. I recommend that you pick one or two and keep the traffic through them consistent.

Technical basics

We are going to review a bunch of technical tips and tricks that you can do within your RapidWeaver projects in order to improve your SEO rankings for web pages.

Simple URLs

Way back in *Chapter 2, Touring RapidWeaver*, when we were taking a tour of RapidWeaver, I talked a little about creating a good folder structure to your pages. If you recall, the folder structure that you give your web pages directly affects your URL scheme. Let's have a look at the URL structure to one of my product pages, and analyze it. You may visit one of the product pages at `http://joeworkman.net/rapidweaver/stacks/letterpress/`.

The first thing that you should notice is how readable and logical the URL is. Just by looking at the URL we can see that there is a simple hierarchy. There should be no question that we are looking at the Letterpress product page, which is a part of the Stacks section on my website. The Stacks section is then a sub-component of the RapidWeaver category on my site. Using a directory structure that organizes your content well makes it easy for visitors, as well as search engines, to know where they're at on your site.

Also note that my URL contains all of the keywords that I want to make sure the search engines associate that page with. The Letterpress product is a stack and is a part of the RapidWeaver family.

[

My URL does not have a page name. Remember that web servers will automatically look for the web page's `index.html` or `index.php` when one is not provided as a part of the URL. This does not have much impact on SEO, but it does make for better looking URLs.
]

The last tip is—*Thou shall not use spaces in your URLs!* Please don't put spaces in your folder names when creating web pages. The resulting URLs look horrendous. The web browser will replace all the spaces in the URL with %20. This not only looks bad but it makes the URL very difficult to read. I recommend using either a dash (-) or an underscore (_) as a replacement for spaces. Have a look at the following URLs and you tell me which one is easier on the eyes:

- `http://joeworkman.net/big%20folder%20name`
- `http://joeworkman.net/big-folder-name`

Here is a glimpse of how the aforementioned, analyzed URL (from my actual website's project file) is set up in the RapidWeaver page inspector:

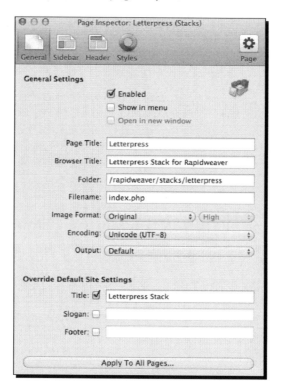

Sitemap

There is a standard file called `sitemap.xml` that all search engines look for on the top level of your web server. This XML file is a special file that contains the structure for your entire website. Search engines will read in this file in order to discover all the web pages contained within your website. Search engines will then take that data and start the process of indexing all the web pages that are contained within.

We will take a more in-depth look at how to create the `sitemap.xml` file, later on in this chapter.

Page titles

The **Browser Title** setting (in **Page Inspector**) for each web page is very important. This setting tells both the users and search engines what the topic of a particular page is. Ideally, you should create a unique title for each page on your site. This helps the search engines to know how the page is distinct from the others on your site.

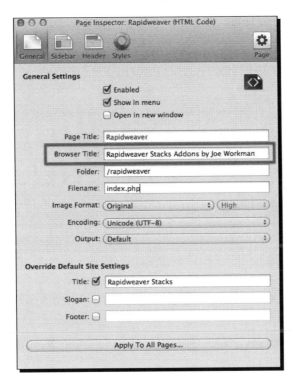

If your web page appears within a search engine's results page, the contents of the **Browser Title** attribute will appear in the first line of the results. Words in the title are bolded if they appear in the user's search query. This can help users recognize if the page is likely to be relevant to their search.

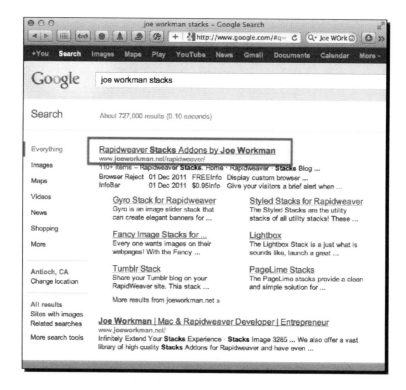

Choose a title that effectively communicates the topic of the page's content. Titles can be both short and informative. If the title is too long, only a portion of it will show in the search results.

Page description

A page's description meta tag gives search engines a summary of what the page is about. While a page's title may be of a few words, the description meta tag might be a few sentences.

In order to add a description meta tag to your web page, you will need to go to the **Header** tab of the **Page Inspector** window. There is a box at the top for **Meta Tags**. Simply click on the + button under this box to add a new tag. Set the name of the tag to **description**. Then simply type the description that you would like to use for this web page into the content field.

 There is a plugin called Sitemap Plus that helps streamline this process a bit. We will have a look at that later in this chapter.

Description meta tags are important because search engines might use them as snippets for your pages. Note that I say "might" because search engines may choose to use a relevant section of your page's visible text if it does a good job of matching up with a user's query. Having a different description meta tag for each page helps both users and search engines, especially in searches where users may bring up multiple pages on your domain.

 There are more meta tags that you can add just as we did the description tag. You can see a full list of available tags at http://www.w3schools.com/tags/att_meta_name.asp.

Anchor text

Anchor text is the clickable text that users will see as a result of a textual link. This text tells users and search engines something about the web page that you are linking to.

Headings

Heading tags are used to present structure on the page to users. There are six sizes of heading tags, beginning with `<h1>`, the most important, and ending with `<h6>`, the least important. Using keywords within your headings is one of the best ways to give your keywords prominence. It informs the search engines about the most important keywords on a particular page that it needs to pay attention to.

Headings in Styled Text

I know that you are a Styled Text guru by now; but just as a refresher, it's really simple to make any text a heading inside a Styled Text area. Simply select the text that you want to make as your heading and from the **Format** menu, select any heading from 1 to 6. You will notice the background color of the text change; this is an indication that the text contains formatting.

Headings in Stacks

There are a few ways to get headings into your **Stacks** page. You can use the Text stack and define your headings exactly how we would with Styled Text. You can also use an HTML stack and code the heading tags yourself, or you can take the easy way out and use the Headings stack!

Simply add the stack to your page and select which heading type you would like, from the setting pane. Type in your text and you are good to go.

Getting geeky with HTML headings

For all you geeks out there, I know that you are too cool for words and already know that you can add your own HTML to your RapidWeaver projects. So I don't need to tell you that you can add your own code into an HTML page, Styled Text (with ignore formatting), or with an HTML stack.

Please don't take it as an insult when I show you the HTML syntax either. I know that you have been doing this since preschool.

```
<h1>Important Geek</h1>
...
<h3>Less Important Geek</h3>
...
<h6>Least Important Geek</h6>
```

Have a go hero – creating headings

We have done exercises in some of the chapters, wherein we have created headings. Just for fun, create a Stacks page and add a Heading, Text, and an HTML stack to your page. Then go ahead and create the same heading in all three stacks. When you preview the page, they should all look identical.

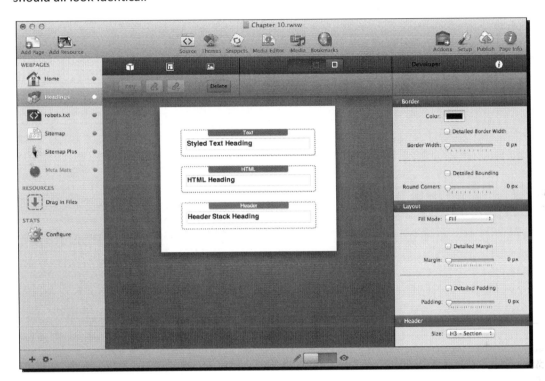

Indexing images

Web pages would be no fun if they were only text. However, search engines don't know what your images contain. This is where the `alt` attribute for images comes into play. The text that you place inside the `alt` tag for an image informs the search engines what the context of that image is. This allows search engines to not only improve your text search indexing but also enables the images themselves to be searchable online.

Images in Styled Text

We all know that you can drag-and-drop images into a Styled Text area. After you have done this, double-click on the image to open the **Media Editor**. You will see a field where you can edit the **Alt Tag** for this particular image:

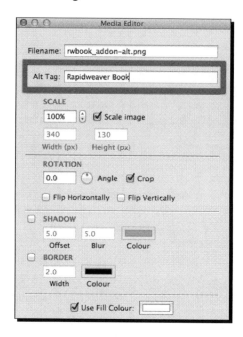

Images in Stacks

When you drag an image onto a Stacks page, double-click it to enter into Stacks' image editor mode. You will notice that there is a field that allows you to edit the image's `alt` tag in the settings pane on the right:

Getting geeky with HTML images

I am going to take all you geeks back to preschool and remind you how easy it is to add an `alt` tag to your HTML images:

```
<img src="images/me.jpg" alt="Proud to be a Geek" />
```

Quality content

This may seem obvious but there is no substitute for quality content. You can implement all the techniques mentioned so far in this chapter, but if you don't have quality content, no one will visit your website. Users know good content when they see it and will likely want to direct other users to it. As mentioned earlier, this could be through blog posts, social media, email, forums, or other means.

When you are writing your content try to keep in mind the key words and phrases that people will be searching for. The search engines will index this and use them to generate better results for search queries.

Try to keep the amount of text to a minimum. If you have three paragraphs of small text, I guarantee you that almost no one will read it. Try to also complement your text with visual images or video. People are more likely to watch a one-minute video than read three paragraphs that could take the same amount of time.

Controlling crawlers

There is another special file for SEO called `robots.txt`. Just like `sitemap.xml`, this file needs to be placed at the root directory of your website. The `robots.txt` file tells search engines which parts of your website they access. This is useful when you don't want search engines to access certain parts of your website.

The basic syntax of this file is pretty simple. The `User-agent` setting defines which agents you would like to apply your rules. You then define multiple `Disallow` settings for all the directories that you want to block the search engines from accessing:

```
User-agent: *
Disallow: /cgi-bin/
Disallow: /tmp/
Disallow: /junk/
```

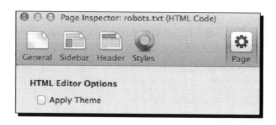

For more information on the `robots.txt` file, I suggest that you check out `http://robotstxt.org`.

 If you want to create this file in RapidWeaver, you can use a simple HTML page. Make the web page name `robots.txt` and set the folder name to be /. You will want to make sure that you don't apply the theme to this file and that it is set to not show up in your navigation menu.

RapidBot

RapidBot is an easy-to-use plugin that can be used to create your `robots.txt`. RapidBot allows you to create your `robotx.txt` conditional logic with an intuitive interface. It then handles all the work of generating the `robots.txt` file with all the proper syntax so that you don't need to worry about it.

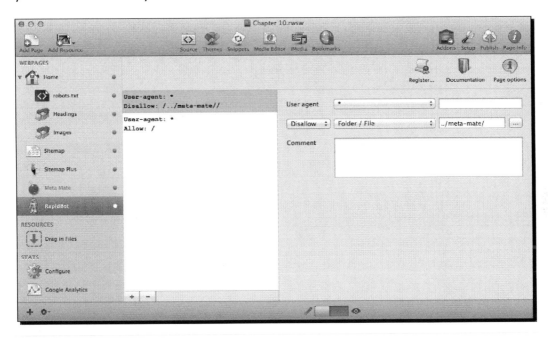

RapidBot is developed by Omnidea, and you can download a free trial at `http://www.omnidea.it/rapidbot`.

Sitemap

The Sitemap page type in RapidWeaver, automatically creates an HTML web page with a list of all the pages in your Page List, so that the visitors to your site may view them. It's sort of like a table of contents for your website. Please note that this is a web page, and not the `sitemap.xml` file.

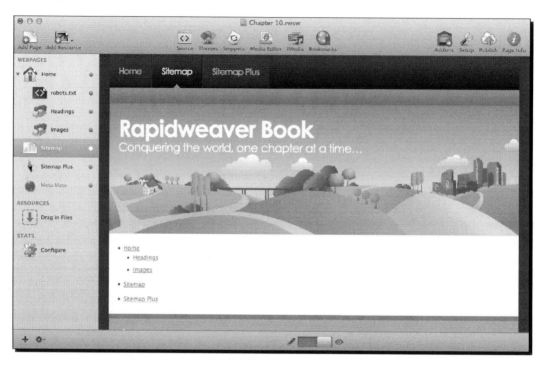

The sitemap links to all the pages in your project, except for those that you choose not to show in the site's navigation menu. To hide a page from the sitemap, simply select the page, open the **Page Inspector** window, and uncheck the **Show in Menu** option on the **General** tab.

RapidWeaver can also create an XML sitemap for you. You can enable this in the **Site Setup | Advanced** settings tab:

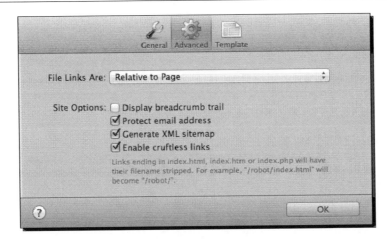

RapidWeaver uses the same logic as the Sitemap page type, in that it will only include those pages in your `sitemap.xml` file that are configured to show up in your website's navigation menu.

Time for action - creating a sitemap page

This is going to be our most challenging exercise yet. Roll your sleeves up and get ready for things to get messy:

1. Add a new Sitemap page to your RapidWeaver project.

2. Preview your web page:

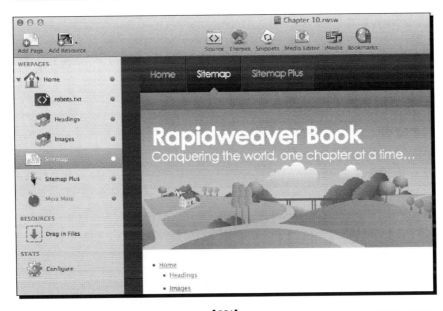

What just happened?

Did you survive that one? I know it was a close call. Jokes aside, you saw how easy it was to create a sitemap for your website. As I said before, this does not generate a `sitemap.xml` file for you. In order to do that you will need to check the setting in **Site Setup**.

Sitemap Plus

Sitemap Plus is a third-party plugin developed by Loghound. Along with Stacks, this plugin is the only other plugin that I use on every single one of my web projects. In essence, Sitemap Plus allows you manage all the key SEO features that we discussed in this chapter, for your entire website in one holistic view.

When you go to the **Site Organization** tab, you will see a list of all the web pages within your project. You will also see all of the SEO-related attributes for each page. This view provides an extremely handy way to edit all of these attributes in one central location. I use this religiously to ensure that I have properly set the titles, descriptions, good URL folder structure, and page names. There is even a checkbox to remove certain web pages from your published `sitemap.xml` file.

Sitemap Plus will create your `sitemap.xml` file for you, by default. If you do decide to use Sitemap Plus in order to create your `sitemap.xml` file, you will want to make sure that you disable RapidWeaver from creating one as well. This can be done in the **Site Setup | Advanced** tab.

Note: The category and keywords fields used to be very prominent tags for SEO. However, over the last few years, search engines have migrated from using these to sourcing your actual page content, heading, and other things mentioned in this chapter.

The **Search Engines** tab allows you to disable search engines from indexing certain pages. Sitemap Plus does this in two ways: It adds a special meta tag to the web page, which alerts the search engine not to index that web page. Sitemap Plus can also create and publish the `robots.txt` file for you, so that you don't need to worry about creating that file at all. However, you will have to enable this in the **Sitemap Plus** settings as it is disabled by default:

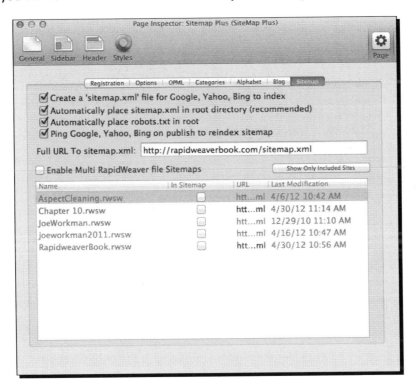

SiteMap Plus can also create sitemap web pages in a variety of styles, similar to how the out-of-the-box Sitemap page can. You can configure this in the **Site Map** tab.

Sitemap Plus is developed by Loghound Software and you can download your free trial version, and get more information about it at `http://www.loghound.com/sitemap`.

Time for action - using Sitemap Plus

In this exercise, we are going to use Sitemap Plus in order to quickly do an SEO audit on our RapidWeaver project. We are also going to configure Sitemap Plus to generate a `sitemap.xml` file for us. In order to complete this exercise, you will need to download and install the Sitemap Plus plugin.

1. Add a new Sitemap Plus page to your RapidWeaver project.

2. Click on the **Site Organization** tab to see the hierarchy list of all your web pages in your project.

3. Verify the following fields are SEO-compliant; double-click the field in order to modify the fields contents:

   ❑ Folder names of your web page are changed to something concise and readable

   ❑ Filename is set to `index.html` or `index.php`

   ❑ Browser Title is a short description of the web page

   ❑ Description is a longer description for search engines

   ❑ Check the **Hide in Sitemaps** for any pages that you do not care to be listed

4. In the **Search Engines** tab, review the change frequency and priority for each web page.

5. In the Sitemap preferences check the following two settings:

   ❑ Automatically place `robots.txt` in root

   ❑ Ping Google, Yahoo, Bing on publish to reindex sitemap

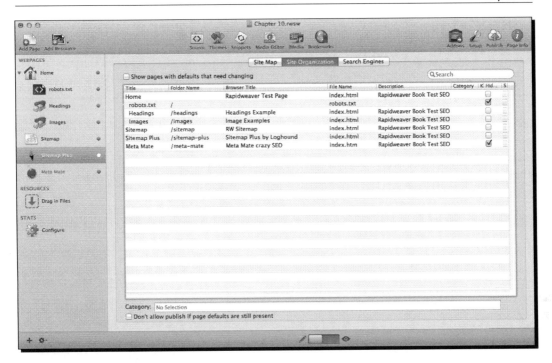

What just happened?

We used Sitemap Plus to do a thorough verification of all of the important page attributes required for SEO. We also configured Sitemap Plus to ping all of the major search engines that there were changes to our website, each time we publish. Sitemap Plus will also create an HTML sitemap file just like the out-of-the-box Sitemap page plugin does. It's probably a good idea to remove this page from your page navigation.

Meta Mate

If you want to go crazy with SEO and truly go the extra mile then the **Meta Mate** plugin may be of interest to you. Meta Mate provides an easy-to-use interface for adding the **Open Graph** meta tags to all your web pages. The Open Graph protocol enables any web page to become a rich object in a social graph. For instance, this is used on Facebook to allow any web page to have the same functionality as any other object on Facebook. For more information about the Open Graph protocol, head over to `http://ogp.me`.

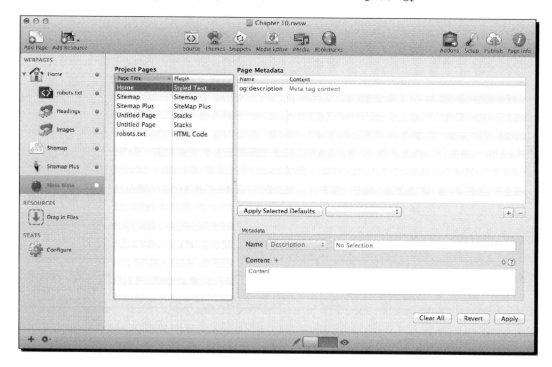

Meta Mate is a third-party plugin and you can get more information as well as download a demo at `http://pagesofinterest.net/shop/meta-mate`.

Analytics

We talked about one of the factors that determines your SEO popularity is the number of visitors to your website. RapidWeaver integrates with two different analytics companies out of the box: *Google Analytics* and *GoSquared*. These analytics services will allow you to track tons of various metrics about who is visiting your website.

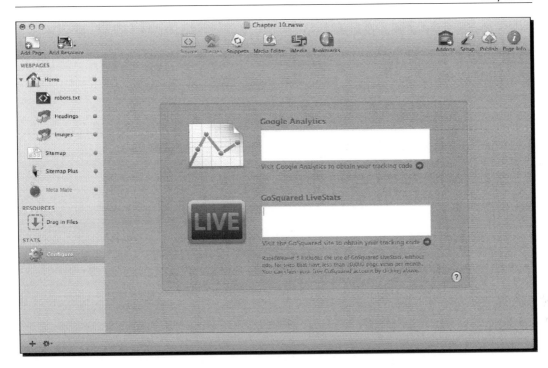

While working on your RapidWeaver projects throughout this book, you may have noticed the **Configure** icon within the **Stats** group in the application pane on the left-side of the page. This is where you configure your analytics service. First, you will need to choose which service you will sign up for and then create your accounts.

Google Analytics was one of the original pioneers in web analytics and it's completely free to use. You can sign up for their service at `https://www.google.com/analytics`.

GoSquared is a relatively newcomer to the analytics game. However, they are definitely the cool kids on the block with the amazing visualizations that they provide to analyze your data. GoSquared has both free and paid-for services. You can sign up and find out more about their features at `http://gosquared.com`.

During the setup process you will probably have to upload a sample HTML file that is provided by the analytics service. This helps them verify if you are indeed the owner of that website.

Once this is done and your account has been verified, you will be provided with a snippet of code that you will copy and paste into the proper service field in the **Configure** applet. In order to get this code working on all your web pages, you will need to republish all the files. This can be done from the **File** menu.

Once you have configured your analytics service, RapidWeaver will add a shortcut in the panel to your account on the left-hand side of the page, so that you can directly access your website metric data directly from within your RapidWeaver project.

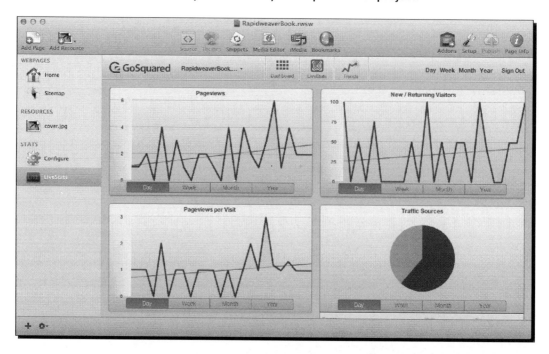

Time for action - adding analytics

We are now going to go through setting up Google Analytics with your RapidWeaver website. This setup will not provide a detailed process for setting up your Google Analytics account. However, this process should be pretty straightforward. In order for Google to verify that you are the owner of a web domain, you will be asked to either upload a file with a certain name or enter in a custom CNAME attribute with your hosting company.

1. Head over to http://www.google.com/analytics and create your Google Analytics account.

2. Once your Analytics account is set up, go to the **Tracking Code** tab in your **Admin** settings.

3. Copy the HTML code in the **Paste this code on your site** section of this web page.

4. In your RapidWeaver project, click on the **Configure** icon in the left-hand side pane of the web page.

5. Paste the acquired HTML code into the **Google Analytics** box in this page:

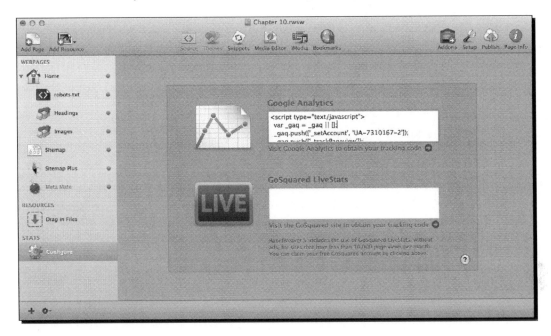

6. Republish your entire website.

What just happened?

We will now be able to track visitors to our RapidWeaver website. Sometimes you will start seeing results within a few hours. However, it has been known to take up to a full day to start seeing metrics for a newly set up domain. Google collects all kinds of data. It's fun to see which web pages your users visit the most, where in the world they are coming from, and if they are still using ancient technology such as the Internet Explorer.

Have a go hero – setting up GoSquared

We added a Google Analytics account onto our web pages. You may want to give GoSquared a try. It has a beautiful interface that is a joy to use. Go ahead and set up a free account and take it for a spin. You may like it more than Google Analytics.

Summary

In this chapter, we learned how to make our websites popular and achieve better search rankings. As long as you are not trying to build the next competitor to Amazon or something, stay away from the black magic. As long as you stick to the basics that we covered in this chapter, you will have an extremely solid SEO implementation.

Specifically, we covered the following:

- How to get popular by linking and getting linked.
- Taking your website social via Facebook, Twitter, and others.
- Making sure your URLs are simple and readable.
- Creating a `sitemap.xml` file to help search engines crawl your site.
- Page titles and descriptions help search engines categorize your web pages.
- Content is king! Quality content and placing keywords in both headings and links are gold.
- You can control where search engines crawl on your website with a `robots.txt` file.
- RapidBot is a good plugin to help you create your `robots.txt` file.
- Sitemap Plus is a valuable plugin, which provides an SEO command center for all your key SEO data.
- Adding web analytics easily into our RapidWeaver projects.

The next chapter will be our last. It will cover a grab-bag of mixed topics along with some tips and tricks.

11
Advanced Weaving

We have reached the final chapter of this book, and I feel that there is still so much to learn about web design. So in this chapter I am going to try to cram in as much of it as I can. Some of these are RapidWeaver-specific topics; however, most are general web design tips and tricks. I hope that you have your geek hard hat on because this chapter is going to be a hard-core-geek-roller-coaster-ride (that's a highly technical term)!

In this chapter we are going to be reviewing the following topics;

- Page automation
- Source view
- Editing content online
- Mobile compatibility
- Custom 404 page
- Tricks with `.htaccess`
- Dev Inspector
- HTML and CSS resources
- Troubleshooting tips

Page automation

As we have seen throughout this book, RapidWeaver has a bunch of settings that can be set on a per-page basis. But what happens if you would like to change a certain setting on all of your web pages at the same time. If you have a small project, going through each page may only take a few minutes. However, if you have a large web project, it may take you a long time to go through each page and adjust the setting that you want. This is also error prone, as you could easily miss a page or fat finger a setting.

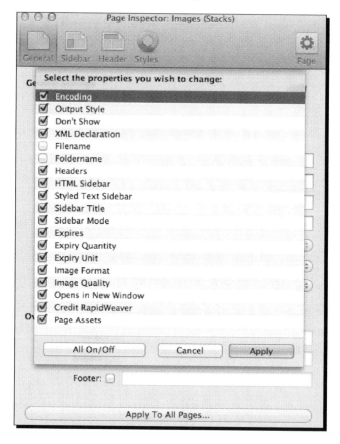

RapidWeaver has a very convenient utility that allows you to take settings from one page and apply them to every single page within your project. At the bottom of the **General** tab in the **Page Inspector** window, you will see a button called **Apply to All Pages...**.

When you click on this button, a list view will drop down from the top. You will see a list of all the available settings that can be applied to all other pages. All that you need to do is ensure that the settings that you would like to sync across all pages are checked. Once you click on the **Apply** button, all of the selected settings from the current page are copied into all of the other pages within your RapidWeaver project.

Time for action – Page automation

Let's play around with the page automation so that you are 100 percent certain how things work:

1. Open up your RapidWeaver project.
2. Open **Page Inspector** on any of your web pages.
3. Uncheck the **Show in Menu** option in the **General** tab.
4. Uncheck the **Credit RapidWeaver** option in the **Header** tab.
5. Go into the **Sidebar** tab, and add some content into the sidebar; just some filler text will work fine.
6. Back on the **General** tab, click on the **Apply to All Pages...** button.
7. Click on the **All On/Off** button at the bottom.
8. Select the following three options: **Don't Show**, **Styled Text Sidebar**, and **Credit RapidWeaver**.
9. Click on the **Apply** button.
10. All the changes that we made on this page should have been propagated to all of your web pages.

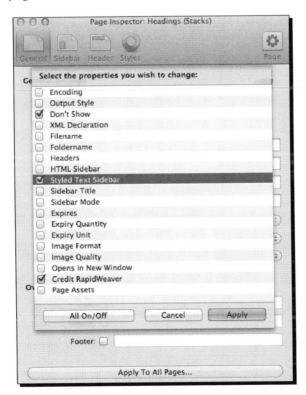

What just happened?

Within just a few seconds we copied settings from one page to all the other pages on our website. This utility is very handy to have in your tool belt. It's probably something that you are not going to use very often. However, when the time comes for you to use it, it could potentially save you hours of boring monotonous work.

Source view

So far throughout this book we have been going back and forth between the **Edit** and **Preview** modes within RapidWeaver. However, there is a third mode that is somewhat hidden by default, called **Source view**. You can access Source view from either the main menu bar (**View | View Source**) or by adding it to your RapidWeaver toolbar. We talked about customizing the toolbar back in *Chapter 2, Touring RapidWeaver*.

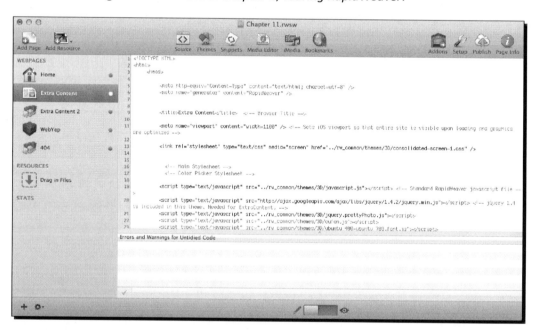

When you look at a web page in the Source view, you are going to see the raw HTML and/or PHP that will be deployed to your server when you publish. Source view is read-only; you cannot modify the page's source code here. Also, having the ability to view the page source, you will also be able to see any page warnings and errors that may have risen for your page.

Have a go hero – surfing through source code

Source view is not rocket science. I recommend that you add it to your main RapidWeaver toolbar if you think that you are going to be using it. Have a look at the source of a few of the web pages in your RapidWeaver project. The more that you look through the code, the better you will understand it over time. This will help you be a better web designer in the long run.

ExtraContent

Back in *Chapter 3*, *Theming Your Site*, when we were discussing themes, we had mentioned ExtraContent and how it can provide a more dynamic and flexible way to add content to your website. You should also be aware that the functionality and locations of extra content areas will vary from theme to theme. There are themes that do not even support it.

 Most of the time, ExtraContent areas will be disabled by default in a theme. You can enable them through the theme's styles settings.

ExtraContent was a standard defined by third-party theme developers. For more information about it, and to download free snippets and stacks for it, head over to `http://extracontent.info`.

HTML snippet

In order to add content into the EC areas, you can use the following sample HTML:

```
<div id="myExtraContent1">
    <!-- Your content goes here -->
</div>
```

This HTML is available as a free snippet at the EC website. The Extra Content container contains an ID `myExtraContentX`, where `X` is an integer that will correlate to the support EC location in your theme.

Once you place the aforementioned snippet onto your page, the content that is placed between the `<div>` tags will be magically moved into its proper location, which is defined by the theme.

If you are going to add this snippet to a Styled Text area, you will need to remember to choose the **Ignore Formatting** option for the first and last lines with the `<div>` tags.

Adding EC via stacks

Adding data into an ExtraContent area via stacks could not be any easier. Simply add the free ExtraContent stack to your page. In the stack settings, you will need to set the number of your EC location for the theme that you are using. Now any stack data that is inserted into the EC stack will be magically ported into the corresponding theme area on your web page.

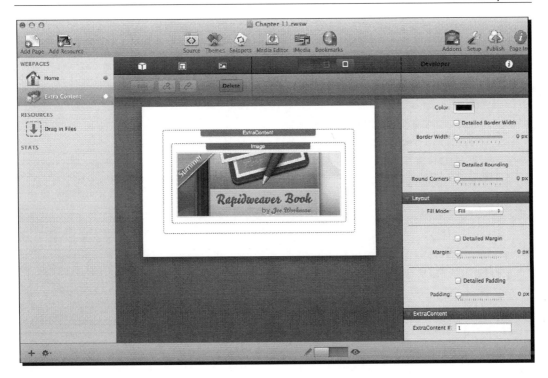

It's very common that you will want to place complex stack data into your ExtraContent areas. However, it cannot be guaranteed that all stacks will function properly when placed into an ExtraContent area.

Time for action - adding ExtraContent

Now that we know how easy it is to implement ExtraContent areas, let's put it into practice. In order to perform this exercise, you will need a theme that supports ExtraContent. Unfortunately, none of the out-of-the-box themes that ship with RapidWeaver supports this. You will need to find a third-party theme if you want to utilize ExtraContent areas. The location of the extra content areas will vary between each theme. You will need to look at the theme's documentation in order to figure out where the ExtraContent areas are located. Some themes will also include a theme style setting that will allow you to preview where each ExtraContent container will be rendered on your web page in the **Preview** mode.

In this exercise, we are going to use a Stacks page so that we can implement both EC methods on the same page. If you do not have the free EC stack, you will want to go download it from `http://extracontent.info`.

1. Open your RapidWeaver project and change the theme to one that supports ExtraContent.

2. Create a new Stacks page.

3. Go into the theme style settings in **Page Inspector**, and enable one or more ExtraContent areas.

4. Add a Text stack to the page and add the following into its contents:

   ```
   <div id="myExtraContent1">
   This text will show up inside the Extra Content area #1
   </div>
   ```

5. You will need to select both the top and bottom lines, and make sure that their formatting is ignored. You can do this via the **Format** menu.

6. Add an EC stack to the page and populate it with some content. You may add an image and text stack inside of it.

7. In the EC stack settings, set the **ExtraContent** number to 2.

8. Preview your web page.

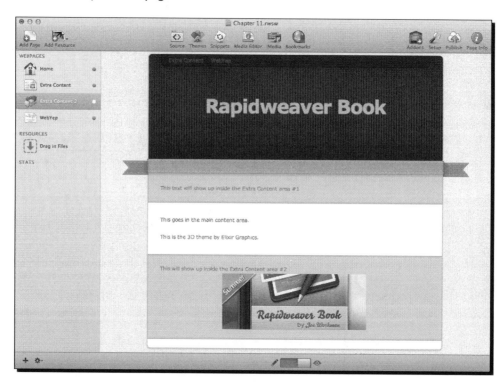

What just happened?

We just added data to two different ExtraContent areas in a theme. As you see, when you preview the web page, the ExtraContent areas are outside the main content. ExtraContent allows us to easily place content inside locations outside the main content area. Without ExtraContent, you would be limited to placing data in either the main content, or the sidebar.

Editing content online

One of the drawbacks of RapidWeaver, especially if you are developing a site for a customer, is that all of the edits need to happen within your RapidWeaver project. However, there are a few good solutions that allow you to edit the contents of your RapidWeaver website online.

I am not going to be giving an in-depth explanation of these solutions. However, I wanted to make sure that you were aware that a solution does exist.

PageLime

PageLime is a service that provides a centralized web console for you and your customers to edit your RapidWeaver websites online. They also have a great iOS app that allows you to edit your websites on the go from your phone. PageLime offers both free and paid plans. For more information check them out at `http://pagelime.com`:

Implementing PageLime into your RapidWeaver project can be easily done through HTML or the PageLime stack set that can be found at `http://joeworkman.net/rapidweaver/stacks/pagelime`.

WebYep

WebYep is a free RapidWeaver plugin that allows you to create user-editable content on your website. WebYep is not a centralized service; the entire WebYep CMS system gets installed alongside your RapidWeaver website.

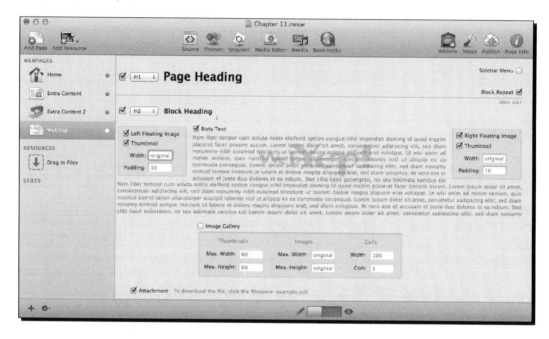

You can use WebYep in any website free of charge, provided that you keep the WebYep logo and product name displayed within the Edit mode.

For more information about WebYep and to download it, go to `http://www.obdev.at/products/webyep`.

Armadillo

We had reviewed Armadillo in *Chapter 8, Blogs, Podcasts, and Going Social*. As mentioned then, you can use Armadillo for more than just creating a blog. You can create as many custom web pages as you would like within Armadillo, and have them be displayed within your RapidWeaver website. One caveat with Armadillo is that you cannot edit web pages created outside of itself. This means that you will not be able to edit Stacks pages, Styled Text pages, and others.

You can find more details about Armadillo at
`http://www.nimblehost.com/store/armadillo.`

Mobile compatibility

Mobile browsing is starting to become a major part of web development. We no longer just sit in front of our computer monitors to surf the Web. We sit in a coffee shop with our iPad or on the train with our iPhone. This is exciting because users can now access our websites from wherever they are.

Mobile browsers do a decent job at scaling traditional websites so that they are displayed properly on mobile devices. However, many times, this leads to users having to zoom into the web page in order to click on a link or even read the text on the page. What if we could dynamically change the look of our website based on the device that people were visiting from?

Responsive web design

While I have been writing this book, a major trend has swept over the Web and RapidWeaver community. This trend is called **responsive web design**. In a nutshell, responsive web design means that you design your website so that the look will be tailored to the device that your user is viewing it on. This means that your website will have a native feel from a 27-inch desktop display, all the way down to a mobile device such as an iPhone. The mobile browsing experience is not what you are accustomed to with the pinch and zoom; your website has a completely native feel as if it were developed for a mobile device.

Building websites in RapidWeaver has traditionally meant a fixed-width website. This means that most of the add ons (plugins and stacks) that have been developed were not designed to be responsive. There has been a wave of some amazing new responsive themes and add ons that will help you build better mobile compatible sites. I am sure that over time, many add ons will be updated to support this growing trend.

If you feel that you are going to want to build a responsive website using RapidWeaver, I encourage that you search through the RapidWeaver Add-ons section for themes and add ons that support responsive design (`http://www.realmacsoftware.com/addons/ search/RapidWeaver?q=responsive`).

For additional information about responsive web design, Ethan Marcotte has written a great book simply titled *Responsive Web Design*. It can be found at `http://www.abookapart. com/products/responsive-web-design`.

Goodbye Flash

If you are reading this book, I probably don't need to inform you about the war on flash. As you probably know, flash is not supported on any of Apple's iOS devices. The reason for this is that flash uses too much system resources and would kill the device's battery life. This means that if you want your website to have a consistent look and feel across all devices, then you need to say goodbye to flash.

Custom 404 page

I am sure that you have at one time encountered a *404 Page Not Found* error while surfing the Web. These 404 pages are pretty simple to create actually. The easy part is creating the HTML page. You can style it and add whatever content you want to it. I suggest that you make sure to add links where the user may want to go. You will also want to make sure that the page is not configured to show up in your navigation menu.

The tricky part is configuring your server to point to our 404 web page. This is done through a special text configuration file called `.htaccess` that is stored at the root of your website directory. This file stores more than just the configuration for the 404 page. We will review a few other tricks later on; however, the following is the configuration that you will need to use in order to get your 404 page working:

```
ErrorDocument 404 /errors/404/index.html
```

The aforementioned configuration tells the web server that when a web page is requested and not found, the defined web page should be sent to the user. You may need to modify the path in this configuration to point to where you have configured your 404 web page to be.

 The aforementioned review requires that your web hosting company should be using the Apache web server. If you are not using the Apache web server, then I suggest that you ask your hosting company how this can be configured in your environment.

Time for action – creating a 404 page

Let's get our 404 on! Creating a 404 page may seem tricky at first. But once you get the trick of editing the `.htaccess` file, it should be a breeze. Every hosting company has different policies about adding the `htaccess` rules. You may want to peruse through your hosting company's online help in order to find their recommended method of editing the `htaccess` rules.

1. Create a new web page inside your RapidWeaver project and title it **404**.

2. You will probably want to change the default folder to `/errors/404`, and leave the page name at `index.html`.

3. Uncheck the **Show in Menu** option in **Page Inspector**, as this is not a page that user needs to navigate to.

4. Add some content to your 404 page. Add a short message that the page no longer exists, and then suggest some links as to where they may want to go.

5. Publish your new 404 page to your server.

6. If a `.htaccess` file already exists on your server, then you can edit that. If not, you will need to create a new `.htaccess` file at the root of your website. This file is a simple plain text file.

7. Add the following rule into the `.htaccess` file: `ErrorDocument 404 / errors/404/index.html`.

8. It may take a few minutes for the changes to take effect. Go to a URL on your website that does not exist. You should now see that newly created 404 page:

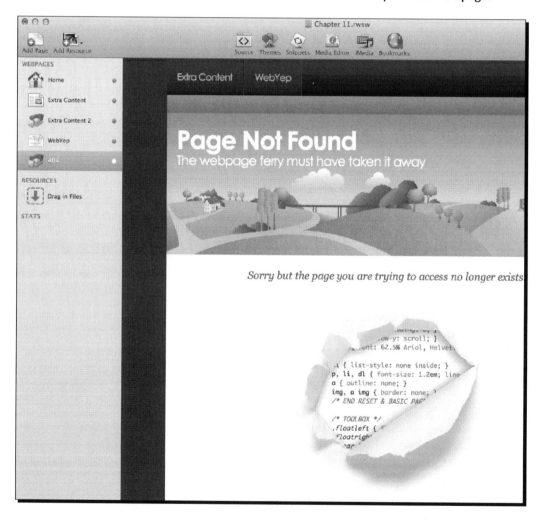

What just happened?

We now have a fully-fledged 404 page that will be displayed to visitors when a web page cannot be found. The trickiest part of this exercise was probably figuring out how to edit the .htaccess file with your hosting company.

Tricks with .htaccess

In the last section, we learned how to configure a .htacccess file to point our web server to our *404 Page Not Found* web page. Let's dive in and learn a few more tricks that can be useful.

For more information on all the things that can be done with your .htaccess file, you can reference http://htaccess-guide.com.

Defining the file types

There are many times when hosting companies might not have all the file mime types configured on your server. These file mime types are used to inform the browser about the format of the files that are going to be used. The following mime types are common settings that will need to be set if you plan on using HTML5 media and custom fonts:

- ◆ AddType font/opentype otf
- ◆ AddType video/ogg .ogv
- ◆ AddType video/mp4 .mp4 .m4v
- ◆ AddType video/webm .webm
- ◆ AddType video/quicktime .mov

Disabling directory access

I am sure that you have visited a URL link where, instead of a web page you saw a list of files and folders. This happens when you enter a directory in the URL and the web server does not have a default web page to display (index.html or index.php). This is common when you have directories on your web server that are solely used to store files and images. There is a simple configuration that you can put into your .htaccess file, which will not allow visitors to browse such directories on your web server. All you need to add is the following simple line to your .htaccess file:

```
Options -Indexes
```

Redirects

Let's say that you are doing a complete revamp of an existing website and you plan on changing the URL structure that exists with the currently published website. The problem with doing that is that if links to your site exist on external websites, those links could be broken. One solution could be to display a 404 page to visitors; however, a better solution would be to redirect users to where you think that they would like to go now.

In order to get your head around this, let's look at a real world example. In 2011, I completely rebuilt my website from the ground up. I had decided to update my URL schemes so that they were better for SEO and prettier on the eye. To make a long story short, my old website had two sections: `joeworkman.net/products` and `joeworkman.net/store`. Both these sections of the website were getting merged into a single `joeworkman.net/rapidweaver` section. The following are the rules that will be added to the `.htaccess` file in order to accomplish this:

```
Redirect 301 /store /rapidweaver

RewriteEngine On
RewriteRule ^products.* /rapidweaver [R=301]
```

I have two different examples in this code. The top line is a very simple redirect, where you can have a one-to-one mapping of the old URL to the new URL. In such a situation, `joeworkman.net/store` will redirect to `joeworkman.net/rapidweaver`.

The second example allows for a more advanced pattern matching of your URLs. The first line enables the `RewriteEngine` within Apache. The remaining lines are the redirect rules. Each rule breaks down into four parts. The only parts that you will need to change here are the middle two arguments:

1. Declare that this is `RewriteRule`.
2. A pattern match for the old URL structure to match.
3. The destination that the user will be redirected to.
4. Redirect the user to the new URL: `[R=301]`.

The pattern that I had used in the aforementioned example `^products.*`, will match `/products` and `/products/anything-after`. I did this for simplicity, so that if anyone tries to visit any of my old product pages, they will get sent to my new main products page. If I wanted to go the extra mile, I could have created a rule for every product page and mapped it to the new scheme.

The pattern matching in the `RewriteEngine` is very extensive. There are also many more powerful things that can be done with rewrites. While it's not a page turner like this book is, there are some great tips at `http://httpd.apache.org/docs/2.0/misc/rewriteguide.html`.

Not all hosting companies enable `RewriteEngine` on their web servers. So, please check with your hosting company if you are attempting to configure your `.htaccess` file and things are not working as you would have expected them to.

More than one .htaccess file

So far we have talked about managing a centralized `.htaccess` file at the root of your website's directory. However, you can place `.htaccess` files within any directory on your website, and the rules that are contained within it will only affect that section of the website. This means that you can set up your global rules at the root level and easily overwrite those rules with strategically placed `.htaccess` files throughout your site.

Dev Inspector

In RapidWeaver's preferences, there is an option **Enable Web Developer Tools**. This unlocks a gem that helps you tweak and troubleshoot your web designs. When you preview a web page, you can right-click on the page and select **Inspect Element**. This will open up the glorious world of the Webkit Dev Inspector:

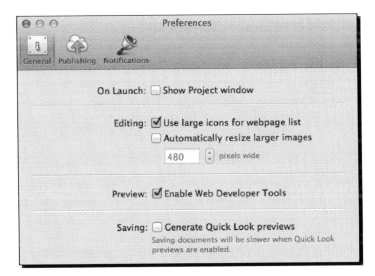

The Webkit Dev Inspector has many wonderful features that can be seen with the tabs along the top. However, we are only going to dive into a few of the ones that I tend to use the most. For a full manual on the Dev Inspector head over to `https://developer.apple.com/library/safari/#documentation/AppleApplications/Conceptual/Safari_Developer_Guide`.

You can also enable the Dev Inspector within Safari's **Advanced Preferences** setting as well. All other major web browsers have similar features as well. Although some browsers require extra plugins to be installed. For example, Firefox has an excellent plugin called FireBug, which is very similar to the Dev Inspector.

When Apple released Safari 6 along side Mountain Lion, a completely revamped Webkit Inspector was also released. In this section, I will be reviewing this latest version. However, if you still have Safari 5 or earlier installed, all of the features described here are still prevalent to your version.

Elements

The default tab that opens for the Dev Inspector is the **Elements** tab. This is by far my most widely used feature. The Elements browser is broken down into three panes—the left-hand pane is the page resource browser, the center is the DOM browser, and the right-hand pane is the style and attribute browser for the selected page element:

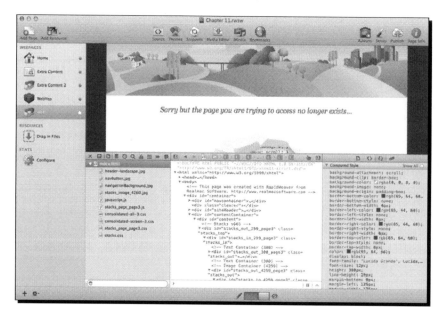

The resource browser

The element browser on the left-hand side, lists all the resources that were utilized and downloaded for this web page you are viewing. This includes JavaScript, CSS, images, and more. This could be useful in verifying if the correct files are being loaded by the web browser. Often, cached files can be used instead of files that could have been recently updated on the server. In order to view a particular resource simply click on it. When the main web page itself is selected in the resources pane, you will see the DOM browser appear in the center.

The DOM browser

At first, the DOM browser looks like it's the web page source; however, it's not. The HTML source that is displayed here is the result of any JavaScript and CSS codes that has been applied to the web page. The source code that is displayed here is what the browser is rendering at any particular moment. If you have a slider on your web page that is actively animating, you will most likely notice the source code changing as you are looking at the element in this browser. *So what can we use this awesome tool for?*

- Analyze classes and IDs of particular elements on our page. We can then use that information to write our own CSS code, to customize the page to our liking.

- Find an element and see its styles in the Style browser (next section). This is very helpful for debugging our CSS code, and figuring out why things may not be styled as we expected them to be.

- Right-click on an element and copy the entire block of HTML to use somewhere else. Remember that this only copies the HTML and none of the CSS or JS codes that may affect that element.

- You can double-click and edit the HTML right there on the spot. This is useful for trying out new things and debugging . Be careful though, any changes that you make are only temporary. Once you reload the page, they will be gone.

Finding elements

There are two ways to find the element that you desire. Right-click on the element on the web page, and select **Inspect Element**. This will navigate to that exact element that you selected within the browser. This is by far the fastest way to find an element.

You can also manually navigate through the element browser by drilling down into the page hierarchy until your find the element that you desire. In order to assist you in verifying that you are correct, the Dev Inspector will highlight the element on the web page, when it gets selected within the browser.

Style and Attribute browser

The **Style** and **Attribute** pane contains tabs along the top. We are going to primarily work in the third and fourth tabs. When you select an HTML element, all the style settings will be displayed in the third tab. This is the style browser, where you can view all the CSS rules that have been applied to the selected DOM element. The style browser itself is broken down into different collapsible lists. Let's review a few of them now.

Computed styles

This section displays the final computed styles displayed in the browser, for the selected element. There is a **Show inherited** checkbox that will display every possible style and its value. Basically, everything that is displayed when this is checked is browser default. This means that particular style attribute was not defined in any of the CSS rules, for this element.

Styles

This provides a potentially long list of all the CSS rules that matched this element, and the order in which they were processed. The style rules at the bottom have less precedence than the style rules defined higher up in the chain. If you find a style that has been stricken out with a line through it, this means that the style has been overwritten by another rule higher up in the chain.

If you double-click on an active style setting, you will have the ability to edit its value. This could be useful if you want to test styles settings out on the fly. You can also completely disable a style setting by clicking on the checkbox to the right of each setting.

 Just as with editing in the element's browser, the changes made here are not permanent. As soon as you reload your page, all your changes will be gone.

Metrics

The last tab in the styles and attributes browser allows us to visually see all the metrics that are used to calculate the size of the selected DOM elements. Essentially, every DOM element is a box. This **Metrics** pane allows you to easily see all of the measurement data for that exact element. In the center, you have the definition of the current width and height for the element. Then outside of that, you have all the other attributes that can add onto the size of the element—padding, border, margin, and position:

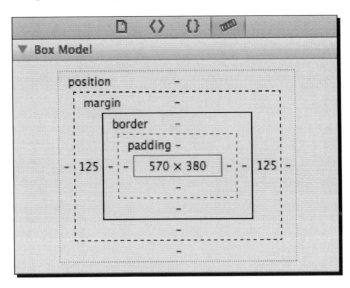

You can double-click on any of the values displayed there, and edit them on the fly. If you see a dash (-) this means that the value has been set to 0. Also, take note that all the surrounding settings (padding, border, and others) are uniquely defined for all four sides of the element.

 Just as I said before with editing in the style browser, the changes made here are not permanent. As soon as you reload your page, all your changes will be gone.

Console

You can find the console at the last tab in the left-hand pane of the Webkit Inspector. The console is a great place to look for any errors that could have occurred on the web page. There are a couple of common issues that can be found here; you may see "404 page" errors, with files and images not being found on the server. If there are any JavaScript errors, they will be displayed here, as shown in the following screenshot:

 If there are JavaScript errors with anything on your website, then all JavaScript on the page will not function. For example, if you have two or three stacks that use JavaScript on your web page, and if any of them have a JavaScript error, then none of them will function properly. We will show you how to troubleshoot this by isolating the problem later on in this chapter.

Have a go hero – using Dev Inspector

I recommend that you take the time to use and learn Dev Inspector. It will really become your best friend when it comes to troubleshooting styles and layout of your web designs. I also encourage that you enable Dev Inspector inside Safari as well. This way when you come across a website or component of a web page that you like, you can easily inspect that element and learn how things were done. You may also want to dive into some of the other features and tabs that we skipped here. There are some valuable tools to help you analyze bandwidth and other performance metrics.

Learning HTML and CSS

In this book, we have learned that you can build some pretty cool websites without ever looking at a line of code. However, having a decent understanding of both HTML and CSS will make you a more versatile web designer. You will be able to tackle more situations, and be able to gets things styled just how you want. While the goal of this book was not to teach you HTML or CSS, I wanted to give you a very basic overview and a couple of resources that I personally use constantly.

HTML basics

HTML is the programming language that defines the structure of your web page. Similar to a word processing document, at the top of the web page may be a heading, followed by some paragraphs, which in turn may have images and sub-headings contained within. HTML is simply a text document that defines all of these elements through a set of predefined tags.

The content for an element must be contained within an opening (<p>) and closing (</p>) tag with a few exceptions such as images. Tags can be nested within each other as well. This is what gives our documents structure and hierarchy. Let's review a few of the basic HTML tag elements.

Document structure

Every HTML document contains a standard set of tags that define the overall structure of the document itself:

```
<html>
    <head>
        <title>This is my page title</title>
    </head>
    <body>
        ...Webpage content goes here...
    </body>
</html>
```

The `<html>` element represents the beginning and the end of the document. The `<head>` element contains information about the web page. A common element added here is the `<title>`, which is the title of your web page. Lastly, the `<body>` element houses the content that is displayed within the web browser.

 If you are going to be using HTML solely within RapidWeaver, you actually don't need to worry about this at all. The theme that you will be using will take care of all this for you. You are going to care more about the content-related elements that we will be going over next.

Headings

We have reviewed the heading element earlier in this book. HTML supports six levels of headings—`<h1>` through `<h6>`. The `<h1>` element is used for main headings. The `<h2>` element is used for sub-headings, followed by `<h3>` and so on, which can be used for further sub-headings:

```
<h1>This is a Main Heading</h1>
<h2>This is a Level 2 Heading</h2>
<h3>This is a Level 3 Heading</h3>
<h4>This is a Level 4 Heading</h4>
<h5>This is a Level 5 Heading</h5>
<h6>This is a Level 6 Heading</h6>
```

Paragraphs

To create a paragraph, surround your text with the `<p>` element. By default, web browsers will place a line break after each paragraph:

```
<p>This is a paragraph. Usually, paragraphs contain more than one
sentence. I hope that you are enjoying this book.</p>
```

Lists

We are going to review the two most common types of lists: **ordered lists** (numbered) and **unordered lists** (bullets). The syntax for these lists is identical with the exception of the surrounding element tag. To create a list you simply create a list element with either the `<ul>` element, or the `<ol>` element. Then within the list container, you can add as many list elements as you like with the `<li>` tag:

```
<ul>
    <li>This is an unordered list.</li>
    <li>In layman terms, this means that we now have a bulleted
    list.</li>
```

```
</ul>

<ol>
    <li>This is an ordered list.</li>
    <li>In layman terms, this means that we now have a numbered
    list.</li>
</ol>
```

 While the aforementioned examples are simple, HTML does support multi-level lists that are nested within each other.

Links

We have discussed links a few times throughout this book. Links are special elements, which when clicked will navigate the user to another web page. Links can also be used to trigger e-mail as well as other functions. The link is created using the `<a>` tag along with an `href` attribute, which defines the location or action that will occur once the user clicks on the link:

```
<a href="http://joeworkman.net">Link to a URL</a>

<a href="mailto:joe@rapidweaverbook.com">Send an email</a>
```

 You can also add links around images. To do this, simply add an `<img>` tag into the `<a>` element instead of text.

Images

We have talked about images frequently throughout this book. An image can be added to your web page using the `<img>` element. There are two required attributes for the `<img>` tag: `src` and `alt`.

The `src` attribute defines the source path to the image file. This will usually be the relative or absolute URL to the image file on your website. The `alt` tag defines the alt text that is used for SEO and assistive browsing. If you want to ensure that your image is constrained to a certain size, you will also want to add the `height` and `width` attributes as well:

```
<img src="images/bookcover.jpg" alt="My Book" width="100" height="150"
/>
```

Notice that the `<img>` element is written with a single tag. In HTML, when a tag is used alone, you will need to ensure that it ends with a forward-slash.

Grouping elements

It's common to group elements together within containers on your web pages. The most common way of grouping elements is with the `<div>` element. You can then target these `<div>` elements with CSS rules, so that you can apply a custom style or position to them. The `<div>` tag is easily the most used element when build web pages:

```
<div>
    <img src="image.jpg" alt="My Image"/>
    <div>
        <h3>My Title</h3>
        <p>With some CSS, we could float the image defined above
        to the left. Then the title and this paragraph could
        be aligned to the right of the image.</p>
    </div>
</div>
```

Have a go hero – playing with HTML

In this section, I went into rapid-fire mode and threw a bunch of HTML code at you without any elaborate examples or walk-through. However, we have done that quite a bit throughout this book. I recommend that you test out each of the elements that we just learned. For simplicity, you can use an HTML page or HTML stack. Happy coding!

CSS basics

Cascading Style Sheets (CSS) allows you to create a set of rules that defines how your content is styled on your web page. Imagine that all the HTML elements are contained within an invisible box; CSS controls how each of these boxes is colored, outlined, and positioned. The style rules defined are cascading. This means that, if a rule for a particular element is defined later in the document, it will override the previous rules, unless the previous rule used a more specific selector (more on that later).

There are three ways to include CSS inside your HTML document—the `<style>` tag, the `style` attribute, or an external textual document linked from within the HTML `<head>` element. Whenever you can, I recommend that you use externally managed CSS files so that all of your style rules are located in a single location. When you use external style sheets, it will also speed up your website, as web browsers can cache your external CSS files so that they don't need to be downloaded for every web page.

```
<style>
    h1{color:red;}
</style>

<div style="color:red;">This text will be red</div>

<link rel="stylesheet" type="text/css" href="css/external.css">
```

ID and class attributes

In order to target certain elements on the page with CSS, there are two global attributes that are allowed on every HTML element—id and class. The id attribute is used to uniquely identify the element from other elements on the page. The class attribute is used when you want to logically group several elements on the same page:

```
<div id="uniqueId"></div>
<div class="card"></div>
```

 You can define multiple classes for an element. You can add multiple class values separated by spaces.

CSS rules

CSS rules are broken down into two parts: *selectors* and *declarations*. The selectors define the target, and the declarations define the style that will be applied.

Selectors

Before we can apply style rules to our content, we need to be able to determine how to target the elements that we want to style. There are three basic ways to accomplish this—through the HTML tag, the id, and class attributes that we just learned about. Let's look at some sample rules. For now, let's simply look at the first part of the rule before the curly braces. This part of the rule defines which elements will be affected within our web page:

```
h1{ color : red; }
.title{ color : red; }
#main-title{ color : red; }
```

Notice that the three CSS rules that we defined earlier have set the color of the text to `red`. As the declarations are identical for all three rules, we can consolidate by defining multiple targets as the selector. This can be done with a simple comma-delimited list of selectors:

```
h1, .title, #main-title { color : red; }
```

Type selectors

To target all elements with a specific tag, simply use the tag name as the selector. The rules below target the `<h1>`, `<h2>`, `<h3>`, and `<p>` elements on our web page:

```
h1, h2, h3 { color : red; }
p { font-family : Helvetica; }
```

Class selectors

To target all elements that have been assigned a particular class, you simply need to use the class name as the selector; prepend it with a dot. The following rule targets all elements that have the `class` attribute set to `title`:

```
.title{ color : red; }
```

Class selectors can be used in conjunction with type selectors, and other class selectors in order to ensure a more precise target. This can be accomplished by combining the selectors with no spaces:

```
h3.title { color : green; }
.title.big { font-size : 50px; }
```

The `h3.title` selector will target all the `<h3>` elements that have the class set to `title`. The `.title.big` selector will target all elements that have both the `title` and `big` class attributes.

ID selectors

To target a specific element, you need to use that element's ID as the selector, prepended with a hash. Remember that the ID attribute for an HTML element must be unique for your web page to be valid. The following rule is the most limiting rule, as it targets the single element that has the ID set to `main-title`:

```
#main-title{ color : red; }
```

Descendent selectors

We've talked about an HTML document being hierarchical. HTML elements can contain other elements, which can in turn can contain more elements. We can target this hierarchy structure by combining selectors, this time separated by a space:

```
.note a { color : blue; }
div.comment .note { border-width : 1px; border-color : black; }
```

The aforementioned first rule will change the font color of all links that are contained within any elements that have the `note` class, to blue. The second rule will add a border to all elements that have the `note` class, and are contained within a `<div>` element that has its class set to `comment`.

Declarations

You have seen quite a bit on CSS rules in this section, so it should be pretty apparent how they function. The declarations are composed of a *property* and *value*, separated by a colon. Properties indicate the aspect of the selector that you would like to style—font, width, height, and so on. The format of the value will change based on the property that you want to use.

Declarations end with a semicolon after the value. You can then start another declaration directly after the semicolon or on a new line. You can define as many declarations as you want within the curly braces for a selector:

```
div.comment .note {
    border-width : 1px;
    border-color : black;
    font-family : Helvetica;
    color : #999999;
}
```

Common declarations

The following is a table that contains the commonly used properties and their commonly used values:

Declaration	Notes
`color : black;` `color : #000000;`	The `color` property will determine the color of the text used. You can specify the color as standard color names, hex codes, or RGB values (not displayed).
`background-color : white;` `background-color : #ffffff;`	This will set the background color to a solid color. You can specify the color as standard color names, hex codes, or RGB values (not displayed).

Declaration	Notes
font-family : Helvetica, Arial;	This defines the list of fonts to use for the content. If the first font in the provided list is not available, the next font is used.
font-size : 15px;	This defines the size of the font. The unit used here can be px, em, pt, or percentage (%).
font-weight : bold;	This will make the font bold.
font-style : italic;	This will make the font italic.
width : 100px; height : 50px;	This will define the width of an element (its invisible box). If you use the px unit, then the element will have a static size. You can also use the percentage unit (%) so that your element will expand and react to its parent element's width. This is an important concept when developing a variable width or responsive sites.
border-width : 2px; border-width : 2px 1px 2px 1px;	This defines the width of the border around the element. This is one property that accepts multiple formats to its value. When only one value is specified, the border will have a consistent width on all four sides. However, you can specify the different width for each side of the element.
border-color : #000000;	The color of the border.
border-radius : 5px; border-radius : 5px 10px 5px 10px;	This allows you to apply a radius to the corners of an element in order to achieve rounded corners. Like border-width, border-radius accepts multiple-formatted values, so that you can define a separate radius for each corner.
padding : 5px; padding : 5px 0px 5px 0px;	This defines the spacing between the element's border and its content. Like border-width, padding accepts multiple formatted values.
margin : 5px; margin : 5px 0px 5px 0px;	This defines the spacing between the elements border and the outside of its invisible box. Like border-width, margin accepts multiple formatted values.
display : none; display : block;	This defines how an element will be displayed. You can even completely hide the element from being displayed. The possible values are: inline, block, inline-block, and none.

Most CSS properties accept many different formats for the value. Based on the format provided, the style could change. I recommend that you study the references mentioned later in this section for a more in-depth look at the different ways to declare your CSS styles.

Have a go hero – playing with CSS

Now that you know the basic concepts of CSS, try to style the HTML page that you created in the last *Have a Go Hero* section. Make sure to add some `class` and `id` attributes to your HTML elements, so that you can use all the available rule selectors that we learned. To make things simple, you can type all of your CSS with `<style>` tags at the top of your HTML document.

HTML and CSS resources

The following are a few great resources that I use on a regular basis, as I am getting geeky with code:

◆ **W3Schools.com**: This website is a great resource to quickly search for a particular HTML tag or CSS attribute, and see the proper syntax and examples. Even though I code in these languages pretty much every day, there are still things that I don't recall, or new attributes that I have never used before. This is one of my most widely used websites. Check it out at `http://www.w3schools.com`.

◆ **Stackoverflow**: This website is an online community of developers for pretty much every language out there. If you have a programming question, chances are that there is already an answer for you at `http://stackoverflow.com`.

◆ **The HTML and CSS book**: While I was writing this book, a ground-shattering resource was published for learning HTML and CSS. Jon Duckett wrote a book titled *HTML & CSS: design and build websites*. This book is like nothing that I have ever seen before. It marks a complete paradigm shift with the format for a programming book. The book looks like it belongs on your coffee table. The examples within the book are so simple and straightforward that even non-geeks can understand it. I really cannot say more about this book other than go get it now at `http://htmlandcssbook.com`.

Troubleshooting tips

It is inevitable that you will come across some issues while developing your first websites. The following is a collection of troubleshooting tips that I recommend you tape to your monitor.

Remove the clutter

I see it all the time—web designers try to pack in way too much data onto a web page. I have seen some pretty crazy web page layout over the years that you would not believe. Sliders inside tabs, inside a lightbox, which itself was launched from a slider inside a tab. I just got a headache typing that sentence! It's ok to spread your content across multiple web pages, I promise.

I try to keep to a simple rule of *one effect per page*. This will make your web pages less complex, load faster, and will ultimately give your visitors a better experience. When users go to a website and cannot find the data they are looking for easily, they will leave and may never come back. So keep things simple.

 Another reason to not clutter you page is that Internet Explorer has a limit of about 30 "calls" per page. This means that after it has loaded 30 resources, it will no longer load any more resources.

Isolate the problem

Maybe you are having a problem with a component of your page, let's say a stack. Create a new page and try to get it working on its own. This will isolate the problem from potentially conflicting with other stacks or elements that you might have on the page. Another good practice is to temporarily change the theme of the page to see if maybe there could be a conflict with the theme.

Watch the spaces

I have said this a few times throughout the book but make sure that you are not using spaces in your page names and folders. Also if an add-on requires that you input sort of unique identifier, it's probably best not to use any spaces.

PHP code displayed

There are times when you view a web page and instead of seeing the finished web page as you would expect to, you see a bunch of code on the page and possibly the page is all mixed up. There are a couple possible solutions to this problem:

◆ Make sure that your page name has a PHP extension and not an HTML extension.

◆ If you are seeing this behavior in RapidWeaver preview mode, then chances are that everything will be fine once you publish your site. RapidWeaver supports only simple PHP codes. Some of the more complex PHP codes may not work properly until you publish.

◆ If you are seeing this behavior on your published website, first check your page extension. If that is okay, then your hosting company may not support PHP. While it is rare, there are some hosting companies that still don't support PHP. I recommend looking for a new host if this is the case. At the time of writing this book, PHP v5.4 was the current stable version. I recommend that you try to use PHP v5.3+.

Mixed up extensions

If you have renamed a web page from `index.html` to `index.php`, you will need to make sure that you go onto your server and manually delete the `index.html` file. If you do not delete the file, it is more than likely the server will serve up the HTML file instead of the PHP file to your visitors.

Blurry images

If you followed the image guidelines laid out in this book, then you should be golden. If you are getting images that are not as crisp as before you added them to your project, it may because you forgot to resize them. Remember that RapidWeaver and Stacks will resize your images, and use their own compression when exporting your site. If you want to ensure your images are as crisp as when you added them, then make sure they are sized properly before adding them into your RapidWeaver project. You may want to review *Chapter 5* and *Chapter 7* for more tips on images.

Ignore formatting

If you added your own code to a styled text page, remember to ignore its formatting. If you do not tell RapidWeaver to ignore the formatting, the code will be displayed as text.

Paste as plain text

As with most OS X applications, beware when you are copying text from a document or other application that has formatted text. The same formatting will be transferred onto your web page. Chances are this is not what you want as it will overwrite the styles that have been defined in the theme. In order to get around this make sure that you use **Edit | Paste as Plain Text**.

Console errors

If things are just not working properly, open up Dev Inspector and look at the console for any errors. You may find that some images or files are missing. There may be some JavaScript errors that are obvious as to what the problem could be.

Check your path

If you are having issues publishing your website, triple check that your path setting is set properly. This is the number one cause of publishing issues.

Republish all files

If your published website does not look the same as it does in RapidWeaver, or you are getting "404 file not found" errors, then try republishing all files. You may also want to empty your web browser cache because it may be serving older cached pages.

Disable CSS Consolidation and Compression

It's been a known issue that **CSS Consolidation and Compression** do not work with some themes. You may want to double check with your theme developer, but disabling one or both of these options may solve your problem.

Update

Most RapidWeaver add ons have the ability to auto-update. It's important that you make sure you have the latest updates. Many times, issues that you may be having could have already been resolved in an update. If you are having an issue with RapidWeaver crashing, the problem may be with a third-party add on. While most of the kinks have been worked out, it is possible that one add on could break the updates for another. Therefore from time to time, you may want to manually verify the versions of the add ons that you have installed.

Make sure to read the release notes for updates as well. There could be important information that you should know about backward compatibility.

Read the manual

Now if you made it this far into this book, I probably don't even have to mention this to you but more times than not, an issue that you are having has already been documented somewhere. Therefore, make sure to read any manuals and FAQs for a product, or watch any video tutorials.

How to submit a good support ticket

So if you are completely stuck with an issue, and you have exhausted all your troubleshooting abilities, feel free to e-mail the developer for support. The following are some tips to ensure that your tickets get addressed, and probably fixed faster:

- Provide a URL to a published page that illustrates the issue.
- Provide an isolated case that has the least amount of other content on the page.

- Say which browser version you are using.
- Make sure to detail the problem that you are having. Explain what you are trying to accomplish. Don't just say, "It's broken!"
- The most important tip is to be nice!

Summary

This was by far the geekiest chapter yet. I hope that you enjoyed it and got some new tips and tricks out of it. If some of these tips did not stick with you right now, I recommend that you come back and evaluate them again later. I find that each time I review complex topics, I pick up new and interesting things that I swear were never there the first time I read them.

Specifically, we covered the following:

- How to automate the changing of multiple page attributes. This could potentially be a huge time saver for you.
- How to look at our page source in RapidWeaver.
- ExtraContent can allow us to add new content to places other than simply the main content area or sidebar of our web page.
- We saw a few different possible techniques for editing our RapidWeaver websites online while our customers or we are out on the go.
- We need to start thinking about mobile compatibility and responsive web design when developing a website.
- Created a *404 Page not found* web page and other `.htaccess` tricks.
- Safari Dev Inspector as a very valuable tool in troubleshooting style and layout issues.
- A few great resources to continue our learning on HTML and CSS.
- Valuable troubleshooting tips and tricks that you should follow whenever you encounter an issue in RapidWeaver.

Well, we have reached the end of the book. I hope that this just marks the beginning of your journey of building websites with RapidWeaver. I recommend that you keep this book and reference it from time to time. You never know when you may learn something new, which you had completely missed before. Never stop experimenting and trying new things; its how we all grow and become better web designers. Now go forth and make your websites great!

Index

About Packt Publishing

Packt, pronounced 'packed', published its first book "Mastering phpMyAdmin for Effective MySQL Management" in April 2004 and subsequently continued to specialize in publishing highly focused books on specific technologies and solutions.

Our books and publications share the experiences of your fellow IT professionals in adapting and customizing today's systems, applications, and frameworks. Our solution-based books give you the knowledge and power to customize the software and technologies you're using to get the job done. Packt books are more specific and less general than the IT books you have seen in the past. Our unique business model allows us to bring you more focused information, giving you more of what you need to know, and less of what you don't.

Packt is a modern, yet unique publishing company, which focuses on producing quality, cutting-edge books for communities of developers, administrators, and newbies alike. For more information, please visit our website: www.PacktPub.com.

Writing for Packt

We welcome all inquiries from people who are interested in authoring. Book proposals should be sent to author@packtpub.com. If your book idea is still at an early stage and you would like to discuss it first before writing a formal book proposal, contact us; one of our commissioning editors will get in touch with you.

We're not just looking for published authors; if you have strong technical skills but no writing experience, our experienced editors can help you develop a writing career, or simply get some additional reward for your expertise.

2314136R00193

Printed in Great Britain
by Amazon.co.uk, Ltd.,
Marston Gate.